Fro Hell...

The Jack the Ripper Mystery

by

Bob Hinton

Old Bakehouse Publications

Abertillery

First published in June 1998
Reprinted in May 2005

ISBN 1 874538 96 4

Published in the U.K. by
Old Bakehouse Publications
Church Street,
Abertillery, Gwent NP13 lEA
Telephone: 01495 212600 Fax: 01495 216222
Email: oldbakehouseprint@btopenworld.com
Website: www.oldbakehouseprint.co.uk

Made and printed in the UK
by J.R. Davies (Printers) Ltd.

British Library Cataloguing in Publication Data: a catalogue
record for this book is available from the British Library.

*This book is dedicated to my brother Andrew
who encouraged and supported me all the way through,
and my long suffering wife Prue
who has had to put up with Jack the Ripper
longer than Scotland Yard.*

ACKNOWLEDGEMENTS

Writing a book is like having a baby, no one person can do it alone. When I first mentioned my theories and that I would like to write a book about them to Brian Marriner in early 1996 he replied with a typical no-nonsense Yorkshire reply *"Why don't you then?"*

Attending the first Whitechapel Murder conference in Ipswich that year I also found a great deal of encouragement from people who are legends in the world of Ripper research. This surprised me as I was half expecting established authors to take the view that *"here was yet another amateur dipping his toe in"*, but nothing could be further from the truth. During my research I contacted Jean Ritchie, the well known author of several crime related books and was most encouraged by the last paragraph in her letter. She wrote *"..the secret is just to keep writing! Lots of people want to write books, but only a few have the sticking power to get it all down on paper."*

It is largely due to these encouraging words that you are reading this today and so I would like to take the opportunity to thank all those who helped me along the way, among them are: Loretta Lay and Cam Wolff of Greyhouse books, Paul Begg, Alan Jones, John Ogan, Betty Davis, the staff at Public Records Office, the staff at Bancroft Road Library, George and Valerie Olifent from The Keyhole (Antique lock specialists), Andrew McNamara Consultant Graphologist at APM Graphologists, Ross Strachan, Malcolm Thomas, Phil Hinton (my son) for his wizardry with a computer keyboard, and of course my sister in law Cherry for her sterling work in editing my manuscript. To all these and others I may have inadvertently overlooked - thank you.

CONTENTS

Key to Map

1.   Number 8 White's Row. Home of Annie Millwood.

2.   Approximately 400 yards along this road was where Ada Wilson was attacked in her home at 19 Maidman Street.

3.   George Yard buildings where Martha Tabram was murdered.

4.   Polly Nichols was found here in Bucks Row.

5.   Annie Chapman died in the rear yard of 29 Hanbury Street.

6.   Liz Stride's body was discovered here in Dutfields Yard.

7.   Mitre Square where Catharine Eddowes met her doom.

8.   Mary Kelly, the last of the Ripper's victims died in her room here in Millers Court.

9.   The only clue ever found in the murders was found here in Goulston Street after the Mitre Square killing.

10.   The Victoria Home for working men was situated here in 1888.

Map of Whitechapel with places of interest

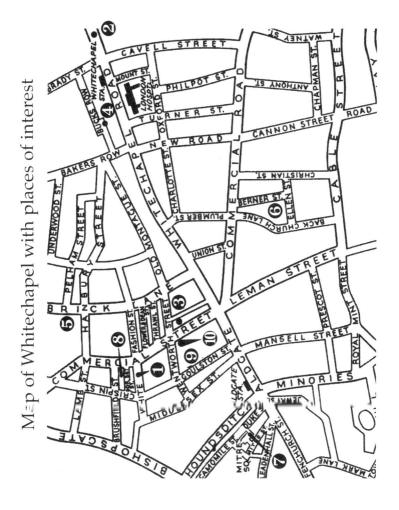

List of illustrations and photographs

Frontspiece

Between pages 111 and 112

Chapter One

"England is an Empire..."
Jules Michelet 1798 - 1874

By the second half of the last century, Great Britain was the undisputed ruler of a large proportion of the earth's surface. The vast tracts of Canada had been pacified by a handful of men wearing the scarlet coats of the North West Mounted Police. When Sitting Bull's band of warriors, fresh from their victory over Custer at the Little Big Horn fled across the border to escape the vengeful wrath of the American Army, they were visited by a lone mounted policeman, Inspector James M Walsh, who rode into their camp and told them that the Great White Mother, Queen Victoria, would let them stay provided there was no trouble. Any problems and he would return. During the Sioux's sojourn in British Territory there was no trouble.

Cetawayo's mighty Zulu armies, reputedly the largest standing army in the world, had been fought and obliterated by sweating redcoats dealing out death and destruction. Certainly there had been drawbacks such as Isandwana, but these reverses were quickly forgotten at Ulundi where the Zulus had been mown down in their thousands for a loss of only a handful of Imperial troops. The Mad Mahdi was causing some bother in the Sudan, but his turn would come, it did just after the turn of the century when the Dervish hordes were blasted into dollrags at Omdurman. India was quiet now, and the Far East was falling into line nicely. The overwhelming power of the British Empire ensured that even if it suffered setbacks, and it did, these would swiftly be overcome, and they were. No one doubted the supreme power of Great Britain. When the Sultan of Zanzibar got a bit uppity, it only required the Royal Navy to hove into view and bombard his palace into brick dust, to convince him that it wasn't such a good idea after all. Still he did make it into the record books as the shortest war on record. He had defied the might of the Empire for all of eight minutes.

If the Nation was proud, so were the Nationals. The British subject was the envy of the World - The Sultan of Zanzibar could testify to the danger of interfering with him. Many people felt the same way as Cecil John Rhodes who said:

1

"Haven't we won the most wonderful prize in life's lottery, to be thirty years old and English!"

The Empire was unshakeable.

Across the world America was just beginning to recover from the awful slaughter of the Civil War, a war that had changed the perception of the American citizen for ever. They saw thousands of their fellow men butchered on the battlefields, they had no illusions of their own mortality, a feeling which lasts to this very day. They were not in an Imperialistic mood, they preferred to stay at home, and punctuate their history with domestic violence, such as the gunfight in 1881 in which three men died, and which entered the history books as the Gunfight at the OK Corral. They started to breed a different kind of killer, the serial killer. Herman Mudgett achieved notoriety as one of the first of his breed. Perhaps if the Americans had vented their need for slaughter on a grand scale in other people's countries, as the British had, possibly this phenomena would not have arisen, who knows.

If Britain was the centre of the world, then the centre of Britain was undoubtedly London. That vast, sprawling incredible mass of humanity and brick, that stretched from the slums of Whitechapel and Limehouse in the east, to the sumptuous elegance and extraordinary wealth of the West End. Life for the upper and middle classes was good, incomes, even directly translating into today's terms excluding inflation, were extremely handsome. Some of the upper echelons were having to struggle by on incomes of half a million pounds a year, close on a hundred million in today's money. Streets were wide and tree lined, swept clean on a daily basis by an army of low paid workers so the ladies dresses wouldn't get too dirty. The air was as clean as could be hoped for, with the only pollution coming from the domestic fires - not the belching factory chimneys that spewed their smoke and filth over the eastern reaches of the city.

Business was conducted at a genteel level, here a hat shop, there a florists with a baker's shop just round the corner. In stark contrast with the poorer parts of the City where slaughterhouses and abattoirs were side by side with human dwellings, where the refuse and the filth built up in the streets

2

so that you had to clamber over heaps of rotting rubbish which were only removed when it rained, and the broken down sewer system flooded into the roads and washed the filthy mess into the river.

If a gentleman required diversion, there were plenty of *'Gentlemen's Clubs'* or sporting houses he could visit. Here he would be offered a selection of women, compliant and eager to fulfil his every desire. He would be entertained in the finest of surroundings, feast on the most succulent of food. If sex was not required then there were gaming clubs, where fortunes were lost and won on the turn of a card. After a strenuous night whoring and gambling, his carriage would take him home to his wife and family. His family he very rarely saw, he had staff to take care of them. He might see his children at breakfast, and he might receive a peck on the cheek when they were taken off to bed by the nanny, but other than that they were usually complete strangers to him. Winston Churchill writes that in all the years he spent living with his parents, he could only recall one conversation he had with his father, on the subject of toy soldiers. His wife might be quite aware of her husband's infidelities in the brothels, but it was tolerated, indeed even encouraged. The more her husband channelled his lustful urges towards a certain type of woman, the less would it be necessary for her to have to submit to them herself. After all that sort of thing was strictly for the procreation of children, nothing more, and once she had done her duty, she wanted no more to do with it.

After a while, the fallen women would begin to lose their looks, and then began the dreaded journey known as *'going East'*. The older and less attractive a prostitute became, the further East she had to work, until diseased, worn out, toothless and old way beyond her years, the stews and the slums of Whitechapel became her last stop. Here the necessities of life were strictly regulated, first was alcohol, normally gin at a half-penny a large glass, then somewhere to doss. A night's bed would cost about fourpence, and a hanging line a penny, and last if possible, some food. Toiletries, medicines, were strictly luxury items, two women would fight with broken bottles for a scrap of soap.

3

Life in the East End was about survival. Children were born, and if they survived (20% didn't past their fifth birthday) they were faced with a life of unremitting hardship. If you were lucky enough to have a trade, carpenter, slaughterman, policeman or similar you might just make it through. If you didn't then you were locked into a system where work was doled out on a daily basis. Labourers, dockers, market porters, and others would start to queue at three and four o'clock in the morning to try and get a day's work, for a day's work might mean a sixpence or even a shilling, and that would put a roof (albeit leaking) over your head and a loaf of bread on the table. If you were a slaughterman or a docker there was always the chance of *'liberating'* a bit of offal, or perhaps even some fruit as a special treat. Men as young as thirty looked sixty, their bodies bent and wasted through bad diet and back breaking work. Their heads were shaved to keep away the lice, but in a pathetic attempt at pride, a lick of hair was kept long at the front, so with a flat cap on, your haircut looked normal.

Your whole existence was different, based on a here today and dead tomorrow fatalism. If you had clothes, you wore them, all of them. Leaving them at home was a bad idea. If you did not raise your rent for that day your landlord might throw you and all your belongings out into the street, and what was in the street belonged to the creatures of the street. Wearing all your clothes made it easier to pawn them, to *'pop'* in the parlance of the time, raising a few coppers to help you survive until tomorrow. Crime was rampant, with assaults, murder and sexual offences topping the list. Stealing was not as common, simply because there was nothing to steal. Those criminals who ventured to the wealthier areas to plunder, ran a whole gamut of risks. If a householder caught you in his house, being shot to death was the least of your worries. Large dogs were the fashion, and two bloodhounds eating you alive was not the easiest way to go. It was no good protesting the householder had used more than the minimum amount of force to protect his property, killing you was generally accepted as the minimum amount of force!!

Even if you did manage to return safe with you ill-gotten gains, what then? A gold tea service worth thousands in the Jewellers of Bond Street, was practically worthless in the East End. What were you going to do with them? Fences paid a few shillings for items worth tens of thousands and sold them on for a few pounds. One of the few ways of making a living from crime was to act as a P.A. or Police Agent, informant or grass in today's slang. It was a precarious living, life was cheap and murdering an informant was the recognised way of dealing with the problem, as Nancy in Oliver Twist found out.

Without the P.A. the Police had very little chance of apprehending the criminal. There were no forensic laboratories to provide scientific analysis of evidence. Fingerprints were still several years away, and bloodstains were classified as animal or human. If a burglar was caught coming out of the premises with the swag on him all well and good, if not and the P.A. couldn't help, then the likelihood was that he would get away with it. In the case of murder, then as now most murders were committed by people known to the victim. If you investigated a killing and found the husband or wife covered in blood, fair enough, stick out your wrists and slap the darbies (handcuffs) on them, if not then the chances of solving it were pretty slim. The other commonest form of murder was the 'killing for gain', such as robbery. If a killing occurs and property is missing and you find someone covered in blood and clutching the missing property, again, case solved. If not then you relied to a greater extent on the public or the P.A. If none of these things happened then it was very unlikely the crime would be solved. The more successful detectives were successful not because of their greater knowledge of crime, but because of their greater knowledge of the criminal. A practical detective (one who actually goes out and arrests the bad guys, as opposed to those who sit in offices and brush their moustaches) might be called to the scene of a robbery, look at the modus operandi of the criminal and say to himself, "Hullo! this looks like the work of Slippery Jim" hop into a Hansom cab or more likely a growler or even more likely on foot, hie yourself round to Slippery Jim's crib and slap the darbies on him. This depth of knowledge took many years to build up, and relied a lot on being accepted by the people you were working with. Lord Peter Wimsey attempting to operate in the East End, would either have been totally ignored, or more likely been bashed over the head and robbed. Even Sherlock Holmes on his information gathering forays would rely heavily on disguise to insinuate himself into the shadowy world of the

East End. This is why most of the successful police officers were of the same working class as the people they arrested. This of course was helpful in most circumstances but became a positive drawback if investigating someone of a higher social standing. Detective Chief Inspector F G Abberline discovered this to his chagrin, whilst investigating the Cleveland Street Scandal. When he made it known that he wished to interview certain extremely well connected people regarding the male brothel, various obstacles were placed in his way until the people concerned could be smuggled out of the country. Before we throw up our hands in horror at such blatant machinations of the upper classes in Victorian times to pervert the course of justice, don't forget exactly the same thing happened in the Lord Lucan case!

Things were gradually changing. On the continent, especially in France, the police were taking a more scientific approach to the investigation of crime. On discovery of a crime, the crime scene was isolated to prevent clues being needlessly disturbed and destroyed. Photographs were taken so that future investigators would not have to rely on officer's memories, clues were collected and their relative positions marked on sketch maps. In England, the discovery of a body usually heralded a stampede of sightseers who crowded as close as possible to the victim, sometimes removing items of clothing and other souvenirs. After they had been cleared away, the press and the police then trampled over everything destroying what little evidence remained. Very rarely was the scene of crime or the body photographed, it was virtually unheard of to make a sketch.

The Police themselves were a mixed bunch. At the bottom was the beat officer or Constable. He was nearly always an ex-soldier or sailor. Ex-servicemen were easier to train, being used to obeying orders, they showed the right respect to their superiors and struck terror into their inferiors. They had a modicum of intelligence and could keep their uniform and kit in good order, thus saving money for the Home Office. Due to the amount of action they would have seen in Victoria's service, they would well be able to handle themselves in a fight. When you have faced four thousand screaming Zulus at Rorkes Drift, a drunken docker would quickly be disposed of. Even so, there were still parts of the East End a uniformed bobby would not go for fear of being murdered by the inhabitants. Dorset Street was one area always patrolled in pairs, if at all.

Above constable came the Sergeants, who were only Constables with stripes. The higher ranks up to Chief Inspector were obtainable, but only with great difficulty. Above that the ranks were nearly always appointed. The Superintendents were chosen from the upper classes, in much the same way officers in the Army were. Theoretically it was possible for a constable to make Superintendent, but like Halley's Comet, we know it's there but you don't see it very often. The highest ranks in the Police force, were nearly always given to very senior Army officers. Commissioner Warren for instance was previously a highly decorated Colonel in the Army, and after he resigned the force, reverted to a being a Senior Army Officer again. These appointments could cause severe problems. A General for instance is not used to dealing with the great unwashed public, he's used to dealing with hordes of Fuzzy Wuzzy's, and his methods nearly always had something to do with Gatling guns and piles of bodies. Now whereas this was all good stuff, and just what you wanted to read over your braised kidneys and toasted muffins, it was damned inconvenient if you couldn't get into town because of great piles of bodies blocking the way. In all fairness it wasn't really the officers' fault, they handled the situation the way they had been trained, and had previously been praised for.

It must be remembered that the last quarter of the 19th century was a time of incredible change throughout Europe. Ideals which had remained in place for a thousand years or more were being challenged. Less than a hundred years before, the French peasantry had rebelled against their betters and had drenched the country with aristocrats' blood (which they were pleased to see was red like the peasants - not blue). English colonists in America had rebelled against their king and declared independence. Unrest and rebellion were for ever present in France, Holland and Germany. In Russia the huge number of downtrodden serfs were beginning to say *"NO! !"*. Almost daily came news of fresh outrages, the King of Italy killed by a bomb, even Queen Victoria herself was the victim of an assassination attempt. Across the water in Ireland, the Fenians were resorting

7

to violence to make their point, and when that didn't work they brought death and destruction to the streets of London. This caused the formation of a select band of Policemen to combat them, known as the Special Irish Branch, they are still doing the same work today, but have dropped the 'Irish' to become the Special Branch.

Even in Great Britain accepted values were being washed away. People from the lower classes were actually making fortunes in wool, cotton, coal, iron, steel and a thousand other ways, all of them contemptuously dismissed by the upper classes as 'trade'. But the writing was on the wall, in trade they may be, but they had the money, what could stop them having the power?

Even the Royal Family were having problems. The Prince of Wales was a notorious rake and libertine. His sexual affairs were well known, and were the subject of gossip from the drawing rooms of the rich to the gutters of the poor. His son, the Queen's grandson, was also a cause for concern. For someone who was to rule the greatest Empire the world had ever seen, he was not showing the right signs, for there were whispers that he preferred the company of his male friends to that of women. He kept company with poets and aesthetics instead of soldiers and statesmen.

In the middle of all this was a press that was beginning to flex its muscles. The power of the press was ably demonstrated during the Crimean War when the *Times* correspondent sent back reports highly critical of the way the war was being conducted. The Charge of the Light Brigade might inspire Tennyson to fine poetry, but when it was revealed to be the product of bungling incompetence, then heads would roll. Reports that we were losing more men to disease and appalling weather conditions, prompted one journalist to write:

'It would make more sense, save more money if we marched one thousand of our men on to Hampstead Heath every week and shot them ourselves. The enemy's losses through their incompetence would still be the same, and we would save the enormous expense of shipping our armies to the Crimea.'

8

The fact that changes were instituted after the war, largely as a result of the press was not lost on the newspaper owners. Here was real power, a power that could cut across the social divide, and stride across the oceans of the world. This emerging popularity of the printed word spawned a new entry into the world of literature, the *'penny dreadful'*!! Magazines with titles guaranteed to catch the public's eye, *The Illustrated Police News, The Penny Illustrated Paper* and others were filled with lurid tales generally of crime, and the bloodier the better. Nothing improves the circulation better than an illustration of a mutilated corpse on the front cover. As Charles Dickens put it *"I want to makes your flesh creep!!"* These papers were eagerly read by the masses, possibly because here was proof that there really was someone worse off than yourself.

This then is the stage on which our drama is to unfold. The scene is set, a country that outwardly displays all the power and confidence, yet inwardly is a seething mass of fears and frustrations, Britannia standing proud, but with a disease-riddled heart. In the wings the actors assemble, ready to walk on and play their part. They are a motley crew, the all powerful monarch, with the wayward children, the chief of police, seen by some as a buffoon, by others as a misjudged hero. The stalwart policeman with his faithful sidekick, the extras, thousands of them, the teeming masses of the slums and rookeries, The People of the Abyss, according to novelist Jack London.

But where is the villain? There he is, hiding in the shadows, a fleeting insubstantial figure, come forward, come into the light. Here he comes, he is almost bathed in the full glow of the footlights, soon we shall see.

But he stops just short, his face is still hidden, but how will the drama unfold if we don't know who it is? Well he has a name ....

"My Lords, Ladies and Gentlemen, please put your hands together and welcome,

Jack the Ripper !!!!!!!!!!"

Thunderous applause, curtain up, our drama begins ....

9

Chapter Two

"Lost is our old simplicity of times,
The world abounds with laws, and teems with crimes"

anon

The East End of London had never been a particularly safe place to be, the sprawling slums with their teeming thousands did not breed many saints, but most of the crime was *'normal'*, understandable, economic. If a drunken sailor was coshed and robbed, it was because someone wanted his money, not because anyone had a particular grievance against sailors. If a man beat his wife, it was probably because he was drunk. All crime was present in the East End, robbery, prostitution, protection rackets and of course, murder. Even wholesale slaughter like the infamous Ratcliffe Highway murders, when a whole family was wiped out was understandable, robbery was the motive. What the public had not really got to grips with was the motiveless, meaningless sort of crime, a crime for crime's sake. That was soon to change.

The year 1888 opened with the usual run of petty crime that the populace had come to expect, street brawls, wife beatings and petty thefts. There really wasn't much to steal in the East End, so most of the thefts fell into the *'petty'* category. On the 8th of February in Backchurch Lane, an out of work Jewish cobbler used a boot finisher's knife to murder his estranged wife and then slit his own throat in a brutal murder/suicide slaying. It caused very little impact, after all she was his wife, that made it almost acceptable. The motive might have been anger, or more likely sheer despair, either way it was something the East Enders could relate too. Later on, all the relevant facts in this case would be given a more sinister meaning.

Towards the end of the month, on Saturday the 25th, another attack took place. This time the victim was the widow of a soldier, a Mrs Annie Millwood, who lodged at 8 Whites Row, Spitalfields. This was a common lodging house and the building still exists today. Now Whites Row is only a few yards from Dorset Street, a name that would soon echo around the Empire, and is still echoing today. To date it has not been established where exactly the attack took place. To the right of the building (as you face it) there used to be a narrow alleyway that was used by the locals as a short cut to Butler Street, it is possible that the attack took place here.

She was admitted to the Whitechapel Workhouse infirmary suffering from *'stabs'*. Her legs and lower parts of her body had been stabbed repeatedly by *'a man she did not know who stabbed her with a clasp knife which he took from his pocket'*. Despite the **Eastern Post** describing her as *'the deceased'* she did recover from her injuries, only to collapse and die on the 31st March from what appeared to be a heart attack. Information on Mrs Millwood is minimal, she was 38 years old, not in a known occupation and might have been a prostitute as she had no other means of support.

The following month in the early hours of the morning of the 28th March, Ada Wilson, a 39 year old seamstress, answered a knock on her door at 9 Maidman Street, Burdett Road, Mile End. She opened the door to a total stranger who demanded that she give him some money, adding that if she didn't do so he would kill her. She refused, whereupon he produced a clasp knife from his pocket and stabbed her twice in the throat. Her screams attracted attention and a doctor was sent for, who after binding her wounds, sent her to the London Hospital. Her condition was extremely serious, the Press commenting *'it is thought impossible that the injured woman can recover'*. But Ada was obviously a survivor, and after thirty days in hospital she was discharged.

Like the Millwood case the police had a description of the attacker, he was about 5 feet 6 inches tall, approximately thirty years old, had a sun-tanned complexion and a fair moustache. He wore a dark coat, light trousers and a wideawake hat. Despite this description, he was never caught.

The motive for this attack, as for the Millwood attack, was baffling. Since the man demanded money, robbery might be considered, but if so, it was the most inept robbery attempt of all time. Why would anyone prepared to use lethal force to achieve their ends knock on a door and demand money? For all the assailant knew it might be opened by a fifteen stone drunken docker very annoyed at having his sleep disturbed. If you were that desperate for money why not just lie in wait for someone in an alley somewhere. At least then you could select your victim with an eye to quickly overpowering and robbing them and then making your escape. If you insisted on robbing someone in their own home, would any half witted burglar do it in that fashion? Firstly, he didn't know who would answer the door, secondly he wouldn't know who else would be present in the house. In any case why announce your intentions of robbing someone on the doorstep, why not try and gain access to the house and then commit the deed? No; using robbery as a motive for this attack does not make any sense at all.

Taking the two attacks together, a pattern is beginning to emerge. Both were made on women of approximately the same age, both possibly in the same profession (seamstress was often used as an euphemism for prostitute) both were stabbed with the same type of weapon, and in both cases the attackers left the scene very quickly. The last point is very important. It indicates that although the motive for the attacks was to injure or kill, it wasn't vitally important that this was carried out. If Mrs Millwood's attacker wanted to kill her he could have done so. If Ada Wilson's attacker really wanted her dead he could have achieved that aim. It was almost as if someone was trying out a new knife, or method of attacking people, and wanted to see if it worked.

During the mid fifties in France, two teenagers were arrested for robbing a post office. They had used a .22 calibre rifle in the hold up, and since they were local boys were recognised and quickly arrested. When they were in custody they were genuinely amazed to also be charged with murder. Although shots had been fired during the robbery no one had been hit, and they could not understand the murder charge. This however related to a local farmer who had been found in a ditch some miles out of town. A reconstruction of the crime demonstrated that he had been shot whilst riding his bicycle. A blood trail showed that he had been shot, continued pedalling and then shot again and again, all the time trying desperately to escape on his bicycle. At this, realisation dawned on the two murderers, Oh yes they remember now, on the way to hold up the Post Office they wanted to try out the gun to see if it worked. Most people would use a tin can for this purpose, they saw nothing wrong in using a human being, an act which meant so little to them that they had genuinely forgotten they had done it. Investigators often make the mistake of trying to attribute normal actions and motives to what are always abnormal people. It is often said that the most successful detectives are those who can think like the criminals they are hunting.

If we accept that the attacker of these women knew exactly who would open the door, is it beyond the realms of possibility to assume that he had targeted them very carefully, like a hunter hunting prey he had stalked his victims, attacked without mercy, then disappeared into the night.

The next attack took place on the 2nd of April. Emma Elizabeth Smith staggered into her lodging house at 18 George Street, Spitalfields, and told the deputy keeper that she had been set upon and robbed of all her money. Her injuries were dreadful, facial cuts, an ear almost torn off and severe abdominal wounds. She was taken to the London Hospital where it was established she had been raped with a blunt instrument that had been inserted into her vagina with such force it had ruptured the perineum. At nine o'clock on Wednesday morning she died.

She told the authorities that she had been set upon by three men in Osborn Street, who had robbed and raped her and made off with what little she had. The brutality of the attack and the sheer viciousness of her injuries, gave rise to speculation that she wasn't being totally frank in her account. There was a rumour that the attack had been carried out by one of the many East End gangs in the area as a punishment for not handing over all her earnings as a prostitute to her *'protectors'*. This is very plausible. There was very little similarity to the other attacks. Her injuries were not reported as being *'stab'* wounds, she was not attacked in her own home, her injuries were consistent of being inflicted as a form of punishment, and there were multiple attackers. Whatever the reason for the attack there was absolutely no reason for her to lie about the number of men involved in the assault. Although the sheer brutality of the attack had shocked the East Enders it was still a crime generally accepted as understandable. What happened next, didn't.

On 7th August at 4.45 am the body of a known prostitute, Martha Tabram or Turner as she was sometimes known, was found on the landing of George Yard Buildings, a scruffy block of cheap dwellings in George Yard off Whitechapel High Street. Doctor Timothy Killeen of Brick Lane was sent for, arriving at about 5.30 am, his initial examination of the body revealed the true horror of the murder.

The body had literally been shredded by no less than thirty nine stab wounds. The ferocity of the attack left hardened policemen shocked, there was absolutely no need for the repeated stabbing, after the first half dozen blows she was probably dead. The doctor concluded she had been dead for about three hours, which placed the attack round about two in the morning. After his brief examination he gave instructions for the body to be moved to the deadhouse belonging to the workhouse infirmary in Old Montague Street.

The results of his post mortem revealed the full extent of the victim's injuries. There were at least twenty two stab wounds on the trunk alone. The left lung had been penetrated five times, the right lung twice. The heart was penetrated once, the liver five times, spleen twice and the stomach six times. The lower portion of the body had also been penetrated once. It was also reported in the *Illustrated Police News* (a publication which despite its name had nothing to do with the Police) that there were also nine wounds in the throat. Death was due to haemorrhage and loss of blood.

Killeen also stated that he thought it possible that two different weapons had been used. He based this on the appearance of one of the wounds on the breast, which he thought differed from the other wounds. The majority of the wounds could have been inflicted with a clasp knife, whilst the one in the breast could have been inflicted with a *'strong long bladed weapon, possibly a dagger or a bayonet'*. It has been suggested in the past that Killeen stated that he thought one of the weapons could have been a surgical instrument and that the murderer *"whoever he was, he knew how and where to cut"*. However an examination of the evidence shows that this was not Killeen's view, a case of editorial license perhaps. The fact was, that the body, far from being carefully dissected, had just been butchered.

It is interesting to pause for a moment and consider the type of weapon that could have been used. Killeen suggests a *"dagger or a bayonet"* and at first glance this seems possible. However if you consider the type of bayonet that was being used at that time, or even for some time previously, this becomes less likely. The standard bayonet of the time was designed to act as a major part of a soldiers armoury. Although magazine rifles had been in use for many years, shooting your enemy was looked upon as almost a sissy thing to do. As a man you were still expected to close with the enemy and run him through with a long length of good Sheffield steel. The first models of the Lee Enfield rifle although capable of holding ten rounds of ball ammunition, were fitted with a *'cut off'*. This slid across the top of the magazine, blocking the ammunition off from the breech, and effectively turning the rifle into a single shot weapon. The inference was clear, although you have bullets, you aren't expected to use them, if the bayonet swept the fields of Waterloo, its still good enough to do the job.

This thinking influenced the design of the bayonet. The standard bayonet of the day, the pattern 1887 Mk I Sword bayonet and the pattern 1887 Mk III Sword bayonet had blades in excess of 18" long. They were heavy and as their name suggests were pointed like a sword. They relied on the combined weight of the soldier, his rifle and the bayonet to penetrate the body of an enemy, and at this they were reasonably efficient. However once the bayonet is removed from the rifle it is an entirely different story. The weapon becomes clumsy, unwieldy and not a very efficient weapon. Think about it. If the blade is 18" long and if the weapon is held 18" from the victim it means the blade is actually touching the body, leaving very little room to build up the required speed to penetrate. What is often overlooked is that human skin is remarkably tough to pierce, once through this layer the flesh underneath offers far less resistance, this is the reason that victims of stabbings often have several minor wounds over the surface of their bodies. In fact to get a really good swing with a long bladed weapon you have to raise your arm an uncomfortable way over your head, and even then the design of the blade makes penetration very difficult. The most efficient design for penetrating the human body is a spike, that's why after the British army did away with sword bayonets it reverted to the 'pig sticker' type of spike bayonet.

So if we can disregard a bayonet as being an unlikely type of weapon in this case, what about 'some kind of surgical instrument'? Tools are generally made with a definite purpose in mind, a hammer is meant for driving nails, a spanner for tightening nuts and so on. There is no surgical instrument designed for stabbing, and in fact most surgical instruments make rather poor stabbing instruments. They are designed in the main for cutting, carefully and precisely. They are made for this purpose, with the strength of the instrument being directly tailored for this need. Even with the heaviest type of surgical knives, amputation knives, the strength of the tool is along the back of the knife, opposite the cutting edge. If you attempt to stab with a surgical knife, because of the temper of the steel and the design of the blade, you stand a good chance of shattering the blade. (It is noticeable that a dissecting knife supposedly the weapon used by Jack the Ripper, has its blade snapped off because someone tried pruning a hedge with it!)

I remember having dinner at my parents one Sunday and whilst waiting at the table I started to fiddle with my knife. It was a very old knife, made in the days when cutlery was individually made, instead of being pressed out of a sheet of steel en masse. The temper of the steel was superb, with the cutting edge firm and strong, but as soon as I bent, ever so slightly, the blade in a way it was not designed to be strained, the blade shattered. My mother was not amused!

If you are trying to establish what kind of weapon was used, I would suggest that the most likely would be a dagger-type knife, something similar to the famous Fairbairn Sykes Commando dagger. Something sharp, pointed, fairly short in the blade (certainly not over 10" in length) and designed for stabbing into an unwieldy body.

So, if we now have a fair idea of what caused the wounds, we know where they were caused, and the outcome, all we have to do now is to find out who caused them.

The police involvement with the case began with PC Thomas Barrett who was brought to the scene of the crime by John Reeves, the labourer who had discovered the body. The first problem was to identify the victim, a mystery that was still not solved by the time the press had learned of the discovery. The issue of the *Star* that appeared on the day of the murder announced dramatically:

A WHITECHAPEL HORROR

A woman, now lying unidentified at the mortuary, Whitechapel, was ferociously stabbed to death this morning, between two and four o'clock, on the landing of a stone staircase in George's buildings Whitechapel.

George's Buildings are tenements occupied by the poor labouring class. A lodger going early to his work found the body. Another lodger says the murder was not committed when he returned home about two o'clock. The woman was stabbed in 20 places. No weapon was found near her, and the murderer has left no trace.

She is of middle age and height, has black hair and a large, round face and apparently belonged to the lowest class.

The *New York Times* for September 1st also carried the story, but anyone reading it may be forgiven in thinking they were describing a different event entirely:

"London Aug. 31. A strangely horrible murder took place at Whitechapel this morning. The victim was a woman who, at 3 o'clock, was knocked down by some man unknown and attacked with a knife. She attempted to escape and ran a hundred yards, her cries for help being heard by several persons in adjacent houses. No attention was paid to her cries, however, and when found at daybreak she was lying dead in another street, several hundred yards from the scene of the attack ....

How they could imagine a woman after being stabbed thirty nine times, (strangely enough they got this fact right,) was able to run several hundred yards, is beyond most observers. It is interesting to note that this crime was really very unusual, otherwise why would a paper printed the other side of the world be interested. The *New York Times* continued to report on all the murders, though with rather a looser style than their

17

British counterparts. The edition for September 9th contains the priceless observation,

"The London Police and detective force is probably the stupidest in the world."

Inspector E Reid of H Division took charge of the investigation. The identity of the murdered woman was established by Henry Tabram, a furniture packer from East Greenwich, who saw an account of the murder in a newspaper. Through him the police were able to piece together the history of the poor woman. Martha White married Henry Tabram on Christmas Day 1869. The marriage was short-lived as Martha's heavy drinking forced a separation in 1875. The break-up was apparently amicable, and Henry gave his wife an allowance of twelve shillings a week, which he later reduce to 2 shillings and 6 pence after she had taken up with another man.

This other man was another Henry, Henry Turner, and they lived together, on and off, for twelve years, her overindulgence in drink causing the occasional rift in their unwedded bliss. By 1888 the couple were out of work and scraping a precarious existence as street hawkers, selling cheap trinkets and other small items of bric-a-brac. When Tom Cullen was researching his famous book on the Whitechapel murders, he appealed for anyone who had any connection with the era to contact him. One gentleman who answered his request was James Bousfield, the son of Martha's last landlady, who still had one of the key chains that Martha Tabram had hawked about the streets.

Turner finally split up with Martha about three weeks before her murder, he last saw her in Leadenhall Street on the 4th August and gave her one shilling and sixpence to buy some more stock *"with which to earn a few ha'pence"*. That was the last time he saw her alive.

Inspector Reid's first task was to interview PC Barrett, the constable who was first called to the body, who gave him some important information. According to Barrett he saw a soldier loitering in the vicinity of George Yard, at about two o'clock in the morning of the 7th August. When challenged the soldier said that he was waiting for a friend who had gone with a girl. A polite way of saying that a mate had gone up an alley with a prostitute for a quick *'knee trembler'*. The constable described the soldier as a Grenadier Guard, age early twenties, height 5' 9" or 10", fair complexion, dark hair and moustache. At a subsequent identity parade Barrett picked out not one but two suspects. It became clear to Inspector Reid that the identity of the suspect wasn't as clear cut as first thought and he dismissed both men.

All was not lost though, for on the 9th August a local prostitute known on the streets as Pearly Poll went to the Commercial Street Police Station, and stated that on the night in question, she had been with Martha Tabram. She and Martha had met with two soldiers, one a corporal and the other a private, and had spent the time from about ten to eleven forty five, walking and drinking around Whitechapel. At this time they had separated into two couples, Poll had taken her beau, the corporal, up an alley, and Martha and her escort had disappeared into George Yard. Apparently that was the last she saw of Martha.

Pearly Poll seemed most anxious to please, offering to attend parades in an effort to identify the soldiers. After a considerable amount of fuss and bother (after the entire garrison of the Tower of London mustered, she forgot to turn up) she eventually did her walk up and down the ranks of soldiery. After being asked if she could identify anyone, she replied, *"He ain't here"*. There was some further mileage to be gained from Pearly Poll when she changed her mind about the regiment her friends belonged to, but all came to nought. Some police officers wondered if Poll hadn't been wasting police time out of sheer mischief, others speculated she might have been frightened off; a more likely explanation is that for once in her entire drab, miserable existence, someone actually took some notice of her, she had had as Andy Warhol would say *'her fifteen minutes'*.

So what did the police eventually end up with? A murdered prostitute, who might or might not have been with a soldier on the night she was murdered. Barrett's soldier said his mate had gone with a girl, but that was at two in the morning. There is nothing to say that the girl was Martha. Pearly Poll said she last saw Martha with a soldier at about midnight, two hours before the accepted time of death. Is it realistic to expect Martha to finish with Pearly Poll's soldier at midnight, and then wait around for Barrett's soldier two hours later? It is most unlikely. What then could have happened? Let us suppose Pearly Poll is accurate in her statement and Martha goes off with her soldier at about 11.45 or midnight. Allowing perhaps thirty minutes for haggling over price, doing the deed, and bidding fond farewells, it might have been thirty minutes later, when she was free and ready to do business again. But this time she is approached by someone who wants a bit more than a furtive coupling in some dark alley. Perhaps Martha or her client knew that George Yard Buildings had a nice relatively private landing, a few more minutes discussion and haggling and its not too unreasonable to find them on the fateful landing at about 1 am. It is not until it is too late that Martha realises that her client has more than sex on his mind.

One thing that did give pause for thought was why no one heard anything. The superintendent of the dwellings lived only 12 feet (measured by a journalist) from where the body was found, yet both he and his wife stated they never heard a thing. There is a possible explanation. If the victim was strangled before being stabbed it would explain why there was no noise, strangling is silent, no noise marks the passage of a soul from this world to the next. One of the newspapers, *The Illustrated Police News*, actually put forward this theory when it wrote:

'The difficulty of identification arose out of the brutal treatment to which the deceased was manifestly subjected, she being throttled while held down and the face and head so swollen in consequence that her real features are not discernible.'

Whether this is an accurate summation of the facts it's not possible to say, it would however explain the absence of noise.

What then was left after the dust had settled. Martha Tabram had probably been strangled, then subjected to a terrifying attack with one knife possibly two. The murderer was in all likelihood right handed.

The attack had taken place in a quiet secluded spot, nobody had noticed anything until John Reeves practically stepped on the body, and the killer had disappeared into the streets of the East End without trace.

The murder had an alarming effect on the population, for here was a crime without any apparent motive. If murder was the reason for the attack, why was it necessary to practically shred the body? If the victim had been strangled first, she would have been already dead. Robbery wasn't a realistic option, she had nothing to steal, rape likewise didn't make sense, if someone had been so desperate why not just rape the woman, beat her up and leave her, besides which Doctor Killeen saw no reason to believe that sexual intercourse had taken place. What the people were seeing, possibly for the first time was a killing that had taken place just for the pure joy of killing. With the previous attacks on women in the same district, this time the press made sure everyone knew about the incident. Having aroused the public's attention, the press noted their reaction in their papers. As the *Police News* reported:

'There have been many visitors to the George Yard Buildings with the rather morbid purpose of seeing the place where the deceased was discovered'.

To cope with the horror of the crime, the killer was starting to be described as a *'lunatic'* a *'bloodlust monster'*. People remembered the story written years ago by Edgar Allan Poe, ***'The Murders in the Rue Morgue'***, where a series of murders executed with similar ferocity were eventually discovered to have been the work of a gorilla. A story from France was published of a pet chimpanzee who had got hold of his master's straight razor, and had proceeded to cut the throats of the entire family. The story was graphically illustrated with a picture of the creature, (though of the size of a fairly robust King Kong) carrying the corpse of the scantily clad lady of the house up the stairs, waving the razor at the terrified children cowering at the top. Then as now, if you can get a story with animals, children, murder and just a hint of sex, you're obviously on to a winner. But out of all these idiotic ramblings came another, more sinister murmur. Such a crime couldn't possibly be the work of an Englishman, it had to be a foreigner, only they were capable of such barbarity, after all look what the Jew cobbler had done to his wife only a few months before. People started remembering another case, the Lipski trial of 1887.

Israel Lipski, a young Russian Jew, murdered Miriam Angel by pouring nitric acid down her throat. The evidence against him was overwhelming, but a lot of people (who bare an uncanny resemblance to the *'free everyone'* section of society today) supported his story that two men had broken into the house and committed the crime. When he was sentenced to death these people gave full and vocal rein to their feelings (Free the Whitechapel Wun). However when Lipski made a full and frank confession to his crimes, the outcome was that this vocal section of the public immediately switched sides. Bitter at being betrayed by their lost cause they now felt that there was nothing so loathsome that a Jew could not be capable of.

The radical press meanwhile, like sharks scenting blood in the water, were getting set to use the apparent inability of the police to either prevent these crimes, or arrest the perpetrator, as a rod with which to beat the largely unpopular Commissioner of Police, Sir Charles Warren.

Sir Charles Warren, was with hindsight, not perhaps the ideal choice for Police Commissioner, but it is all too easy to overlook the very real fears of the establishment of the time. Britain's place on the world stage was won with one thing and one thing only. Discipline. Discipline straightened the backs of redcoats everywhere, and enabled the Imperial Armies to impose their wills across the globe. It was discipline backed with the British bayonet that had stopped and turned the Zulu hordes at Rorkes Drift, it was discipline which enabled an Empire to be ruled by a handful of men thousands of miles from the far flung borders.

The enemy of discipline was anarchy, and all over Europe anarchy was raising its ugly head. Two of the great nations of the world, America and France had been born out of anarchy, a throwing off of old traditions and masters. Karl Marx's daughter, Eleanor, was actively involved with the East End poor. In July of 1888 the Bryant & May match girls withdrew their labour and marched through the East End to Hyde Park. William Morris, an ardent Communist urged, *'all workers to combine to bring about a Social Revolution, which will place the means of production and exchange in the hands of the producers'*.

It wasn't just talk, even Queen Victoria herself had been the subject of an assassination attempt, an act which mentally scarred her for life. The Irish Fenians were exploding bombs in London, even at the epitome of Law & Order, Scotland Yard. Political activists flooded into the East End as refugees, escaping the pogroms of their native governments. The previous Commissioner, Sir Edmund Henderson had been forced to resign when a demonstration in Pall Mall got out of hand and a mini riot ensued, with shops being attacked and looted. The shopkeepers demanded protection. The following Wednesday, 10th February 1886, Scotland Yard ordered West End shop-keepers to close up and barricade their premises, they had received intelligence that a mob was going to attack. When the threatened attack failed to materialise the Home Secretary censured Sir Edmund so strongly, that he packed up and left.

Thus did Sir Charles Warren arrive. Sir Charles had several good points - for a soldier. He was a disciplinarian, stern and humourless, and with an unpleasant temper. Now while these are just the qualities required of a man who has to tame the untameable, perhaps they are not quite what is required of a police officer. His style of command was ably demonstrated by an incident which later became known as *'Bloody Sunday'*. On the 13 November 1887, some 20,000 demonstrators tried to enter Trafalgar Square, despite Sir Charles closing the Square to all such demonstrators.

Opposing the marchers were some 4,300 Police, 300 Grenadier Guards with bayonets fixed, and 300 Life Guards. During the inevitable clashes, some three hundred demonstrators were injured and one killed. It is very easy from the comfort of an armchair to criticise the police action in this case, but to five thousand police and army, 20,000 demonstrators are an awful lot of people. Having been in riot situations myself I can assure the reader that it is the most terrifying thing I have ever experienced. You are faced with an entity that has no mind, no reason, no purpose other than that of crushing you beneath its feet. There is no reasoning with a mob, if it runs out of control people will die. Bearing in mind the enormous amount of people involved, and the way tempers were running, I think controlling a situation like that with only one fatality, has much to commend it. We only have to look at a similar situation in Northern Ireland in the early seventies, which left thirteen dead, to realise how easy it is for the death toll to rise.

In spite of this, Warren's name was mud, to be used with hate and venom for ever more in the East End. Rabble rousers like William Morris used the incident to raise the status of the dead man to that of martyr.

Warren made few friends within the force by ensuring that five new senior police posts were filled by Army Officers. Again there may have been sound reasoning behind his methods. In 1877 police found that operations against a swindle perpetrated by a gang of con men were being hampered by the fact that the criminals always seemed to know what the police intended to do. An internal investigation discovered that senior police officers were in league with the criminals, and as a result Chief Inspector Palmer, Detectives Meiklejohn and Druscovitch were tried and jailed. It was always rumoured that these were just the unlucky ones, and others escaped justice. As a result of this the Detective department underwent a complete re-organisation, becoming the Criminal Investigation Department, the CID. Any hint of cover up or scandal was ruthlessly investigated - the CID had to be Caesar's wife beyond suspicion. It is very likely that Warren being the new broom wanted to ensure that everything was now swept clean, and to aid him in this he imported his own new brooms.

Sir Charles also had problems of his own in the hierarchy of the Home Office, for the new home secretary, Henry Matthews, was described by his own private secretary as *'.... an exceedingly able lawyer, but quite incapable of dealing with men'*. Any chance of an able overseer curbing the excesses of the police Commissioner were nullified by the appointment of Matthews as Home Secretary, in effect the Commissioner's direct boss. It became a matter of honour for the two of them to be ever scoring points off the other. If Matthews said one thing, Warren supported the opposite view. This bickering in a time of normality could be highly counter-productive and frustrating, in the storm that was about to burst upon them, it would be disastrous, and end with the ignominious resignation of one of them, hounded from office by the jeers and catcalls of the public, and the unrelenting animosity of the press.

One of the first casualties of the battles between the Commissioner and the Home Secretary was James Monro, the

Assistant Police Commissioner, in charge of the CID. The basis of the trouble was that Monro had been allowed to organise a special intelligence section in Scotland Yard, which was known under different names, but was commonly called The Special Irish Branch. (Today just known as Special Branch) Because of the nature of the work carried out by this special section Monro was allowed to report directly to the Home Secretary, instead of going through the Commissioner. Monro believed that the CID should operate in the same way, and was constantly at loggerheads with Warren over this matter. Warren quite naturally insisting that all police departments should report directly to him. Monro, although beloved by all who served under him, was nonetheless not quite as popular with his equals and superiors. He often played the prima donna card, offering his resignation at the drop of a hat. Unfortunately for him he did it once too often and Warren accepted his resignation just as the most infamous series of murders the world has ever known started. His replacement was Robert Anderson, a Warrenite, who promptly went on sick leave the day before the first of the so called Jack the Ripper murders.

This bickering and childishness right at the very top of the police force led a lot of observers to comment that if Monro had been left in place and given a free hand, the killer may not have been so lucky, we will never know. Years after his retirement Monro talking to his grandson, made a very telling remark, he said:

"the Ripper was never caught, but he should have been".

As the days dragged on nothing more was learned about the brutal slaying of Martha Tabram. There were very few leads for the police to follow, those that did exist were followed as best as they could. There was a distinct lack of witnesses, there was no weapon, no suspect, and no information to be had from the PAs (police agents - snouts). The case was closed, the summer dragged on.

That changed in the early hours of the morning of the 31st August 1888.

Mary Nichols, or Polly as she was known to her friends, was a pathetic drab, old before her time, with her front teeth missing

25

and what little dignity she possessed, long since gone, she was on the streets willing to sell herself for the fourpence she required to buy herself a corner of a filthy room for the night, even so she didn't deserve the fate that awaited her.

She had been ejected from her lodgings earlier that night because she lacked the pennies required, all mates together they might have been, but it was still cash up front for your flop. Polly was a tough one, only 5 ft 2 ins, she still had the unquenchable confidence needed to survive on the mean streets of the East End. *"I'll be back. Look what a fine bonnet I've got"*, she told the lodging house keeper. What she expected to do with the hat was anyone's guess, it was too late to pop (pawn) it now. Perhaps she thought it added something to her well worn charms.

Emily Holland, a friend, spoke to Polly at about 2.30 am on the corner of Whitechapel Road and Osborne Street. The two friends talked for a few minutes, then Ellen left Polly Nichols to walk off into history.

It was just after 3.30 am when Charles Cross on his way to work walked along the narrow street known as Bucks Row. The morning was chilly and it was still very dark, and he almost missed seeing the bundle lying in the entrance to the stable yard on the South side of the street. At first he thought it might be a tarpaulin which had blown off some passing cart. As a carrier himself (he worked for Pickfords) he appreciated the value of a good canvas tarpaulin. He was half way across the street when he realised that what he was looking at was the body of a woman. He stood for a moment in the middle of the street, unsure as to what to do next. He heard the footsteps of Robert Paul, another car man on his way to work, thankful that he wouldn't have to act alone he went up to him:

"Come and look over here," he said, *"There's a woman lying on the pavement."*

They crossed to the body, which was lying on its back, its skirts raised almost to her stomach. They checked to see whether or not she was still alive, Cross thought she was dead, his companion thought he could detect faint signs of life. In the darkness neither of them could see any signs of injury, and possibly thought she had merely collapsed from natural causes.

26

In any event the finding of a body on the streets wasn't that unusual in Whitechapel, and they dare not be late for work. They attempted to pull her skirts down for modesty's sake and continued on their way. After they had gone perhaps 300 yards they met PC Mizen in Bakers Row and told him of their discovery.

Meanwhile PC John Neil patrolling East along the south side of Bucks Row had also found the body. It was approximately 3.45 am and when he had made the same patrol about thirty minutes earlier he had noticed nothing. Unlike the two car men, PC Neil had his bullseye lantern to illuminate the corpse, and by its light he could see what the two workmen could not - the woman's throat had been savagely slashed. He felt the woman's limbs and was sure he could detect some warmth in her upper arm. While he was inspecting the corpse he heard another constable, PC Thain, patrolling up Brady Street which runs at right angles to Bucks Row at its Eastern end. He called out and informed him of his find and then sent him to fetch the doctor. When PC Mizen arrived soon afterwards, Neil sent him for an ambulance (a two wheel handcart) and assistance from Bethnal Green Police station.

When he was satisfied that he had done all that could be done, Neil started to look around. He rang the bell of the building directly opposite the gateway, Essex Wharf and inquired of the manager, Walter Purkis, if he had heard anything. At that moment Sergeant Kirby arrived and knocked on the door of New Cottage, the house immediately to the East of the gateway and therefore only a few feet from where the body was lying. The houseowner, a Mrs Green, didn't hear anything either. An examination of the road revealed no cart tracks or any other clues.

Dr. Llewellyn of Whitechapel Road, arrived on the scene very quickly. He made a preliminary examination of the corpse, noted the injuries to the throat and pronounced life extinct. Dr. Llewellyn also detected some warmth still in the body, and estimated that she had been dead for about half an hour. By now the scene was beginning to attract sightseers, and Dr. Llewellyn decided that the body should be moved to the mortuary.

Whilst waiting for Inspector Spratling to examine the crime scene, Mrs Green's son decided to wash the blood away from the pavement. This unfortunately was typical of the kind of chaos that reigned at the scene of a crime. Sightseers often trampled the crime area so badly that there was very little hope of retrieving any clues that might have been left. Souvenirs were routinely spirited away from under the gaze of the police, and evidence such as patches of blood, casually destroyed. Unfortunately the janitorial efforts of Master Green, led to speculation that because there was so little blood at the scene of the crime, the body must have been murdered elsewhere and dumped in Bucks Row. Such is the stuff myths are made of.

In fact Dr. Llewellyn later stated that there was small pool of blood there when he made his examination, and PC Thain later spoke of the woman's blood saturating her clothes. It would appear that the evidence pointed to the poor woman being murdered where she was found.

If the police thought the surprises were over for the night, Inspector Spratling soon corrected that idea. After examining the crime scene he went to the mortuary in Old Montague Street to examine the body. When the clothes were removed he discovered to his horror that the abdomen had been savagely ripped open and her large intestines were protruding through the stomach wall. He immediately sent for Dr. Llewellyn to acquaint him with his find. This new, gruesome discovery guaranteed a good press coverage, as evidenced by this report in the *Star*:

*'No murder was ever more ferociously and brutally done. The knife, which must have been a large and sharp one, was jabbed into the deceased at the lower part of the abdomen and then drawn upwards not once but twice. The first cut veered to the right, slitting up the groin and passing over the left hip, but the second cut went straight upward along the centre of the body, and reaching to the breast bone. Such horrible work could only be the work of a **maniac**.'*

What the *Star* didn't report was the likely cause of death, which were the injuries to her throat. Her throat had been slashed twice, one cut being about four inches long and the other eight inches. Both carotid arteries had been parted and the tissues down to her vertebrae severed. In other words someone had cut her throat so deeply the blade of the knife had reached her spine, there was also some bruising on her face. One thing that was remarked upon was the relative absence of blood staining to the front of the body. For example if the victim had been seized from behind and her killer slit her throat from a standing position, it would be natural to expect the blood to gush out forwards and to fall down the front of the victims clothes. From the evidence however it would appear that his did not happen. All the signs pointed towards the victim lying on her back, most of the blood was found soaked into her clothes underneath her body. Even so, when the carotid artery is punctured the blood spurts, unless of course the heart has stopped beating, in other words she was already dead when her throat was cut!

Taking into account all the physical evidence of the blood stains, the complete absence of noise and the fact the victim was lying on her back when she had her throat slit (prostitutes did not lie on the floor to service their clients, especially not in the streets) and the marks of bruising about her face and neck (police reports state her face was discoloured and her tongue slightly lacerated) it becomes exceedingly likely that Polly Nichols was strangled before the knife slashed and ripped her body. This being so, once again the East End was witness to a killing where the murderer, not being content with merely taking the poor woman's life, had been driven my some unknown horror to mutilate the sad remains. Surely the *Star* had got it right, this must be the work of a maniac.

The police questioned several of the residents of Bucks Row, but could find no-one who had even heard anything suspicious. A Mrs Harriet Lilley who lived two doors away from the scene of the murder said she thought she heard something at 3.30, but couldn't be sure. A nightwatchman, Patrick Mulshaw, who was on duty some one hundred yards from the vital spot said he was standing in the street having a smoke between the hours of 2.30 and 3.30, and yet heard nothing nor did he see anyone enter or leave Bucks Row. Since it has already been shown that between those times at least three people, the two workmen and PC Neil had passed that way, perhaps not too much reliance should be placed upon his testimony, it did however serve to endow the killer with supernatural like powers.

It is of course possible that the killer was seen, but not recognised as such by the people on the spot. For example while PC Neil was inspecting the body, several slaughtermen from a nearby slaughterhouse crowded around to see what was going on. At the same time an unknown man passed along Bucks Row. Who this mystery man was no one could say, but a statement made by the watchman, Mulshaw, at the inquest poses more questions than it answers. He states:

"... another man then passed by, and said, 'Watchman, old man, I believe somebody is murdered down the street..'"

First of all if he had seen no-one pass by, how could the person be *'another man,'* surely he would just have been *'a man'*. Secondly the choice of words *'somebody is murdered'* is very strange. Why, seeing a body lying on the floor, do you automatically assume murder is involved, surely a drunk would be the logical first guess. Of course it can be argued that perhaps the stranger pressed in close to get a good look, but this is rather negated by the fact that PC Neil took the names of everyone who was in the near vicinity of the body. PC Neil did however mention seeing an unknown man pass down the street whilst he was engaged in examining the body. Again this is very strange behaviour. Imagine walking down the street at 4.00 am and seeing a knot of people surrounding a police officer examining what looks like a body on the floor. You would have to be the most un-inquisitive person in the world to walk on by, and if you were that type of person, why stop off to tell a nightwatchman that there had been a murder?

I believe that unknown man was the killer. Put yourself in his place, you have just murdered a woman and the time is about 3.35. Before you can make your escape from the scene the two workmen, Cross and Paul are coming towards you. You cannot walk west out of Bucks Row because you know that a constable (PC Neil) will shortly be entering that end of the street and you would find yourself trapped between the two men and the police officer. You do the only thing possible, and hide yourself in the shadows of the stable yard. You hear the two men discuss their find, and note their reluctance to do anything about it, soon they leave, walking west. You leave the yard and start

walking east to avoid PC Neil who must soon enter Bucks R
Keeping close into the houses, hidden in the shadows, all goes
well until you hear PC Neil find the body behind you. You press
yourself against the wall as Neil shouts to PC Thain who has
appeared at the Eastern end of Bucks Row. PC Thain is sent to
get help, you dare not continue on your way because you might
run into Thain and re-enforcement's coming in the opposite
direction. You look back, you see Neil examining the body, but
you also notice there are three other men crowding round.
Now's your chance, it takes ice cold nerve, but of that you have
plenty. You walk briskly back down Bucks Row, crossing the
street so that you will be on the north side. As you pass the scene
your heart misses a beat as PC Neil looks up and sees you, but
he has more important things to do and you pass by. You are
almost clear and the relief is incredible, you can almost taste it.
At the last moment and old man you recognise as the watchman
from Winthrop Street, asks what the fuss is, you are almost
laughing inside as you tell him and note the look of amazement
cross his face. You have been lucky, but there is no point in
pushing your luck. You climb over the wall and drop down onto
the tracks of the Metropolitan District Railway, within minutes
you are well away from the scene.

Did it happen that way, who knows? The only thing we do
know for certain is that someone walked down Bucks Row at
the relevant time, and to this day he has not been identified.

Inspector Spratling, the senior officer who made the initial
enquiries into the murder, was soon replaced by Inspector
Helson who took charge of the enquiry. This was no reflection
on Inspector Spratling's abilities, merely the fact that as the body
had been found within the jurisdiction of the newly created
J Division, Bethnal Green, it landed on Helsons desk so to speak.
However it did not go unnoticed that this was the third murder
of a prostitute in the same area within a very short space of time,
and so it was almost a forgone conclusion that Scotland Yard
would get involved. Their involvement took the portly form of
Inspector Frederick George Abberline.

Chapter Three

"It made our hair stand up in panic fear"
Sophocles 495 - 406 BC

Inspector Frederick George Abberline was born in 1843, at the time that railways were just becoming an accepted mode of transport, and died in 1929 when aircraft were beginning to span the world. During his lifetime he saw changes that we today cannot envisage, the standard weapon of the day at his birth was the muzzle loading musket, when he died aircraft flying hundreds of miles to drop bombs and defending themselves with machine guns firing 800 rounds a minute, were the norm.

During his career in law enforcement he was the officer in charge of detectives in the Jack the Ripper Murders, led the investigation into the Cleveland Street Scandal, and after his retirement from the Metropolitan Police became the European agent for Pinkertons' Detective Agency. He was above all things, a practical detective.

He was twenty when he joined the Metropolitan Police in 1863. He must have impressed his superiors with his ability because he was promoted to Sergeant in 1865, an almost unheard of rapid promotion. He was then attached to the plain clothes branch, working against the Fenian terrorists. Such work would have honed his skills in blending in to the background, but at the same time being able to operate efficiently as a police officer. He married in March 1868, but his wife tragically died of consumption two months later. He re-married in 1876, and this time his wife, Emma, outlived him by one year, dying in 1930.

In 1873 he was again promoted and took over as Inspector of H Division (Whitechapel) where he remained for 14 years. During that time he built up a phenomenal knowledge of the district and the criminals who inhabited it. In 1887 he was transferred to Scotland Yard at the special request of James Monro, the head of the CID. It was whilst he was serving at Scotland Yard that he was brought in to take charge of the detectives working on the Whitechapel Murders.

Physically his appearance gave a hint of his Dorset stock (he was born in Blandford). At 5ft 9ins, his dark brown hair, thinning on top, hazel eyes and portly build, gave him the appearance more of a bank manager or solicitor, if Abberline had been a dog, he would have been a bulldog. In the fashion of the time he had a large bushy moustache and thick side whiskers. He was soft spoken and modest, and much admired by his colleagues who described him as *'even handed and meticulous'*. His ability, judging by his extremely rapid promotion, was undoubted, and unlike a lot of policemen, did not have a military background, before he joined the police he was a clockmaker. This then was the man chosen to spearhead the attack on one of the most baffling series of crimes the world has ever known, and truth be told, it is doubtful if a more able officer could have been chosen.

He also had one other great asset to bring to the investigation, the people of Whitechapel knew and trusted him. When he left Whitechapel on transfer to Scotland Yard, the citizens of Whitechapel, together with his ex-colleagues honoured him with a presentation dinner. They gave him a gold watch inscribed *'Presented, together with a purse of gold, to Inspector F G Abberline by the inhabitants of Spitalfields, Whitechapel, etc. on his leaving the district after fourteen years' service, as a mark of their esteem and regard.'*

The investigation into this latest killing got under way. The day of the murder saw several police officers making a careful search of Bucks Row and its vicinity. PC Thain, the officer sent to get a doctor by PC Neil, personally searched Essex Wharf, The Great Eastern Railway, the East London Railway and the District Railway, but found nothing. It is interesting to note that it had obviously occurred to the police that the killer had used the railway tracks to make a speedy and effective escape from the area. Inspector Spratling returned to the scene to look for clues, and returned later with Sergeant Godley to search the railway yards, all to no avail. The care with which these searches were made can best be illustrated by the report of Inspector Helson who said that he saw a stain that *'might have been blood'* in Brady Street. Anyone who was searching that thoroughly certainly was not skimping the job.

However, what all the police failed to grasp was that searching an area that has been contaminated by passers-by was worse than useless. If for instance they had found something, how could they possibly know it was connected with the murder, valuable time would be wasted tracking down supposed clues. They had not yet learnt the lessons that their colleagues on the Continent had learned, and that is, as soon as possible cordon off the crime scene and restrict access to it. This basic lack of investigation procedure was to return to haunt them in the trouble-filled weeks ahead. Before we get too smug about the inefficiency of the police in those days to appreciate clues, just recall the Whiteway murder case of the early fifties.

The prime suspect was arrested and taken to the police station for questioning. Due to a complete lack of evidence he had to be released. Later a police officer found an axe in the very car the prisoner had been transported in, and put it in a locker in the police garage. Returning from leave and finding the axe where he had left it, he took it home and used it for chopping firewood. He had in fact been using it for several days, when he saw a notice asking the public to be on the lookout for such a weapon.

Rather shamefacedly, he went home, retrieved the weapon and handed it to the investigating officers. The suspect, a man named Whiteway, admitted the axe was his, but commented that when he last saw it the edge had been razor sharp, now it appeared as if someone had been chopping wood with it! Luckily the careless police constable hadn't completely destroyed all the forensic evidence and a conviction was secured, but as they say, if you had written that as fiction who would have believed you?

Nothing was obtained in the way of physical evidence, and nothing was obtained from door to door inquiries, the investigation looked as if it was going no-where. The police spread their net wide, asking at lodging houses, coffee stalls, pubs, in fact anywhere anyone might know something, all to no avail. The Officer who had overall charge of the case (as opposed to just the Detective branch which was Abberline's job), Chief Inspector Swanson, wrote on the 19th October that the

> '*absence of* **the motives which lead to violence** *and of any scrap of evidence either direct or circumstantial, left the police without the slightest shadow of a trace*'.

Here then was the essence of the problem, the police were just not used to dealing with what appeared to be a motiveless crime, they could not grasp the concept of a killer who kills just because he enjoys doing it. That is quite understandable, we often have difficulty in accepting that today, in 1888 this was an unheard of concept. Ask any policeman and he will say that the most difficult crime to solve is that which is done on the spur of the moment, without any discernible motive and without any logical connection.

There were a few minor grumblings about the investigation, mainly by armchair pundits armed with large doses of malt whisky and even large doses of hindsight. Why wasn't the area sealed off so that a proper search could be made for clues? Because generally that was not police practice, and besides it would have been a near impossible task to seal off the entire area as it extended to Commercial Road, one of the busiest roads in the East End. Why was the body not taken to a proper mortuary and attended to by a professional mortuary attendant instead of a pauper inmate? Because Whitechapel couldn't afford a proper mortuary, that's why the body was taken to the workhouse mortuary. Why didn't the police notice the injuries to the woman's abdomen at the scene of the crime? Because there was only one street light in the area, and the initial investigations had to be done by the light of the officers' lamps.

It is very noticeable that if all the criticisms of this nature were acted upon, new public buildings, better street lighting, disruption of trade etc. the very people who originally made them, would now be spouting forth about the terrible waste of public money etc. etc.

The truth was that what could be done was being done, unfortunately to no avail. At the end of all the questions and investigations, what were the police left with? A middle aged prostitute, probably strangled then stabbed through the throat.

Severe mutilations on her body, possibly done with a sharp, fairly long bladed knife (about 8"), the killer in all likelihood right handed. What was worrying though was that faced with yet another brutal, apparently motiveless murder, people were now beginning to wonder if the same man could be responsible for all of them, was there really a blood thirsty deranged killer stalking the streets of the East End? The effects of these crimes began to be seen in daily life, the people were edging closer to panic; local traders were noticing their trade, small though it was, beginning to drop off as more and more people from the neighbouring districts gave Whitechapel a wide berth.

Then just when the police thought they were looking at another dead end their inquiries started to turn up some very interesting information. Apparently a number of Whitechapel prostitutes walked in fear of a man who would try and extort money from them. A refusal earned them a savage beating. They only knew him by his nickname *'Leather Apron'*, so named for the leather cobblers apron he habitually wore. This is just what the police needed, a sinister suspect with a reputation for violence against prostitutes, things just didn't get any better - but they did! When the police started investigating *'Leather Apron'* whose real name was John Pizer, they found that in July 1887 he was sentenced to six months hard labour for **stabbing** a man named James Willis. On the 4th August 1888 he also appeared before Thames Magistrates charged with indecent assault, the case however, was dismissed. Here was a man the police urgently wanted to interview, but before they could close in on him the worst possible thing that could happen - happened - the press got hold of it.

The *Star* was at the forefront, in the absence of any hard facts it just filled in any gaps that the editor felt necessary. On the 5th September the edition was headlined:

'LEATHER APRON'

THE ONLY NAME LINKED WITH THE WHITECHAPEL MURDERS

A NOISELESS MIDNIGHT TERROR

The story continued in much the same vein, with one important addition. *'Leather Apron'* was Jewish!! He was described as having a *'sinister expression'* with eyes that are *'small and glittering'*. His lips were of course *'parted in a grin which is not only not reassuring, but excessively repellent.'* The fact that his victims usually ended up battered and bruised, and not cut or stabbed didn't really enter into the equation. The killer used a knife ergo *'Leather Apron'* had to have a knife and so it was reported that *'he was supposed to carry a sharp knife, the sort used to trim leather, and that he frequently menaced women with it'*.

In putting forward a Jew as a candidate for the killer the press were only pandering to the subconscious desires of the populace. The crimes were bestial, completely without motive, vicious and violent to an unimaginable degree, therefore they could not possibly be the work of an Englishman, Englishmen simply didn't do that sort of thing. After all, didn't the Lipski case prove that only Jews were capable of such atrocities?

Unfortunately the press interest in John Pizer, caused an immense amount of frustration to the police. Just when they thought they had a lead, the first real bit of information they had got hold of; the papers had broadcast it everywhere. The result was obvious. If he was the killer he had now been effectively warned off; and if he wasn't he was probably so scared of being lynched he would go to ground and become impossible to trace. In the event that's exactly what happened. When Pizer heard about the stories in the press he immediately went into hiding with his relatives, unfortunately a great deal of police effort was now directed towards finding him. Officers that could have been better used pursuing inquiries or patrolling the streets were now off on a *'wild Pizer chase'*.

For some reason of all the papers involved, The **Star** seemed to be the most virulent in its pursuit of *'Leather Apron'*, with their informants stating that they had seen the suspect recently *'crossing London Bridge as stealthily as usual'*. How you *'stealthily'* cross a busy bridge in broad daylight is not explained, but it all added to the veritable barrage of hate being directed at John Pizer. Two women reported seeing him in Commercial Street and added *'It will be necessary to look into all the shadows, as if he is there he will surely be out of sight.'* Few of the **Star's** readers could have any doubt at all that John Pizer, aka *'Leather Apron'* was definitely the Whitechapel Murderer. However for those members of the public who bothered to check any of these so called *'facts'* with the police, they would have been told that there was absolutely no evidence against Pizer at all, other than the fact that he seems to have extorted money from prostitutes. Inspector Helson wrote on the 7th September, *'there is no evidence whatever against him.'* On the 19th Abberline in his report wrote, *'there was no evidence to connect him with the murder.'*

Apart from whipping up hysteria about a possibly innocent man, the press also had the effect of alienating the police. In certain circumstances the media can be valuable allies in the fight against crime (as evidenced by our modern Crimewatch UK series) but at other times they can cause tremendous difficulties. A story that breaks too soon can give a suspect ample warning that the police are on his trail, evidence that the police want keeping confidential is blazoned all over the front pages of a hundred newspapers. The journalists used all sorts of dubious tricks to try and get a story, from plying constables with drink and bribes, to shadowing detectives during the course of their duties. Without doubt the police force was extremely *'leaky'* at that point, information that landed on senior officers desks sometimes seemed to have come via an editors.

With a coincidence that bordered on the eerie, the **East London Advertiser** wrote on the morning of Saturday 8th September,

'The murderer must creep out from somewhere, he must patrol the streets in search of his victims. Doubtless he is out by day and night. Three successful murders (the papers were beginning to link the Emma Smith, Martha Tabram and Polly Nichols murders) will have the effect of whetting his appetite still further, and unless a watch of the strictest be kept, the murder of Thursday will certainly be followed by a fourth'.

Before the edition containing those words could appear on the streets another body was found, at 6.00 am the name Hanbury Street was forever etched in the annals of horror.

Hanbury Street in 1888 was about seven hundred yards long, stretching from Commercial Street by Spitalfields market in the West, and ending where it met Bakers Row in the East. Today only about half is still left, before it can meet what was once Bakers Street it finishes, in limbo, going nowhere, a whim of the district planners.

Number 29 is only a few hundred feet from the start of the street, next door but one to the Black Swan public house. It was a three storeyed house with the unusual feature of having two front doors. One door led into the small cats meat shop run by Mrs Hardiman and her son, another part of the house was rented by a Mrs Richardson, who lived in some of the rooms, and sub-let the rest. Altogether seventeen people lived permanently at number 29, with others employed on the premises, coming and going. The other front door led into a passage way that traversed the entire house, front to back, leading to a small yard. The 1967 James Mason film, *'The London Nobody Knows'*, contains what I believe is the only film shot of a Ripper murder site, when Mr Mason enters the very yard at the back of number 29. The passageway was there to give access to all the other rooms leading off it, and so the front door was permanently left open. This fact was known to the local prostitutes who often used to take their clients out to the yard. It was in this backyard that John Davis, an elderly carman employed in Leadenhall market made a discovery that would haunt him for the rest of his life.

He had spent a restless night in the third floor front room which he shared with his wife and three sons. Awake from about 3.00 am to 5.00, he then dozed intermittently for another half an hour before he got up at 5.45 (timed by the chimes of Spitalfields church clock). After drinking a cup of tea he went out to the backyard, he got as far as the top of the two steps, the backdoor (a stable, two piece type of door, with both halves nailed together) wouldn't open flat against the wall, a fence prevented it, and it was between the steps and the fence that he saw the body of a woman.

Davis noticed a few details about the woman, her head was nearest the house, her feet pointing towards the little woodshed and her skirts had been pulled up. He didn't wait to see any more, he turned back into the passageway, went through the front door, and out into Hanbury Street. In the street he saw three workmen, Green, Kent and Holland who were waiting to start their day's work. The sight of a wild eyed elderly man bursting out into the street must have made them start, before they could say anything he called out to them, *"Men,"* he shouted, *"come here!"*

The three men followed Davis back through the passageway out to the back yard. Davis stood with Kent and Green on the top step, and Holland bravely went to examine the body. A quick look at the horrendous injuries convinced him that murder had been done, joining the other men they set off to find a policeman. Kent only made it to the front door of Number 29 and not seeing a policeman in the street he fortified himself with a brandy before searching his workshop for a piece of canvas to cover the body. When he finally returned to the crime scene a small crowd had gathered.

Inspector Joseph Chandler was on duty in Commercial Street, when several men ran up to him shouting that another murder had been done. When he arrived at the scene of the murder there was no one else in the yard, so it is quite possible that he was the first police officer to view the body. The true horror of what he found can best be summed up in his official report made later that day.

"I at once proceeded to No 29 Hanbury Street, and in the back yard found a woman lying on her back, dead, left arm resting on left breast, legs drawn up, abducted, small intestines and flap of the abdomen lying on the right side, above right shoulder, attached by a cord with the rest of the intestines inside the body; two flaps of skin from the lower part of the abdomen lying in a large quantity of blood above the left shoulder; throat cut deeply from left and back in a jagged manner right around her throat".

The murderer had gone one step further with his latest victim, instead of just slashing the abdomen as he had done with Polly Nichols, this time he had reached inside her body and disembowelled her.

The local divisional surgeon, Dr. Phillips arrived at about 6.30 to examine the body. After certifying that life was extinct,

Dr. Phillips had the body removed to the Whitechapel Mortuary. He thought the woman had been dead for about two hours, possibly longer. After the body had been taken away, Dr. Phillips and Inspector Chandler made a thorough search of the yard. The yard was only twelve feet by fifteen feet and surrounded by a wooden fence some six feet high. *The Penny Illustrated Paper* shows the fence as being about four feet high and slatted, i.e. with gaps between the fence boards, but that was wrong the fence was in good repair and close boarded, there were no gaps.

There were no obvious signs of a struggle. Some blood stains were noticed on the wall of the house about eighteen inches above the ground, just about where the head would have been. These blood stains were clear enough to be counted, Chandler noted the number as six, varying in size from a sixpenny piece (about the size of a modern 5p coin) to a *'point'* which we can take as being the size of a pin head. On the fence, again near the head's position, he also found other smears of blood about fourteen inches from the ground. Since these were the only traces of blood found it was concluded that the murder had taken place where the body was found.

Later on blood smears were found on the passage walls, leading some newspapers to speculate that the victim had been murdered elsewhere, and the body carried through the passageway and dumped in the yard. Later on however it was revealed that these smears had been caused by carrying the body out not in.

They weren't the only clues to be found in the yard. Further down the fence, approximately where the woman's foot would have been, the Inspector made a bizarre discovery. In a heap were a small piece of cloth, a comb, and another comb in a paper case. There has been much speculation about this pathetic heap of belongings, were they merely found on the ground or were they carefully arranged? Dr. Phillips thought they had been placed there deliberately. He told the inquest:

*"They had apparently been placed there in order, that is to say, **arranged there**,"*.

The *Pall Mall Gazette* asserted that

"her three rings had been wrenched off her fingers and placed at her feet".

The Daily Telegraph contributed:

"two farthings polished brightly, and, according to some, these coins had been passed off as half sovereigns upon the deceased by her murderer".

Both stories are untrue. What is true is that the woman was known to wear two brass rings and these were missing, though a mark on her finger indicated that they had been roughly removed, there was absolutely no way of telling when they had been removed. The police instigated inquiries among pawn-brokers to see if anyone had tried to pawn them thinking they were gold, something they would hardly have done if they had been found at her feet. As for passing off polished farthings as sovereigns, someone is overestimating the cost of an East End whore, most of the poor wretches were satisfied if they could raise fourpence for their somewhat dubious favours, a whole sovereign would have seen the recipient disappear into the night as fast as her legs could carry her.

However never let the facts stand in the way of a good story and even today you can still find serious authors regurgitating the *'rings and half sovereigns'* fable.

The yard still had further mysteries to reveal, near the steps a scrap of paper was found. On examination it proved to be a part of an envelope containing two pills. The envelope appeared to hold out the chance of a real clue, for on the back was embossed a crest and the words *'Sussex Regiment'*, on the front was the letter *'M'* in handwriting, and below that the letters *'Sp'*.

It appeared that the original letter had been addressed to someone whose name or title began with *'M'* and who possibly lived in *'Spitalfields'*, the postmark was London, Aug. 23, 1888. As a clue no doubt the police had seen better, but they made a determined effort to establish exactly where it had come from and who it had been addressed to.

42

A visit to the depot of the First Battalion Royal Sussex on the 14th September by Inspector Chandler, elicited the fact that the envelopes were on sale in the canteen and that most of the men used them. A check of the men's paybooks failed to match the handwriting to anyone in the battalion. A visit to the post office where the letter was posted, Lynchford Road, also established that the envelopes were on sale there to anyone who wished to buy them!

The mystery of the envelope was finally resolved when William Stevens a lodger at 35 Dorset Street, Crossinghams Lodging House, stated that he had seen the victim on the morning of her murder. She had some tablets that had been given to her by the hospital but the box she had them in had disintegrated. The woman picked up a scrap of paper off the floor and wrapped them in that.

Stevens was sure that the scrap of paper was in fact the torn envelope. Once more a promising lead went nowhere.

The yard was to reveal one more clue that for a moment gave rise to speculation that the net was finally closing in on the killer. As Chandler looked around he saw something which must have made him catch his breath - for there on the fence was a leather apron!

With the furore over the suspect known as 'Leather Apron' still fresh in his mind Chandler must have thought his luck was in, and proceeded to examine the article in company with Dr. Phillips. The apron was soaking wet, but did not seem to have been used recently. Neither of the two investigators could discern any connection between the apron and the crime. A Mrs Amelia Richardson, who rented the first two floors of 29 Hanbury Street, came forward and claimed the apron belonged to her son, John.

She had found the apron in the cellar some days before and seeing that it had started to mildew, had washed it and hung it on the fence to dry. She also claimed other objects found in the yard, an empty tin, a piece of steel and other bits and pieces belonged to her. With no physical evidence to go on, the police fell back on questioning witnesses about the victim.

The body was quickly identified by the lodging house keeper at Crossinghams, a Mr. Timothy Donovan, as one Annie Sivvey, who had lodged at Crossinghams since May of that year. In this he was only half right, her name was Annie, but not Sivvey (she adopted the name of a man she had lived with) it was Chapman. Once again it was the familiar tale of a marriage wrecked by alcohol and immorality. She supported herself by hawking matches and flowers in the streets, and when trade was slack, by prostitution. She was only 47 years old at the time of her death yet Dr. Phillips reported that

'she was undernourished, with chronic diseases of the lungs and brain membranes which would have killed her before long'.

The details of the last few days of her poor life were soon revealed.

Some time before her death Annie had got into a fight with another occupant of Crossinghams, Eliza Cooper, over a scrap of soap that Annie had borrowed and failed to return. During the fight Annie had collected some bruises on her face and chest. A friend of hers, Amelia Palmer, met Annie on Monday the 3rd September in Dorset Street, and remarked on her injuries. They talked of Annie going hop picking, a popular working holiday for the East Enders. The following day Amelia met Annie again and noted how ill she looked, she gave Annie 2d to get something to eat and admonished her not to spend it on rum, an indication perhaps that Annie liked a drop when she was in funds.

Amelia last saw her friend alive on Friday 7th September at about 5.00 pm. She looked very ill, unable to even move from where she was standing. She professed to her friend that she was going to pull herself together and get hold of some money for her lodging that night. Later that night another lodger saw her in the kitchen of Crossinghams drinking beer, so her search for funds must have been partially successful.

At about 1.30 am she was sitting in the kitchen warming herself; and eating a baked potato, when she was asked for her doss money. She confessed she hadn't got it and Donovan wasn't the sympathetic sort. She was soon out in the streets again looking for a customer who could fund her night's board.

She left Crossinghams and walked down Dorset Street heading West. She crossed over to the small alleyway known as Little Paternoster Row which led onto Brushfield Street. Her route is strange as anyone looking for custom and therefore people would naturally turn and go east into Commercial Street.

It is not known which way she went then because the next sighting of her is in the area around Spitalfields market at about 1.50 am. Mrs Elizabeth Long who lived in Church Street left home at about 5.00 am to go to Spitalfields Market. At about 5.30 am (by the clock of the Black Eagle Brewery) she was walking along Hanbury Street going west, when she noticed a man and a woman outside No 29. The woman was facing her and the man had his back to her, they were talking.

When Mrs Long (who also used the name Darrell for reasons best known to herself) gave evidence at the inquest she stated that she could positively identify the woman she had seen as being Annie Chapman. The man she described as being dark complexioned, wearing a brown deerstalker hat and possibly wearing a dark coat. His age she gave as *'over forty'*. She described his height as a little taller than the deceased, which is interesting. Annie Chapman was five feet tall, so if the man was *'a little taller'* we could be forgiven if we estimated his height at about five feet two or three. However when a short person talks to a taller person, the shorter of the two stretches to his or her full height, and the taller tends to stoop. Next time you see a couple talking, watch and see. So it is possible that if we now estimate Annie's height to be 5' 1" or 2", then the man's height could easily be 5' 5" or 6". It would also depend on the angle the couple were viewed. Mrs Long concluded by saying she thought the man had a *'shabby genteel'* look about him and looked like a *'foreigner'*.

How much credence can we give Mrs Long's statement. It is quite possible that she could recognise Annie. With dawn just breaking, there should have been enough light to see and recognise someone, providing they were facing you and you walked right past them. As for the description of the man, this is less certain. There were no street lamps outside number 29, the only two lamps on that stretch of Hanbury Street were several yards away, one on the corner of Wilkes and Hanbury, and the other on the corner of Brick Lane and Hanbury, neither positioned to shed much light on the scene.

It seems unlikely therefore that Mrs Long could have seen very much of the man, bearing in mind that she only saw his back. Her references to a dark complexion and the man being a foreigner could be a mere pandering to the popular opinion (foreigner was a euphemism for Jew). Out of her entire description I believe we can only place real credence on the reference to height (or is it a coincidence that this suspect is described as dark complexioned and the man who attacked Ada Wilson is described as *'face sunburnt'*?). She finished her testimony by saying that as she walked past them she heard the man say *"Will you?"* and heard the woman reply *"yes"*. She didn't look back and carried on her way.

When considering her testimony we must remember that sunrise on the 8th September was at 5.28 am, so anything she could have seen is open to conjecture. Not that I am suggesting for one moment that Mrs Long tried to deceive the inquest, but there is a natural trait of wanting to be involved in any noteworthy incident. It is however more than likely that if she did see Annie Chapman with a man at 5.30 am, that man was her killer.

Amelia Richardson's son John also gave evidence at the inquest. Because of some local thefts, John had been in the habit of checking the premises on a fairly regular basis. Sometime between 4.45 am and 4.50 am on the morning of the murder he was in the backyard on just such an errand. After checking that the cellar door was padlocked he sat down on the steps to cut a piece out of his boot that was rubbing his toe. Even though it was still half an hour to sunrise the night was fine and clear and in the false dawn he had enough light to accomplish his task.

What was important about this testimony was not what he did see, but what he didn't - he didn't see a body! There were three steps down to the yard, and he sat on the middle one. In that position the door, because it opens level with the top step would not obstruct his view of the body *if it had been there*. It has been suggested that he had the door held open using his left arm, because the weight of the door made it naturally want to close. However sitting on the middle step his arm would have come into contact with the door at about its mid point, meaning he only had about 18" of door blocking his view, and whereas this might have very well have hidden the top half of the body, the rest of it would have been unobstructed. The body would have been less than eighteen inches away from him and it is highly unlikely that if there was enough light to attempt a bit of DIY cobbling, it was too dark to see a body.

Another witness, Albert Cadosch a carpenter living next door to number 29, stated that at about 5.20 am he went into his backyard (in case anyone is wondering why the attraction of backyards - that's where the WC was) and could hear voices apparently coming from next door. He went back into the house unable to hear anything of any importance apart from the word 'No'. He returned to the yard a few minutes later and heard something apparently falling against the fence. Shortly afterwards he left work, passing Spitalfields Church at about 5.32 am. In examining this testimony we must ask ourselves why did he return to the yard? A plausible explanation would be that knowing of the practice of prostitutes to take their clients into the back yard of number 29, he might have returned to do a bit of eavesdropping, and hearing nothing of interest left for work. This also raises another important point, that since he didn't hear anything out of the ordinary, and since he obviously didn't place any significance on the word 'No' whatever was happening behind the fence there wasn't a violent struggle or any apparent resistance.

However when we look again at the timetable of events, discrepancies start to creep in e.g.:

5.00 approx.	John Richardson trims his boot sees nothing
5.30 approx.	Annie Chapman seen in street by Mrs Long
5.30 approx.	Noises heard in backyard by Albert Cadosch
6.30	Body examined by Dr. Phillips who estimates time of death at approximately 4.30 possibly before

Can the apparent discrepancies be explained? I believe so. Inspector Chandler neatly solved the problem by dismissing Richardson's testimony by saying that the body was there, but

Richardson didn't see it. He then attaches no importance to the testimony of Mrs Long or Albert Cadosch. Why does he do this? Because Dr. Phillips stated that the woman had been murdered at about 4.30 am and she had been killed where she had been found. For a mere policeman to have disagreed with the learned opinion of a Doctor was unheard of in those days, however let us look at how Dr. Phillips arrived at his estimate of time of death.

Nowadays any pathologist will tell you that in a lot of cases where a body is found in similar circumstances, time of death can be fairly accurately estimated to within four or five hours. After extensive tests are carried out such as analysing stomach contents and rectal temperatures this might be further narrowed down. However this is only after the most careful note is taken of conditions prevailing at the time and place of the murder. The air temperature is taken, humidity measured, dampness of the ground etc. etc. In 1888 this just didn't happen. The doctor merely guessed the external temperature and estimated how far rigor mortis had progressed. Bearing in mind that the body was eviscerated, her skirts thrown back and the air temperature was cold, it is hardly surprising that the body cooled down more rapidly than might have been first thought. In fairness to Dr. Phillips he did point this out at the inquest and admit that he could be very wrong. Bearing all this in mind, I think we can quite safely say that the true sequence of events now looks like this;

5.00 approx.	Richardson sits on step - doesn't see a body
5.30 approx.	Mrs Long sees Annie Chapman with her killer
5.30 approx.	Albert Cadosch hears the murder being committed
6.00 approx.	John Davis finds the body

We must accept that it is impossible to be any more precise than that, don't forget this is in the days before ownership of a personal watch was commonplace, and most people relied on church clocks, or any others in public places, and it is impossible to say how accurate they were.

The inquest did however reveal for the first time the extent of the injuries suffered by poor Annie Chapman, possibly because the killer had more time with the body than he had with that of Polly Nichols, the injuries were more severe. It is very probable that she was strangled first. None of the residents of number 29 heard anything, and Albert Cadosch certainly didn't hear anything that caused him alarm. Dr. Phillips was confident that he could detect signs of strangulation. Disregarding bruises probably inflicted during the fight with Eliza Cooper, he noted:

'the face was swollen, the tongue was swollen and protruding.'

Unfortunately no report or post mortem notes now exist, and no official records of the inquest survive, so we are reliant on the reports printed in the press for the details. However no less an authority than the Lancet confirms Dr. Phillips' suspicions reporting on the 29th September:

'for not only were no cries heard, but the face, lips, and hands were livid as in asphyxia, and not blanched as they would be from loss of blood.'

As for the mutilations to the body they were truly horrendous. The throat had been severed by two cuts which tracked from left to right. These were so deep as to cause Dr. Phillips to suggest that an attempt had been made to remove the head completely. As for the injuries to the abdomen, here again we can refer to the article in the Lancet of the 29th September:

"the abdomen had been entirely laid open; that the intestines, severed from their mesenteric attachments, had been lifted out of the body, and placed by the shoulder of the corpse; whilst from the pelvis the uterus and its appendages, with the upper portion of the vagina and the posterior two thirds of the bladder, had been entirely removed. No trace of these parts could be found, and the incisions were cleanly cut, avoiding the rectum, and dividing the vagina low enough to avoid injury to the cervix uteri. Obviously the work **was that of an expert - of one, at least who had such knowledge of anatomical or pathological examinations as to be enabled to secure the pelvic organs with one sweep of the knife...**"

This was bombshell stuff indeed, for here was a Doctor (the article in the Lancet was unsigned, but we have to assume it was the testimony of Dr. Phillips) who was actually suggesting that this horrible murder could have been committed by one of his own profession! He went on,

'The whole inference seems to me that the operation was performed to enable the perpetrator to obtain possession of these parts of the body. I myself could not have performed all the injuries I saw on that woman in under a quarter of an hour'.

This evidence is important, because for the first time the theory of the *'Mad Doctor'* has surfaced. This idea was to fuel more outlandish speculation that just about anything else, if your suspect did not have a medical background, he was instantly dismissed, and conversely if you found someone with a medical background why then of course he was the killer! But let us examine the statement more closely and see if we can place any other interpretation on it.

When you shoot a rabbit, the first thing you must do is to *'clean'* it, i.e. remove all the internal organs. You do this straight away for two reasons, first, if you leave it the body will stiffen, and trying to skin a board is very difficult, secondly you stop the spread of bacteria from the gut of the animal into the meat. To clean a rabbit is very simple, lay it on its back, head away from you, pierce the belly near the back legs with a very sharp pointed knife (being very careful not to cut too deep and puncture the animals gut) and slit up the body as far as you can go. Now take the animal by the neck, reach inside the cavity and draw everything inside, out. Give a sharp tug with the hand and everything comes away in one heap. Now this takes remarkably little time, I learned the skill from my father who learnt it from his father before him, and an expert can completely clean a rabbit in under half a minute.

The point is this, if I asked a vet to remove a rabbit's bladder or other organ, how long do you think he would take? His estimate of the time would be based on an entirely different set of guidelines. He would estimate the time for a careful incision, finding the required organ and delicately removing it. In other words different people view various tasks from different angles. If you asked a hunter to remove a rabbit's bladder he would simply clean it, point to the heap of entrails and inform you that

50

it was in there somewhere. A vet would be scrupulous about the whole operation.

If you look at human anatomy the same circumstances apply. If you ask a surgeon how long it would take to amputate a leg, he would probably estimate a half to three quarters of an hour. However the fastest surgical procedure in the Guinness Book of Records is just such an amputation, and that took less than a minute! The difference between the two operations is the quickest one took place in the days of *"quickest done soonest mended"* school of surgery (needless to say not many people survived this type of operation).

Bearing in mind that although the killer managed to quickly sever the uterus in one piece possibly using medical training, he seems to have made a right hash of securing the bladder, as he left a third of it in the body!

On balance then I believe we must reach the conclusion that no special skill was used here, but rather the killer reached inside the body cavity and just cut away with his knife until bits came free. Of course the inference in stating that certain body parts were missing, was that they had been removed by the killer, and their removal was the motive for the killing. There is however not one scrap of evidence to support this theory. It has been a constant source of amazement to me that several authors have apparently jumped to the same conclusion, and in some theories the theft of body parts is central to the murders. The only thing which is definite is that the bits were missing. So could there possibly be another explanation as to their whereabouts? I think so.

My wife and I were walking through the capital of a third world country in the early seventies. My wife was eating an apple and when she had finished threw the core into the gutter (which was the only method of refuse disposal available) I still swear to this day the core didn't actually hit the ground before a rat the size of a cat leapt out of a drain, seized his prize, and disappeared down the drain again. The thing about rats is that they will seize a morsel of food and take it back to their lair, a cat or a dog will eat it where he finds it.

Now if you take into account the number of slaughterhouses in the immediate vicinity of Hanbury Street, add to that the fact that the front room ground floor of number 29 was used as a cats' meat shop, wouldn't you expect that the rat population of the immediate area would be quite large? Accepting that, can't we now come to a more realistic conclusion as to what became of the missing body parts?

Dr. Phillips did have some important information as to what type of knife was used. He describes it as a very sharp weapon, with a thin blade at least six to eight inches in length. He makes the very important point that it was not a bayonet and not the type of knife commonly used by cobblers. When asked by the coroner, Mr. Baxter, whether it was the type of knife to be found in a post mortem set of knives, Phillips replied:

"The ordinary Post Mortem case does not contain such a weapon"

much to the chagrin no doubt of Baxter who for some reason seemed determined to *'pin'* this on the medical profession! It is possible that this desire arose because of what he had been told by the curator of a pathological museum.

The curator stated that some time before he had been approached by an American who had wanted to obtain specimens of a female uterus. He needed them to accompany the sale of a medical work he was writing, and he was willing to pay £20 for each specimen. However since an entire corpse could be purchased for far less than £20 this seemed unlikely, a fact borne out by a report published in the British Medical Journal which stated that the story had grown out of a misheard conversation the previous year when a well known foreign physician of the highest reputation had made inquiries at two medical schools into the possibility of obtaining anatomical specimens.

Once again it was a case of not letting the facts stand in the way of a good story. The coroner's summing up does mark another milestone, suspicion was now firmly placed on the medical profession, and the finger now pointed, however tenuously, at an American, a fact that would be remembered in the coming weeks.

What seems clear is that Annie Chapman, in an effort to scrape together her doss money met a prospective client outside 29 Hanbury Street at about 5.30 am. She took him through the passage out into the back yard, where she was seized by the throat and strangled. She might just have been able to gasp out the word 'No' before death overtook her. Her killer lowered her body to the ground, and taking out a very sharp knife slit her throat twice. He then slit open her abdomen, pulled out her intestines, sliced off a couple of pieces, threw the whole mess down on the ground and left. Because the heart had stopped, the actual amount of blood spurting out would have been minimal, evidenced by the very few traces on the fence. His hands would certainly have been covered in blood and other bodily fluids, but merely thrusting the hands into pockets would have hidden any traces. He walked out of the passage into Hanbury Street and disappeared once more.

As Hanbury Street lay within the jurisdiction of H Division, Inspector Reid, who had investigated the Tabram murder, would normally have headed the investigation. He was enjoying a well earned leave at the time of the Chapman murder, so it fell to Inspector Chandler and Sergeants Thick and Leach to make the inquiries. Superintendent West thought it would be a good idea to secure the services of Inspector Abberline, who had an almost encyclopaedic knowledge of H Division, and who was also engaged in the investigation of the Nichols murder. Abberline had already been seconded to the Chapman investigation, due to the common belief by the police that the Nichols and Chapman murders had been committed by the same man.

From the start though the police were doomed to get nowhere. They had very little to go on, a vague description of a man seen talking to the victim, who according to the medical evidence had already been killed so it couldn't have been the victim anyway! Every tangible clue had been followed up with no positive result. The envelope was a red herring and the leather apron was at the scene of the crime by pure coincidence. No one had witnessed anyone leave the murder scene, no one had noticed anyone with bloodstains on their clothes or person. Inquiries among the lodging houses had drawn a blank, and John Pizer aka. 'Leather Apron' had vanished from the face of the earth. Just when it seemed the inquiry would go nowhere, the streets started buzzing with the news; *'Leather Apron'* had been arrested!!

On the morning of Monday 10th September, Detective Sergeant Thick went to 22 Mulberry Street and arrested a Polish Jew called John Pizer, aka. Leather Apron. Depending on what version you believe he was either arrested with dignity and decorum, or had a hand clapped to his shoulder followed by the words *"You are just the man I want"*, obviously the Victorian equivalent of *'you're nicked.'* In either event Sergeant Thick acted with considerable cool cunning by strolling into Leman Street police station with his charge at his side with no more fuss and bother than if he had been delivering sandwiches. The ruse worked, and the considerable crowd that had gathered outside failed to realise that their quarry was now safely in custody.

Initial jubilation at the arrest of London's most wanted man, soon turned to dismay when it turned out that Pizer had nothing to do with the murders. He was able to account for his movements on the nights of the killings, and on checking with other witnesses, these alibis were confirmed. On the night of the Nichols murder Pizer returning to his lodgings, noticed a glow in the sky over the docks where a fierce fire was raging. He stopped to discuss this with another man, who just happened to be a police officer. So convinced were they that the infamous *'Leather Apron'* had nothing in fact to do with the murders, the police released him on the evening of the 11th September.

The following day John Pizer attended Chapman's inquest as a witness. When asked by Baxter why he had not come forward knowing as he must have done that the police were looking for him, he replied that he was afraid of being lynched by a mob if he left the safety of his relative's house in Mulberry Street. In stating this, Pizer was merely pointing out the incredible hatred that had been whipped up by the press against him. On the day of his arrest one paper printed the following doggerel,

> *'They've captured Leather Apron now, if guilty you'll agree;*
> *He'll have to meet a murderer's doom, and hang upon a tree.'*

hardly the sort of thing to inspire confidence in the general public. It is difficult to imagine today the tensions that were present in the streets at this time.

Crowds of young boys would surround some perfectly harmless person demanding money, if none were forthcoming they would start to chant *'Leather Apron, Leather Apron'* and watch with glee as the poor citizen was pursued by a howling mob. Anybody who looked even slightly suspicious was in very real danger of being lynched by the citizenry of the East End.

Walter Dew, the policeman who later arrested Crippen, tells the story of a vicious East End villain named Squibby. Squibby was extremely violent and seemed to have the aim in life of crippling as many police officers as possible, he was a genuine bad man. When Dew was given the task of arresting Squibby on the charge of throwing a half brick at a policeman he didn't relish the job. Spotting his suspect who turned and ran, they immediately gave chase. This time however the East End was awash with murderer fever, and the passers-by seeing a man being pursued by two police officers immediately took up the chase with the cry *'Murderer, murderer'*.

When Dew and his colleague finally caught up with Squibby trapped in a house, they were amazed at the change that had come over him. Normally faced with a vicious brutal villain who took at least four officers to subdue him, they were now faced with a cowering, sobbing wretch who begged the police to protect him from the mob. He had every reason to be afraid because by now the house was surrounded by a large crowd who were screaming for blood. The arrival of a large force of uniformed men saved the day, but even these reinforcements didn't stop the crowd from charging the police in an attempt to get at their prey.

Even when he was lodged in Commercial Street Police station, the mob tried to break in and lynch him, and it wasn't for many hours that they were finally persuaded to disperse. One point of interest for those of a liberal disposition towards criminals, Dew reports in his memoirs that ever since that incident, Squibby's entire attitude to the police changed, and he never failed to thank Dew for saving his life whenever they met. Perhaps the threat of a really horrible fate does alter criminals' attitudes after all!

The most worrying aspect to the whole attitude of the public was this virulent hatred that was being whipped up against the

Jews. There was absolutely no evidence to link a Jew with the murders, but what with the press campaign against *'Leather Apron'*, it was hardly surprising that crowds were now beginning to form with the express intention of attacking Jews. Once again the old story of *'No Englishman could possibly do that to the woman in Hanbury Street'* was making the rounds. Rumours of medieval Jewish blood sacrifices and ritual murders were circulating. To try and counter act this unreasoning hatred, prominent members of the Anglo Jewish community became the first to introduce methods to assist the police in capturing the murderer. The Jewish MP for Tower Hamlets, Samuel Montagu, offered a £100 reward for the killer's capture. The Mile End Vigilance Committee largely consisted of Jewish tradesmen, the president of this committee, George Lusk, was destined to make his own appearance on the gruesome stage of the Whitechapel Murders.

The police were forbidden to help in the promulgation of the reward as it was against official Home Office policy. It was explained that the old practice of the government offering rewards was discontinued when it was found that bounty hunters weren't too fussy who they turned in for the cash.

During this time the press had been having a field day. Another murder coming so soon after the Bucks Row killing was guaranteed to boost circulation. So many papers were sold that crowds collected outside newsagents in a desperate attempt to get a copy, when all available stock had been sold, they milled around outside waiting for more to be delivered. The cry was out, papers and yet more papers, the accuracy or otherwise of the contents took second place to sheer volume. Editors and sub editors swamped by the demand took less and less time checking the stories and just rushed copy to the print room. If you waited to check whether or not the reporter had got it right, your competitor might get the story first into the streets. Print and be damned was the order of the day, or to be more accurately, be damned if you don't print. Thus readers were treated to such treats as:

'London lies today under the spell of a great terror. A nameless reprobate - half beast, half man - is at large, who is daily gratifying his murderous instincts on the most miserable and defenceless classes of the

community. There can be no shadow of a doubt now that our original theory is correct, and that the Whitechapel murderer, who now has four victims to his knife, is one man, and that man a murderous maniac. The ghoul like creature who stalks through the streets of London, stalking down his victim like a Pawnee Indian, is simply drunk with blood, and he will have more.

This was the offering from the ***Star***, but even the quality press were quickly learning to play the *'popular'* card. Thus readers of the ***Telegraph*** were regaled with tales of the

'baleful prowler of the East End alleys, of beings who look like men, but are rather demons, vampires....'

Papers spoke of the strange occurrence of crowds forming at the murder sites, at the mortuary even outside police stations, mindless aimless crowds, as if they were waiting for some mystic revelation that the horror that had visited their world had returned to the hell from whence it had come.

An article in the ***Morning Post*** seemed to restore some sanity to the situation when it pointed out the fact that horrible as these crimes were, they had at least woken the rest of the country up to the appalling conditions that existed in the heart of their great nation's capital. It made the very valid point that without these murders few would have known of the conditions and even less care. Since the ***Morning Post*** was generally accepted as being the voice of the Conservative party this was strong stuff indeed. Other more radical papers, such as the ***Gazette*** made the same point in a different way when it wrote:

a murder sometimes touches a heart indifferent to less violent reminders'.

Other papers were even more barbed in their comments, what if the victims had been wealthy ladies of the West End instead of poor prostitutes of the East End? In all honesty the results would have probably been the same, but the feeling that the police weren't particularly bothered about catching the killer still remained.

The days dragged on, various sightings were followed up, supposed clues examined but all to no avail. The crowds that roamed the streets during the day evaporated during the hours of darkness. After 12.30 am the streets were practically empty apart from patrolling policemen. Sales of locks soared and some prostitutes even left Whitechapel. Gradually things began to quieten down. Groups started gathering in the Whitechapel road, laughing and joking, a sort of community whistling in the dark. Prostitutes started to walk the streets again, though the younger ones didn't tarry long after midnight, only the older, starving desperate ones carried on through the night. A brittle, artificial sort of normality had settled over the East End, with the terror still lurking just below the surface. Thus a drunk acting in any way suspiciously could still find himself surrounded by a mob trying to lynch him.

In true entrepreneurial spirit the inhabitants of Hanbury Street found a new way to make a quick copper. The occupants of the houses next door to 29 Hanbury Street were charging sightseers one penny to view the murder scene from their windows. The *Police News* decided that what was really needed was a round up of all the available facts, and so obliged with a penny pamphlet called *'The Whitechapel Murders; or The Mysteries of the East End, A Thrilling Romance'*, hardly the sort of document to be studied by serious researchers.

Annie Chapman's remains were laid to rest early in the morning of the 14th September. Her funeral was paid for by her family and all the arrangements were kept confidential to avoid crowds of morbid sightseers flocking to the cemetery. The coffin plate read: *'Annie Chapman, died Sept. 8, 1888, aged 48 years.'* The *Advertiser* noted *'All the arrangements were carried out most satisfactorily, and there was no hitch of any kind'*.

Towards the end of the month things were gradually getting back to normal, no other bodies were found and the inhabitants began to wonder if it all had been a bad dream, then on the 27th September a pebble was tossed into a pond and the ripples are still felt to this very day.

Chapter Four

"from Hell"
Return address given on Lusk letter.

The amount of mail received by the Central News Agency was quite staggering. Every day hundreds, if not thousands, of letters, reports, stories and press cuttings arrived from all over the globe. Sorting through this mountain of paper was what the agency was all about. If the story seemed fairly minor, it was taken at face value and re-distributed to all the subscribers with the appropriate by-line. If it seemed that a major story was in the offing then it was up to the head of the agency, Mr Moore, to decide whether or not to send one of the agency's own reporters.

One letter received on the 27th September at the Bridge Street office of the Central News agency was definitely going to attract the attention of the head of the agency. It was written in red ink in a neat scholarly hand. It read:

Dear Boss

I keep on hearing the police have caught me but they wont fix me just yet. I have laughed when they look so clever and talk about being on the <u>right</u> track. That joke about Leather Apron gave me real fits. I am down on whores and I shant quit ripping them till I do get buckled. Grand work the last job was. I gave the lady no time to squeal. How can they catch me now. I love my work and want to start again. You will soon hear of me with my funny little games. I saved some of the proper <u>red</u> stuff in a ginger beer bottle over the last job to write with but it went thick like glue and I cant use it. Red ink is fit enough I hope ha ha The next job I do I shall clip the ladys ears off and send to the police officers just for jolly wouldnt you. Keep this letter back till I do a bit more work then give it out straight. My knife's so nice and sharp I want to get to work right away If I get a chance. Good luck.

yours truly

Jack the Ripper

Don't mind me giving the trade name.

and underneath at right angles to the rest of the letter:

wasnt good enough to post this before I got all the red ink off my hands curse it No luck yet. They say I'm a doctor now ha ha.

There had of course been letters before this one, but what guaranteed this letter a place in history was the signature - the murderer now had a name - Jack the Ripper!!

In fairness to the head of the News Agency he did hand it over to the police after a couple of days delay during which time he assumed the letter to be a hoax. He forwarded it to Scotland Yard on the 29th September, together with a note to that effect. Their first and most important task was to try and establish whether the letter was genuine, in other words was it written by the murderer. The term of address, *'Boss'* was thought by some to be an Americanism, and with memories of the American doctor trying to purchase body parts still fresh in the minds of many police officers, a serious effort was made by the police to track down the author of the letter.

At the beginning of October the police had thousands of posters printed showing both this letter and a postcard which they had also received. These were displayed outside every police station and anywhere they could be seen by the public. The day after several papers published facsimiles of both the letter and the postcard. It was a brave attempt at trying to establish who had written them, and the public were urged to contact the police if they recognised the handwriting.

However this was to have an unfortunate side effect. By publishing an exact representation of the handwriting, any crank that wanted to send similar letters now had something to copy. In hindsight it might have been more productive to hold the handwriting samples back for use as evidence should an arrest ever be made. The other problem was that by publishing the writer's *'trade name'* it now gave something for cranks to latch on to. Publishing this was inexcusable. For if it could be established that the letter was genuine, by withholding the nom de plume it would have given an instant check on the veracity of further correspondence. It would be a similar case today if the police were to play a tape from a terrorist bomber giving the password that they use to authenticate bomb warnings.

The police made mistakes, but in fairness they had very little experience of this type of case. The murders were bad enough, motiveless, brutal and vicious, but the idea that the killer would want to write to them was totally unheard of. So we are left with the same old question, was the letter genuine or not?

When I first saw the letter two things struck me, first, there was something there that shouldn't be there, second, there was something not there that should have been.

Firstly, the letter is beautifully written, the handwriting neat and precise. The layout is perfect, with well drawn margins, salutation, date and farewell all exactly where they should be. The spelling and grammar are acceptable, punctuation reasonably accurate, and that is all wrong. The neatness, the very perfection shouldn't be there, this is a letter supposedly from a cold blooded killer, not an English teacher. It is the writing of someone who has taken a considerable amount of care and control with his writing, this isn't just fluid writing, this is copybook. It is almost as if a sixth form pupil had copied it out as part of a penmanship lesson.

Secondly, there was something missing - passion! There is absolutely no passion in the letter. Here is a man who is revelling in his achievements and how does he describe it, *'Grand work the last job was'*. No memories of the frantic, ecstatic stabbing and slashing as he wiped the whore from the face of the earth. No sentences that trail away into incomprehension, no scratched out words as mistakes are made, no blots, smudges or miss-spellings. Whatever evil force drove this man, there would have been passion in every line, exultation that he had managed to murder, not once but twice or even thrice, still they can't catch him, but how does he describe this supreme triumph over society? *'I keep on hearing the police have caught me but they won't fix me just yet'*. Compare this to other communications written by killers:

'Hello from the gutters of NYC which are filled with dog manure, vomit, stale wine, urine and blood. Hello from the sewers of NYC'.

(written by David Berkowitz, the Son of Sam murderer) or how about this from William Heirens

'For heavens sake catch me Before I kill more I cannot control myself'

in both these extracts there is a power, a passion that is missing from the Jack the Ripper letter.

Another pointer that leads me to suppose this is a fake is the reference to trying to save *'some of the proper red stuff in a ginger beer bottle'* meaning the killer tried to save some blood from Annie Chapman in a ginger beer bottle. This is ridiculous, how on earth was he hoping to direct a jet of blood with sufficient accuracy to fill a bottle? This idea is clearly a non starter for practical reasons, (it would mean a killer stalking his pray armed with a razor sharp knife and a ginger beer bottle) but makes an excellent horror story.

There is also the strange choice of addressee. The majority of killers who feel the need to advertise their crimes (or as they see it their cleverness) by writing do so by writing directly to the person or persons they see as their direct *'enemy'*. For instance when Jimmy Breslin a reporter on the New York Daily News wrote about the Son of Sam murders, Berkowitz wrote directly to **him**. When Captain of Detectives Joseph Borrelli was interviewed about the killings, a letter addressed to him personally was found at the scene of the next murders. When Eliot Ness of the Untouchables fame was pursuing a serial killer he received postcards from the man he was hunting. Heirens wrote his message in lipstick on a wall at the scene of one of his murders, knowing that the police would be the first to see it.

If the Jack the Ripper letter had been addressed to Inspector Abberline, or Commissioner Warren it might have made sense, but it seemed totally pointless to send the letter to the head of a news agency unless whoever wrote the letter wanted to be sure that it would get the widest possible distribution in the shortest possible time, in which case a news agency is tailor made. In later years senior police officers thought so as well. Anderson and Swanson writing over thirty years later stated that the letter was written by a journalist who wanted to keep the story going. The journalist has been variously identified as one Mr. Best, who supposedly confessed to writing the letters in the 1930s, a Tom Bullen who worked for the Central News Agency, or a Mr. Charles Moore, his boss.

I don't believe that the letter did come from the killer, there are just too many things which don't fit. It is possible that it was written by a journalist, although I would have expected a more blood curdling effort from a member of the press. My personal guess is that a bored ledger clerk (red ink wasn't the sort of thing that just anyone had a supply of lying about the place) decided to spend an interesting afternoon, if it was, then by the invention of the name he has assured himself a place in history!

Apart from mocking letters the police were also getting a hard time from more conventional forms of the written word - the press. The apparent inability of the police to apprehend the culprit was generating a stream of vitriol in the papers. What was worrying about this was some of the most strident of attacks were launched in the very papers that might have been considered very pro establishment. The *East London Advertiser* categorised Commissioner Warren, as a

'martinet of apparently a somewhat inefficient type, who by imbuing his own sense of militarism into the police, had drastically reduced their effectiveness, the detectives seemed unable to detect, and the beat bobby seemed helpless to protect the public.'

The attack continued in the *Daily Telegraph* which spoke of Sir Charles as an

"'admirable commandant of gendarmerie' which nonetheless left the CID without an effective head of operations at this most critical time and had reduced it to an 'utterly hopeless and worthless condition'".

Unfortunately the police lacked a strong champion to fight their corner. The Home Secretary, Charles Matthews, was hardly the man to support the Commissioner, as they were constantly at loggerheads over one thing or another. Charles Matthews did manage to distinguish himself in one field however - unpopularity, apparently none of the political parties liked him, not even his own! His answer to the criticism of the press and the public was to try and resign, something that Lord Salisbury wouldn't let him do. It hardly boosts your morale to know that when things start to get tough, your head of departments only answer seems to be to run away!

The constant sniping at the police did nothing to improve relations between them, and it is arguable that the failure to work together hampered the investigations to an unnecessary degree. When journalists were (quite rightly) refused immediate access to the murder site at 29 Hanbury Street, the *Daily News* commented,

'If the London police were as capable in other respects as they are in holding their peace, no criminal in the realm would pass undetected.'

On the other hand the police complained that the press did hamper their investigations, detectives were followed by reporters trying to scoop a story, witnesses inexpertly questioned by reporters instead of police thus muddying the waters even further. The situation deteriorated so much that in the end Warren was forced to bring the situation to the attention of the Home Secretary. When he called on the Home Secretary, neither he nor his private secretary were available to see him, but another official noted his comments:

'He remarked to me very strongly upon the great hindrance, which is caused to the efforts of the Police, by the activity of Agents of Press Associations and newspapers. These 'touts' follow the detectives wherever they go in search of clues, and then having interviewed persons, with whom the police have had conversation and from whom inquiries have been made, compile the paragraphs which fill the papers. This practice impedes the usefulness of detective investigation and moreover keeps alive the excitement in the district and elsewhere.'

Even this did not go far enough. The police force was full of leaks, the pay collected by a constable was not so great that he felt able to turn down the odd shilling offered over a pint of beer for a bit of inside information. This practice brought forth its own problems, for if the constable didn't have anything worth repeating, why then make something up as long as the reporters were happy. Most of them were quite happy to print any story no matter how wild and unlikely. However since printing alarmist details only stirred up the public, other items could have serious repercussions for the investigation.

The *'Leather Apron'* debacle is a point in case, if the press hadn't gone overboard on their condemnation of *'Leather Apron'*, it is likely that John Pizer could have been brought in for questioning and subsequently eliminated much sooner. Instead he was forced to take refuge, and was only discovered after a considerable amount of police resources had been expended looking for him. It was no wonder then that the police were very tight lipped about anything they discovered, and this in itself caused problems, as a properly managed media can be of inestimable help in the solving of crime, our current Crimewatch series is an excellent example.

It is a fact that none of the papers seem to give credit where it was due, and acknowledge that the police were doing all they could. Certainly mistakes were made, they always will be, but on the whole there wasn't a lot more that could be done. Abberline and his men were beginning to realise that the killer was either being incredibly clever or incredibly lucky. The slim file of facts they had mustered about him so far revealed:

He generally struck in the early hours of the morning, using darkness to his advantage.

He chose the scenes of his attacks very carefully.

No one had ever witnessed an actual attack, and there were only vague reports of sightings of him.

He killed in a brutally efficient way. His method of murder was apparently strangulation. This ensured the killing was carried out quickly and quietly, evidenced by the fact that despite people being within a matter of feet from the killings, no one heard anything. Strangulation also ensured that the amount of blood spurting out and possibly marking the killer would be kept to minimum.

He knew the area extremely well, his ability to disappear completely was causing problems to the investigation.

It is very likely that he lived not far from the scenes of his crimes, this also enabled him to get off the streets quickly thus avoiding any cordons thrown round the area in an attempt to trap the killer.

He left no weapon and no clues at the scene.

It was extremely likely he was a local man. Given the generally nervous and excitable state of the public at large, a stranger would attract immediate attention. For the same reason it was also deduced that he made his way on foot, a carriage would be very noticeable, in much the same way as a Ferrari driving round an area like Brixton would today.

Now given that was all the information the police had, and that largely by deduction rather than hard fact, a modern police force would have extreme difficulty in doing any better; even with all the advances of modern technology. A brief look at the Yorkshire Ripper, Sutcliffe, will confirm this. Sutcliffes's reign of terror lasted several years. During that time some of his victims had actually recovered and were able to give police descriptions of their assailants. The police had physical evidence in the form of a five pound note found on one of the victims and traced back to the firm where Sutcliffe worked. During one attack he came close to being caught when the boyfriend of his victim came to her aid and drove him away. Despite all of this, and the most intensive police operation this country has ever seen he still evaded capture. His arrest finally was a pure accident. In the back of his car with another prostitute, Sutcliffe was questioned by two police officers during a routine sweep of the area. It was only the fact that the car he was in had false number plates that led to his arrest. It is frightening to think that if he had not fitted false number plates, his final toll could have been much higher.

One interesting point of this investigation was that like the Whitechapel murders, police in the Sutcliffe case received both letters and tapes supposedly from the killer. After a great deal of police time and effort was wasted on these, it was finally revealed that they were fake, recorded by an ex-police officer who had a grudge against Chief Inspector George Oldfield. (Interestingly Robert Ressler, the FBI profiler, had already denounced these tapes as fakes, but was ignored by the Yorkshire police who resented anyone else getting in on what they saw as exclusively their act).

One thing that was suggested to Abberline's men at this time was the use of tracker dogs. This wasn't as silly as may at first appear. Bloodhounds had been used in a murder in Lancashire in the 1870s. Mr. Ashforth, the dog handler involved in that case, wrote to Sir Charles Warren offering him the use of the dogs for the present case, but after Dr. Phillips had been consulted about the efficacy of using them, the offer was politely refused.

The police did have a number of leads to follow, and a great many arrests were made, but as always the suspects were always eliminated purely through lack of any evidence that would link them in any way to the murders. One very promising suspect, a butcher called Isenschmid had actually been detained in Colney Hatch Lunatic Asylum the previous year, but was eventually cleared. His wife in answer to questioning said *"I don't think my husband would injure anyone but me!"* A touching testament to his innocence. Undoubtedly the police were under great pressure to secure a conviction in this case, even Abberline spoke of a need to *"allay the strong public feeling that exists."* The satirical magazine **Punch** summed up the situation in its *'Detectives Diary'*:

Monday - Papers full of the latest tragedy. One of them suggested that the assassin was a man who wore a blue coat. Arrested three blue - coat wearers on suspicion.

Tuesday - The blue coats proved innocent. Released. Evening journal threw out a hint that the deed might have been perpetrated by a soldier. Found a small drummer boy drunk and incapable. Conveyed him to the station house.

Wednesday - Drummer boy released. Letter of anonymous correspondent to daily journal declaring that the outrage could only have been committed by a sailor. Decoyed Petty Officer of Penny Steamboat on shore, and suddenly arrested him.

and so on throughout the week. At this point the police were still placing their bets on the killer being some form of lunatic. Anyone who had any connection with insanity, or who had actually been committed was therefore attracting a great deal of attention. Then again anyone who had any anatomical knowledge, however slight was also put under the spotlight. A lunatic medical student or butcher would possibly rate a top score in their hunt for the elusive killer, and bearing in mind the popular perception that the killer must be foreign, a Jewish lunatic medical student or butcher would definitely get top billing.

As the month wore on, and the nights were closing in, the East End gradually began to return to normal. Passers-by were questioned about the killer and gave their opinion that he had left the district. Then on the night of the 29th to 30th September, Jack came back with a vengeance - as noted on a blood smeared post card, *'double event this time!'*

Elizabeth Stride was born Elisabeth Gustafsdotter on 27th November 1843 near Gothenburg, Sweden, she died in Berner Street on the 29th September 1888. In between these two dates she had led an interesting, if somewhat uncomfortable life. She came to London in 1866, and three years later married John Stride, a coffee house keeper. At some point her marriage broke down, she threw herself on the mercy of the parish in an attempt to get assistance, telling the board of guardians that her husband had been drowned in the Princess Alice tragedy. (The pleasure steamer Princess Alice was rammed by a barge in the Thames in 1878 and sank drowning between 600 and 700 people) This however was not true but merely a ploy to explain her single status.

For the next few years she moved between lodging houses, supporting herself as best as she could, no doubt with an occasional foray into prostitution. In 1885 she met a dock labourer by the name of Michael Kidney, and she stayed with him for the last three years of her life, though occasionally living apart. The reasons for these separations are not clear, according to Kidney it was because of her drinking, but according to Liz's friends it was because of his uncontrollable temper when drunk.

She moved to 36 Devonshire Street with Michael Kidney and apparently set up home with him there, but on the 27 September she turned up at the lodging house at 32 Flower and Dean Street saying that she had quarrelled with her partner and had moved out. Elizabeth Tanner, the deputy at 32 Flower and Dean, spoke of her as a quiet, sober, woman. This may have been perfectly true, but there is no doubt that Long Liz, as she was known on account of her height, was a different person when she did succumb to the demon drink. She frequently appeared before the local magistrates on charges of drunk and disorderly conduct.

She did however seem to have made an impression on her fellow lodgers. The watchman spoke kindly of her saying,

"when she could get no work she had to do the best she could for her living, but a neater and cleaner woman never lived".

She earned a precarious living sewing and charring, but when that was not available, she resorted to prostitution.

On the last day of her life, she had managed to get a cleaning job which paid her sixpence. Mrs Tanner met Long Liz in the Queens Head in Commercial Street and they had a drink together, afterwards they walked back to their lodgings at 32 Flower and Dean Street. Long Liz was in the kitchen between six and seven, preparing to go out for the evening. She was dressed in her best clothes and asked a fellow lodger if she might borrow his clothes brush. She asked a woman who worked there to look after a large piece of green velvet for her, and showed her the sixpence she had earned that day, although she did not tell her where she had got it.

Just after 11.00 pm two labourers named Best and Gardner, went for a drink in the Bricklayers Arms in Settle Street, just off Commercial Road. As they were entering a man and a woman, whom they later identified as Long Liz, came out. The couple stood in the doorway for a few moments cuddling and kissing obviously oblivious to the spectators. The two men started to barrack the unfortunate lovers, but just to show there was no hard feelings, invited them back into the pub for a drink. The couple, obviously embarrassed walked off in the direction of Commercial Road. The man was described as wearing a morning suit and coat and a bowler hat. The man was described as short and with a dark moustache.

At approximately 11.45 pm a William Marshall was standing outside his house at 64 Berner Street, when he noticed a man and a woman talking together. They were kissing and carrying on and he overheard the man say in a quiet, educated voice, *"You would say anything except your prayers"*. He later identified the woman as Liz Stride and described the man as *'middle aged, about 5ft 6ins, decently dressed in black cutaway coat and trousers with a clerky appearance. The man wore a round cap with a small peak.'* Unfortunately he didn't get a good look at the man's face so was unable to say whether he had a beard or moustache.

There was another sighting which was reported by a man called Matthew Packer, a shop keeper who had a small shop in Berner Street. Unfortunately Mr. Packer altered his story so often that little credence can be placed on it. His first statement said that he saw Liz Stride and a man at about midnight, but later on alters this to 11.00. There is possibly no intention to deliberately deceive, but more likely an altering of the story to please whoever was listening to it, because of this Matthew Packer's tale should be treated with caution.

The next sighting was made by PC William Smith, who saw Long Liz with a man at about 12.30 am. He describes them as being near the Infants school, talking to each other. The man is described as being of respectable appearance, about twenty eight years old, five feet six or seven, with a small dark moustache. He wore a dark deerstalker type hat, white collar and tie and a black cutaway coat. He did notice one other thing, the woman was wearing a red rose in her coat.

It was almost 12.45 when Israel Schwartz turned into Berner Street from Commercial Road. He lived in Ellen Street which ran West to East across the bottom of Berner Street. As he approached the gateway to Dutfields yard (which was on the West side of the street) he noticed a man walking in front of him a little unsteadily, as if he were the worse for drink. He saw the man stop and speak to a woman who was standing in the gateway. The man then grabbed hold of the woman and tried to pull her into the street, when he failed to do this he threw her to the ground, the woman didn't appear to be too frightened by this behaviour, because although she screamed three times, its wasn't very loud and failed to attract any attention.

Not wanting to get involved in what seemed to be a domestic argument, Schwartz crossed to the opposite side of the road. On the western corner of Berner and Fairclough streets was a public house, and Schwartz states that a man came out of this pub and stood for a minute lighting his pipe. The man who was struggling with the woman called out, apparently to the pipe smoker, 'Lipski'. Schwartz was beginning to feel very uncomfortable about the situation and moved away rapidly, only to find himself being pursued by the pipe smoker. Seeing this he started to run, still however, with the pipe man in pursuit. After a short distance the man stopped chasing Schwartz, much to his undoubted relief.

Schwartz could not say with any certainty if the two men knew each other, or even if they were working in concert. It is obvious he was distinctly unhappy with the whole situation and decided to leave the area as soon as possible. He described the man struggling with the woman as being, about thirty, height 5ft 5ins, complexion fair, hair dark, small brown moustache, full face, broad shouldered; and wearing a dark jacket and trousers and a black cap with a peak. The pipe smoker was described as being about thirty five, height 5ft 11ins, complexion fresh, light brown hair with a brown moustache. He was dressed in a dark overcoat and wore a black hard felt hat.

However before getting too excited about this seemingly important evidence it is as well to remember the following. Schwartz couldn't speak English, both the statement he gave to police and subsequent interviews he gave to newspapers were through an interpreter. His state of mind at the time of the incident can best be described as agitated, this is borne out by his unwillingness to *'get involved'* in anything, and his obvious desire to quit the scene as quickly as possible. Under these circumstances how much reliance can be placed on his descriptions of the men?

Consider the following facts. The nearest lamp was on the corner of Berner and Fairclough Street. It was about forty feet from the public house and about ninety feet from the scene of the struggle, *and on the opposite side of the road*. The weather that night had been cloudy with rain, although it did start to clear after midnight. Taking all these variables into account I think that it is unlikely that Schwartz could have given so detailed a description of both men. Don't forget he was unwilling to get involved, so it is highly unlikely that he would have stared for any length of time at either of the men, he actually crossed the road to avoid getting entangled in what he assumed to be a domestic dispute, and when the second man turned to follow him ran off.

I am sure we have all been in a similar situation. The drunk at the bar who becomes more aggressive and belligerent. What do we all do? Huddle over our drinks and turn away from him, hoping we won't be noticed. The last thing we do is to stare at him long enough to be able to furnish the police with a detailed description of him later. So why did Schwartz make such a statement, was he deliberately trying to mislead the police? I think the answer is far more likely to be a willingness to please whoever is asking the questions. Schwartz had recently come from a country where if the police asked a question you had better have an answer, the validity of the answer wasn't that important, but woe betide you if you sat there and said you didn't see anything. Imagine the state he must have been in, going to the police station to make his statement, I think nervous would not adequately describe it. Notice he has answered all the questions: complexion? answer fair, moustache? answer brown, and so on. If you look closely at the statement you start to see cracks appear.

He states the man was wearing a peaked cap, and yet describes his hair as dark. How much hair could he reasonably be expected to see, on a wet cloudy night, ninety feet from the dismal illumination from a gas lamp (assuming it was working) at one in the morning? The same reasoning applies to the second man, he too was wearing a hat but apparently showing enough hair to describe it as light brown, and this was whilst Schwartz was supposedly fleeing from him.

The struggling man was presumably in animated conversation with the woman, in which case he would be facing her, and with his back towards Schwartz. Where then do the details of the man's moustache, complexion, type of face and style of cap come from?

Another minor point is that the two descriptions are different in every detail. Let me explain, if you are questioning someone about two people, and the person you are questioning is going to fabricate his story, it is quite often the case that the descriptions will be very dissimilar. The liar always thinks you will believe him if he doesn't repeat himself. Try it yourself, ask a friend to invent descriptions of two people, and its a fair bet all the points will differ. In real life of course there are many points about people which do coincide. Listen to a genuine description on Crimewatch, it is peppered with average this and average that.

Compare this description with that of Marshall's. Now Marshall wasn't in any way agitated, in fact he was perfectly relaxed, in his own words *'loafing in his doorway'*. He saw the couple three doors away, where they stood talking, and he watched them for about ten minutes. Then they walked past him *in the middle of the road*, so they were about ten feet away from him at the closest point and walking towards a lamp about twenty feet away. Yet despite all this, the relaxed nature of the witness, the time he had been watching them, the nearness of the pair to the witness and the fact that the lamp was only twenty feet away at one point, Marshall still maintains he didn't get a good look at the man's face, and couldn't possibly say whether or not the man had any facial hair!

There is one final incident that points towards Schwartz's willingness to say whatever the questioner wanted to hear. The statement made to the police is as already mentioned, however when subsequent to this he was tracked down by reporters (the police did not release Schwartz's name or give any clue to his identity. He didn't even give evidence at the inquest) a slightly different version appears in the *Star* on October 1st, the day after the murder. Incidentally this is a perfect example of how the papers did get hold of any information the police had, and had no hesitation in publishing it in the interests of a good story. In the *Star's* version the second man no longer had a pipe in his hand but a knife! One can almost hear the reporter getting all worked up at hearing the tale, but then being quite deflated upon hearing the second man was only armed with a pipe. *"Are you sure it wasn't a knife"* he asks, *"Ah yes"* Schwartz replies *"now you come to mention it, I believe it was a knife".*

It is also very noticeable that the descriptions of the two men have now changed. The struggling man is now described as rather stout, instead of broad shouldered, brown moustache instead of a small brown moustache and is now wearing a felt (trilby type) hat instead of a peaked cap. The details for the second man have now completely disappeared, he is now taller than the other man but not stout, and his moustache has now changed colour to red from brown. No mention of complexion, hat, clothes and the pipe has changed to a knife.

No, once you start to examine the statement of Schwartz it just doesn't ring true. I honestly believe he didn't mean to deceive anyone, he just agreed with whatever was put to him, he said whatever he thought they wanted to hear.

The next incident happened at about 1.00 am, when Louis Diemschutz, a market trader and steward of The International

Working Mens Educational Club, was returning after a day selling cheap costume jewellery. He lived on the Club premises with his wife, and wanted to deposit his unsold stock before stabling his pony in Cable Street. As he turned into Dutfields yard, which was adjoining the Club building, his pony shied at something on the ground.

It was too dark to see properly, but he could just about make out an object lying on the ground. He prodded it with his whip and found it yielded slightly. Getting down from his cart and using a match he could just make out the shape of a woman. For some reason he got it into his head that the woman was his wife, and he ran into the club to get help. However, once inside he found his wife safe and sound, so getting a candle and some reinforcements he returned to the yard.

Even before they reached the body they could see a large pool of blood. Mrs Diemschutz even went so far as to say that it was still flowing, and later events proved her correct. The body was lying facing the wall, on its side. Diemschutz and his companion wisely made no attempt to disturb the body (the large gash in the woman's throat told them that she was beyond help), but immediately set off to get help. They ran down into Fairclough Street yelling for the police, running as far as Grove Street. Finding no one they retraced their steps. When they reached the Beehive Tavern, on the corner of Christian and Fairclough, they were stopped by Edward Spooner who was standing outside with a woman, and asked what all the fuss was about. Upon being told that a woman's body had been found in Dutfields yard, Spooner returned with them to the scene of the crime.

When they returned they found a small crowd had gathered around the body. Spooner bent down and examined the woman by the light of a match. He noticed the woman's face was still warm and that blood was still flowing from a large gash in her throat. Morris Eagle, one of the club members attracted by the commotion in the yard went down to investigate. The sight of all the blood upset him, and he turned away to fetch the police. Whereas Diemschutz had turned South to Fairclough, Morris Eagle turned North to Commercial Road, the main highway. PC Lamb was walking his beat with another constable, when they were accosted by two men running towards him and shouting. At the time PC Lamb was in between Christian and Batty Streets on the Commercial Road.

When they reached the body, PC Lamb displayed obvious detective qualities by asking all the people to keep back, otherwise as he told the inquest *"they might have their clothes soiled with blood and thus get into trouble"*. Kneeling down he noted that the woman's face was still warm, and that the blood which had flowed onto the ground had not yet congealed. He sent his colleague for a doctor and the athletic Morris Eagle to Leman Street police station about four hundred yards away.

The nearest doctor, Dr. Blackwell, was at 100 Commercial Road, and it wasn't long before the constable was knocking at his door. The doctor was asleep and whilst he was dressing his assistant, Edward Johnston, accompanied the officer back to Dutfields yard. The first thing that Dr. Blackwell did when he arrived at the scene was to consult his watch, it showed 1.16 am.

By the light of the policemen's bullseye lanterns he made his examination. Working out the times taken to do all the various running around, fetching people etc., and working back from Dr. Blackwell's arrival time of 1.16 am, it is very probable that Diemschutz is fairly accurate in his estimation of the time, if anything it may have been about 12.55 am rather than 1.00 am when he drove into the yard.

Dr. Blackwell's examination was very thorough and amongst the things he found were a small packet of cachous (little breath fresheners like Tic Tacs) in her left hand. Around her neck was a scarf which had been pulled extremely tight, the bottom edge of which was slightly frayed, as if it had been cut with a knife. The fatal wound started on the left side, just nicking the carotid artery, passed through the windpipe, and ended on the right side of her neck, without severing the arteries. The woman's clothing had not been disturbed. Within a few minutes, Dr. Phillips, the divisional police surgeon arrived, and commenced his own examination. By this time Chief Inspector West and Inspector Pinhorn had taken charge of the body.

With one minor exception (concerning the packet of cachous) the two doctors agreed in their findings. The time of death was estimated as between 12.36 am and 12.56 am, with a definite leaning towards later rather than earlier. If you consider that it was a chilly night with a minimum of 6 degrees centigrade, and that the body was still warm when Dr. Blackwell arrived at 1.16 am, a later rather than earlier estimation does make more sense.

When Edward Johnston (Blackwell's assistant) had arrived on the scene, PC Lamb had the large double gates to the yard closed, and posted a man on the small wicket gate. He then started a search of the club premises, checking the hands and clothes of the club members and searching rooms. He next checked the few cottages at the end of the yard, but found nothing of importance. It is interesting to note that in this case where the crime scene had been quickly attended by a police officer of above average ability, more care had been taken to preserve any evidence that might exist. The yard had been sealed off and a man posted at the gate to stop unauthorised persons gaining access. Care had been taken to avoid innocent bystanders being contaminated by blood. The police surgeon and the nearest doctor had been summoned and preliminary investigations had commenced.

All that could have been done was done, and still the killer had escaped. Because of the sealed off nature of the crime scene the body wasn't moved until 5.30 am, but by then the horrors of the night had multiplied, at 1.44 am in Mitre Square, a mere quarter of a mile away, another body had been found, Jack the Ripper had murdered twice in one night - or had he?

Serial killings bring with them their own special problems. For a start the first killing is very rarely spotted as being the start of a series, and the police are very often caught unawares when the next body turns up. The most worrying aspect about investigating a serial killer is that the inquiries gather their own momentum and all is swept before it. For instance, if a body is found with similarities with other bodies in the series it is all too easy to sweep it up in the net and count it as one of *'theirs'*. This can prove disastrous for the police, for if their suspect can prove he had nothing to do with the spurious killing, he is generally discarded. It has almost become a hallmark of serial killer investigations that the culprit will have been interviewed, and might at one time been a suspect. At one time the police investigating the Yorkshire Ripper, Peter Sutcliffe, had assumed that Jean Harrison was one of his victims, based on the facts that she was a prostitute and had been murdered in Preston. They overlooked completely the fact that she had been raped (which none of the others were). It is possible that because Sutcliffe was able to provide an unshakeable alibi for the Harrison murder, and in spite of being interviewed on several occasions, he was always released.

Another equally worrying feature is that if a body is discovered without the hallmarks of the killer they are seeking, a lot of the time it is discounted as being one of the series. David Berkowitz, the Son of Sam killer, started attacking his victims with a knife. His first victim screamed so loudly that he ran away. With the second victim he was determined to *'finish the job'* but despite badly stabbing and puncturing a lung, this girl also survived. Convinced then that a knife wasn't an efficient killing weapon he changed to a large calibre revolver, but even this allowed some of his victims to live, so he further refined his murderous ways by adopting a two handed grip on his pistol to ensure maximum lethality. The police never linked the botched knife attacks with the ruthlessly efficient murders later committed. What they failed to realise was that the killer was trying out various weapons to find the most lethal, refining his search even down to adopting a different grip.

Other circumstances seem to conspire against the police in such cases. Because of the widely publicised nature of the crimes, you often get copy-cat crimes. Murders that are committed to resemble as closely as possible the real serial killers' crimes. The publicity also attracts a large following of cranks. Possibly the most infamous being the ex police officer who taunted the investigators with letters and tapes supposedly from the Yorkshire Ripper. How much police time and effort was wasted on these bogus items is impossible to calculate, is it also outside the realms of possibility that without them Sutcliffe may have been caught earlier and lives saved?

We must bear all these things in mind when we look at the Jack the Ripper murders, for by the time Stride's body was found the police and the public had stopped asking the most important question in any murder investigation - **WHO DID THIS ?** - they thought they knew.

If we were to look at the Stride killing in isolation, discounting the other killings entirely, what path would the police follow. First of all let us look at the situation. Liz Stride is living with a man, who when drunk becomes violent and beats her up. She has twice had him in court for this offence, once she failed to turn up and the charges were dropped, the second time she gave evidence and he was gaoled. A few days before her murder she apparently has another violent quarrel with Michael Kidney (he denied this) and moved out to lodgings of her own. On the night of her murder she is in high spirits and is apparently getting ready to go out on a date. She pays extra attention to her appearance (asking a fellow lodger for a clothes-brush) and leaves a piece of velvet (possibly a gift from her intended date) with a friend. She has money in her pocket and is looking forward to a good time.

Presumably before being seen by the two labourers, Best and Gardner, she had something to eat (the autopsy showed the remains of a meal) possibly with the man who was accompanying her, described as about 5ft 6ins, decently dressed in dark jacket and trousers. About fifty minutes later William Marshall saw her with a man who fits this description, and at 12.30 am PC Smith sees her in the company of a man who again fits this description, apart from his age which the officer believes to be about 28, and the others place at about middle aged (whatever that means). At this time he also notices Liz Stride is now wearing a flower pinned to her dress. All witnesses agree that the couple seemed very much *'wrapped up'* in each other, with lots of kissing and cuddling.

Given the time scale, and the fact that all the descriptions are very close, it is a fair assumption that Liz Stride was with the same man throughout the evening. Following on from this it is also acceptable to assume this man was her *'date'* and not a client. Prostitutes do not waste time canoodling and talking to their clients, they meet, the business is done, and off they go again. Everything points to this conclusion, the corsage pinned to the dress, the cachous to sweeten the breath, the time spent walking and talking, kissing and cuddling. Who is this man? The simple answer is we do not know, but we can take an educated guess.

Liz Stride as we know worked as a charlady when she could. Is it outside the realms of possibility that the man she was with was someone she met whilst charring? We are told that most of her work was done for the Jews, and most of the Jews in the Whitechapel area had some connection with the clothing or footwear trade. What better present to give your lady love than an offcut of material. We know that on her return from the Queens Head with Mrs Tanner at 6.30 p.m. on the Saturday evening she gave Catherine Lane a piece of green velvet to look after. This indicates that she obtained the material whilst she was out, if she already had it in her lodgings, why take it out of its hiding place? She then got ready to go out, but this time taking extra care over her appearance. Could we now write a timetable of events for that evening, filling in the gaps with informed guesswork?

Previous to 6.30 pm Liz meets boyfriend (married?) and tells him she has funds for a night out. Boyfriend gives her a piece of material as a present and arranges to meet her later that night. Liz goes to Queens Head for a drink, meets Mrs Tanner there and together they return to the lodgings, arriving at about 6.30 pm.

6.30 pm to 7.00 pm Liz gets ready to go out, asking to borrow a clothesbrush to spruce herself up. Before she leaves she gives her piece of velvet to a friend to look after, knowing that it is likely to be stolen if left unattended. She meets boyfriend and together they go for a meal.

11 .00 pm Liz and boyfriend are seen by Best and Gardner, kissing and cuddling at the Bricklayers Arms, Settle Street.

11.45 pm Liz and boyfriend seen by William Marshall in Berner Street, talking, kissing and generally carrying on. They walk off at about 11.55 pm.

12.30 am Liz and boyfriend seen by PC Smith who notices that she now has a flower on her dress. It is possible that at about this time they cross the road to go to the pub on the corner of Berner and Fairclough. Whilst in the pub she hears the very news she doesn't want to hear, her erstwhile ex-lover Michael Kidney has found out about the new man in her life and is furious. We know that Kidney was violently jealous of Liz Stride, before when he thought she had another man he beat her and padlocked her in their lodgings. *Liz parts from her boyfriend and starts to hurry home, wishing to avoid having her (married?) boyfriend caught up in a slanging or fisticuffs match with Michael Kidney. She leaves the pub and turns left, making for Commercial Road. As she walks up the road she sees Kidney weaving his way down towards her, he is drunk and at his most dangerous. She turns into the entrance of Dutfield's yard hoping that Kidney hasn't seen her and will walk by, it is very dark there and she hopes the darkness will protect her.*

Unfortunately he does see her and stops to talk to her, she notices there is another man behind Kidney (Schwartz) who crosses the road. Kidney starts on her. Telling her to stop this nonsense and come home with him, he starts trying to pull her out into the street Liz won't have it and fights back, she tells him to go away and he throws her to the ground. She tells him to go away again but he takes no notice. She isn't particularly frightened by all this, she has been here before, he'll beat her up and then leave her alone. She is afraid that if she screams for help and causes trouble, the beating will be more severe, so she meekly awaits her punishment. A man comes out of the pub on the corner and asks what's going on, Kidney hesitates for a minute, then pointing to Schwartz on the opposite side of the road replies that the 'Lipski' over there had attacked the woman. The newcomer starts off after Schwartz who rapidly leaves the scene. Liz takes advantage of the interruption to try and escape, this infuriates Kidney, who grabbing hold of her scarf uses it to pull her to the ground, he is almost beside himself with drunken rage now, furious that she had tried to escape, he pulls out his rigging knife that he carries, and holding her head down to the ground, slashes her throat. As the blood begins to flow from the horrible gash, he realises what he has done. The slash has severed her windpipe so she cannot cry out. Fear sobers him up rapidly, he realises if he is found he stands a good chance of being lynched by a mob. He scuttles up Berner Street and turns left at the Mission Hall about a hundred feet away. He knows that if he can get over two backyard fences he will find himself in Battys Gardens, and then into Back Church lane, away from the scene as quickly as possible. He has just turned by the Mission Hall when he hears the pony and cart of Diemschutz turn into Dutfield's yard.

Now according to the edition of the *Star* printed the day after the murder, a man walking up Church Lane at about 1.30 am on the night in question, saw a man sitting on a doorstep wiping his hands. The man looked at the stranger with a certain amount of suspicion, whereupon the man concealed his face. Described as wearing a short jacket and a peaked sailor's hat. Unfortunately because Jack the Ripper was at that time engaged in another murder half a mile away, the report was dismissed, and no attempt was made to verify or disprove it. This graphically illustrates the dangers of assuming every murder is the work of the same person. The interesting thing is that this description is very close to that of Schwartz's i.e. dark jacket and peaked sailor's cap, *but was printed before Schwartz had made his statement.* If you had to pick anything from Schwartz's statement that could be accurate, the jacket and hat the man wore would be it.

I must emphasise that the account written in italics is pure supposition, there is not one scrap of evidence to say this actually happened, however there are certainly a lot of pointers.

• Schwartz says the man was walking down the street in front of him and stopped to talk to the woman. In other words the encounter took place there and then, and yet within seconds the man was pulling the woman about. It is almost impossible to imagine an argument *between strangers* deteriorating so quickly into physical violence, but as any battered wife will tell you a lot of men will beat their wives within minutes of coming home drunk.

• The man tried to drag Stride out into the street, not back into the yard as anyone intent on murder would have done. Don't forget it was pitch black in Dutfield's yard, Diemschutz couldn't make out it was a woman even when he was prodding it, he had to use a match. What murderer would drag his intended victim out of the dark into whatever light there was?

• The woman called out three times, but not very loudly. We not only have Schwartz's testimony on this but there was a public house only feet away, and the International Mens Club only inches away and they heard nothing. Given the circumstances, the murders, the hysteria, the tales of Leather Apron etc. etc., any attack like this on a woman committed by a stranger, would have brought forth screams to waken the dead out of hell. The only conceivable reason for Liz Stride not to have screamed the house down was that she knew what was going to happen next, a beating probably followed by protestations of love and remorse.

• The actual killing was completely unlike the other killings. The woman wasn't strangled to death first and the knife wound only knicked one of the arteries and completely missed the other. In other words, if he hadn't have severed the windpipe she still would have been able to scream. According to the autopsy, the weapon used was unlike those used in the other killings.

• Berner Street, unlike the other murder sites was not known for its prostitutes, it was a respectable area of shops, public houses and private dwellings. It was a very unlikely place for a murderer intent on killing prostitutes to hunt in.

This does not fit in with the MO of the other murders *in any respect.* The other murders were committed with brutal efficiency. There were no witnesses, no struggle - the women were strangled to death and then their throats completely severed, and all attacks took place in quiet out of the way places. A busier place than Berner Street on a Saturday night is difficult to imagine. Another point is that the time does seem a little early. Polly Nichols was killed at about 3.45 am, Annie Chapman at about 5.45 am and Mary Kelly at anytime between 4.00 am and 5.00 am. The exception to this is Kate Eddowes, but as we shall see there is a very good reason for this.

Given all these indicators I believe that we are justified in saying that if we were to examine Liz Stride's murder in isolation, the police would have wanted to interview Mr. Kidney. Because the police wanted to keep Israel Schwartz and his testimony secret, he never gave evidence at the inquest, an inquest where we know Michael Kidney was present, it is interesting to know what would have happened if they had met.

One last point, many victims of drunken abuse tell the same story, that after they have been battered into unconsciousness, the batterer is often full of remorse, swearing undying love and promising never to do it again etc. etc. On the evening of October 1, Michael Kidney turned up drunk at Leman Street Police station shouting about how if he was the constable who was on duty when his poor Liz had died, he would have shot himself. He went on to say that if he had been given detectives he could have prevented the murder. Sounds like remorse to me!

The mystery of who killed Liz Stride will never now be solved, but I believe there are enough indications to say that whoever did do it, it probably wasn't Jack the Ripper. Did Michael Kidney do it? Well all I will say on the matter is that if the murder is looked at in isolation, and the case dealt with in normal circumstances I know who I would be wanting to question if I was a detective assigned to the case!

At about the same time the body of Liz Stride was being discovered, Catharine Eddowes (although calling herself Mary Anne Kelly) was being released from the cells at Bishopsgate Police Station. In less than an hour her butchered remains were found on the streets, but this time the killer had struck not in Whitechapel or Spitalfields, but in the one square mile of the City of London.

Chapter Five

"Ill met by moonlight, proud Titania."
Shakespeare, A Midsummer Night's Dream

Catharine Eddowes was born on the 14th April 1842 in Wolverhampton, to her family she was known as Chick, to everyone who knew her in the last year of her life she was Kate. After many trials and tribulations, Kate ended up moving in with an Army Pensioner called Thomas Conway, she was then aged sixteen. Although they never married they stayed together for over twenty years, and she bore him three children, one girl, Annie, and two boys. They eventually split up because of bad drinking habits, apparently the arrival of the army pension heralded a departure to the nearest pub where they both drank to excess and rounded off the evening with Conway beating up Kate. It seems a familiar story but one with an unusual twist, according to Kate's sister, it was Kate who drank to excess and provoked the quarrels. Even Kate's own daughter, Annie, states that it was all her mother's fault, explaining that her father was a teetotaller and *"lived on bad terms with Kate because she drank".*

Notwithstanding this Kate soon found someone else, and in 1881 she took up with a man called John Kelly whom she met at the lodging house at 55 Flower and Dean Street. Whatever her faults, Kate seems to have had the knack of engendering genuine affection for herself, three days after the murder John Kelly told the *Star*:

"We got throwed together a good bit, and the result was that we made a regular bargain. We have lived here (55 Flower and Dean) ever since, as the people here will tell you, and have never left here except when we've gone to the country together hopping". (Hop picking in Kent was a popular way to escape the city for a while, the chance to breath some clean air and earn a bit of money).

In a show of loyalty reminiscent of Liz Stride, Kate's friends insist she was not a prostitute. She worked at various jobs, charwoman and hawker in the winter, and the summer saw her and Kelly travelling around the country fruit picking, hop picking and any other labouring jobs they could get. Her sister later stated that she would not do anything wrong, a view shared by Frederick Wilkinson the lodging house deputy. Although he accepted that Kate did have a drink problem, he had not heard or known of her being intimate with anyone else but Kelly. In fact the only thing that could be said against Kate was that she was a hopeless scrounger. She was so bad that even her own children kept their whereabouts secret from her. Kate's daughter Annie, moved from King Street Bermondsey, to Southwark Park Road in an attempt to prevent her mother borrowing money from her.

The autumn of 1888 saw Eddowes and Kelly in Kent, *'hopping'* again. The pay must have been good, for on their way back to the East End they stopped off in Maidstone to buy John a new pair of boots, and Kate a jacket. However by the time they got back on Thursday the 27th September, they were broke again. They managed to get a bed in the casual ward at Shoe Lane on the night of the 27th, but this was good for one night only, the following day they had to make other plans.

Kelly managed to earn himself sixpence at some job, and being a gentleman and obviously fond of Kate, offered her the money to get herself a single bed for the night at Cooney's Lodging house, 55 Flower and Dean Street. He would go to the Mile End casual ward, where in return for a days work, he could get a bed for the night. Kate was obviously the brighter of the two, and gave him the money for the bed while she went to the casual ward, being a woman she would only have to perform some menial task for a bed.

The next morning, Saturday the 29th they met up again. This time they were completely out of luck and out of funds, and John insisted on popping (pawning) his new boots. Kate protested, but John was adamant, and he waited barefoot outside the pawn shop while Kate went inside to collect her 2s 6d. Unfortunately once they were in funds they do what so many people do when faced with unexpected wealth, they squandered the lot.

After buying their breakfast at Cooneys and some tea and sugar, by two in the afternoon they were flat broke again, so presumably certain public houses benefited in the general blow out. It is from this point that the exact circumstances get a little hazy and confused. Kate stated her intention of going to borrow money from her daughter. Now just why Kate should say that is not known. She knew that her daughter had moved the previous year to get away from her, and she did not know where she now lived. Incidentally when you look at the extreme lengths the couple went to raise funds, it does add credence to the proposition that Kate was not a prostitute, if she was a working girl it is very strange that her boyfriend would go barefoot rather than see her ply her trade!

Anyway just before she left Kelly reminded her of the crazed murderer on the loose and advised her to take care. Kate promised to be back by four, and with a cheerful;

"Don't you fear for me. I'll take care of myself and I shan't fall into his hands."

she walked out of his sight and into history.

The next time she was seen was by a crowd in Aldgate High Street, who apparently didn't appreciate her impersonation of a fire engine and called the police. An officer arrived on the scene and stood her against the wall, but she promptly slid back down to the pavement. It was obvious that he could not leave her there and summoning assistance from another police officer he took her to Bishopsgate Police Station, just opposite Liverpool Street Station, and booked in at about 8.45 pm. When asked what her name was she replied, *"Nothing"*. She was taken to a City Police Station because Aldgate was inside the boundaries of the City of London.

The routine with drunks in those days was to lock them up until they were judged fit to take care of themselves, and then they were released. Very rarely were formal charges ever brought against anyone. It saved time and money and was remarkably effective, the drunks knew that if they were picked up, in they went. The police knew that provided they didn't get any trouble, in the morning they could empty the cells and not be bothered by paperwork, and the public knew that if they were bothered by a drunk he would be removed from the streets pretty sharpish. Before our legal system got too tied up in red tape, a similar system was in operation in most garrison towns right up to the early seventies. All in all a system that worked remarkably well.

Shortly before 1.00 am PC Hutt was sent down to the cells to see if anyone was fit to be released. He thought Kate had sobered up and took her upstairs. She seemed very worried about the time,

"What time is it?" she asked

"Too late for you to get any more drink," was the reply *"Well,"* she insisted, *"what time is it?"*

"Just on one"

"I shall get a damned fine hiding when I get home then" she observed.

At the front desk she gave her name as Mary Ann Kelly and her address as Fashion Street. Giving a false name was quite a common practice in those days as drunk and disorderlies worked on a totting up system, if you got too many you found yourself in the workhouse picking oakum. It also again lends weight to the argument that she wasn't a prostitute as most of the working girls were well known to the local police. She was shown out to the passageway that led to the outside world, and as she reached the street door, Hutt asked her to pull the door to after her. With a cheerful *"All right, good night old cock"*; Kate Eddowes walked off into the streets.

At approximately 1.35 am three men, Joseph Lawende, Joseph Levy and Harry Harris saw her standing in Church Passage, a small covered alleyway that led into Mitre Square in Aldgate. She was apparently talking to a man. She appeared to have her hand on his chest and they appeared perfectly amicable. Lawende and Levy identified her by her clothes, neither saw her face.

Ten minutes later, PC Watkins, City Constabulary, entered the square by the carriageway that led from Mitre Street. Turning right he started to walk around the perimeter of the square when in the beam of his lantern he saw the body of a woman. At the coroners court four days later he described what he had seen:

"I next came in at 1.44. I turned to the right. I saw the body of a woman lying there on her back with her feet facing the square her clothes up above her waist. I saw her throat was cut and her bowels protruding. The stomach was ripped up. She was laying in a pool of blood".

The actual injuries suffered by the poor woman were even more horrifying than this. The medical report to the inquest noted:

'The body was on its back; the head turned to the left shoulder; the arms by the sides of the body as if they had fallen there, both palms upwards, the fingers slightly bent; a thimble was lying off the finger on the right side; the clothes drawn up above the abdomen; the thighs were naked; left leg extended in a line with the body; the abdomen was exposed; right leg bent at the thigh and the knee; the bonnet was at the back of the head; great disfigurement of face; the throat cut across; below the cut was a neckerchief; the upper part of her dress was pulled open a little way; the abdomen was all exposed; the intestines were drawn out to a large extent and placed over the right shoulder; they were smeared over with some feculent matter; a piece about two feet was quite detached from the body and placed between the body and the left arm, apparently by design; the lobe and auricle of the right ear was cut obliquely through; there was a quantity of clotted blood on the pavement on the left side of the neck, round the shoulder and upper part of arm, and fluid blood coloured serum which had flowed under the neck to the right shoulder, the pavement sloping in that direction; the body was quite warm; no death stiffening had taken place; she must have been dead most likely within the half hour; we looked for superficial bruises and saw none; no blood on the skin of the abdomen or secretion of any kind on the thighs; no spurting of blood on the bricks or pavement around; no marks of blood below the middle of the body; several buttons were found in the clotted blood after the body was removed; there was no blood on the front of the clothes; there were no traces of recent connection'.

Once again a woman had been murdered on the streets of London and mutilated with almost unbelievable barbarity. Although it was not known at the time, the Mitre Square victim had not yet given up all its horrors. Already the hallmarks of a true Ripper killing were evident:

Victim probably dead before her throat was cut. Note the reference to no spurting of blood.

Complete absence of any sound. A police officer was asleep in his house at number 3 Mitre Square a mere sixty-two feet away from where the murder was committed and yet heard nothing! This is equal to about four large saloon cars length. From his bedroom window he had a clear view of the body.

No witnesses to the actual assault.

No sign of a weapon.

There were however two important differences to this crime. First of all the killer had strayed from his patch, all the other killings were committed on territory belonging to the Metropolitan Police, for the murder of Kate Eddowes he had crossed the boundary into the one square mile of the City of London, and that belonged to the City of London Police. Secondly, for the first and last time he actually left a clue. An hour later in the doorway of Wentworth Model Dwellings in Goulston Street an alert police officer found what he first took to be a piece of old rag, but later was identified as part of Kate Eddowes apron.

Wentworth Model Dwellings were built as a means of providing cheap housing for the mainly Jewish immigrant population of the area. They consisted of four blocks of flats on the east side of Goulston Street where it meets Wentworth Street. The block right on the corner consisted of seventeen flats (numbers 90-107) and the other three contained eleven flats each. The piece of apron was found in the entrance to the next block down, numbers 108 to 119. (The actual doorway is still there today, but the entrance has been blocked using a roll shutter. It is right next door to a Fish & Chip shop). But the bloody piece of apron wasn't the only secret to be revealed in the entrance way, there on the wall above the piece of cloth were written the words:

"The Juwes are the men that will not be blamed for nothing".

At least that is one interpretation. It is unfortunate to note that in this instance where the killer might have actually left a genuine clue there is so much disagreement about it. Not only can no one apparently agree over its meaning, but more unforgivably there is considerable argument over the actual

89

words! For amazing as it may seem, the words were not photographed or even accurately copied down before they were obliterated. It should be noted that the words were extremely small, the largest letter according to one police officer was less than an inch in height!

It has long been a mainstay of conspiracy theorists that the Commissioner himself ordered the writing to be obliterated, but this is not strictly true. Superintendent Arnold briefed Sir Charles at Leman Street Police station on the two murders at about 5.00 am. He also told him of the discoveries in Wentworth Dwellings and advised that the writing should be obliterated at once. He gave as his reasons the recent unrest in the East End and the tremendous amount of bad feeling that had been whipped up against the Jews. He was afraid that if the graffiti was spotted by anyone, the area was now getting very busy with people going to work, the resulting problems could quickly get out of hand. The area was mainly peopled by Jews and the spectre of a riotous mob attacking looting and burning was not to be ignored. Superintendent Arnold had already dispatched an officer with bucket and sponge to Goulston Street to await his instructions.

Sir Charles, to his great credit, realised that such a decision should be correctly made by himself and not a subordinate. This does show the Commissioner to be a man of great moral courage, it would have been easier for him not to get involved in this matter, thus having a handy scapegoat should things go wrong. He decided therefore to visit Goulston Street personally, before going on to Berner Street. This was the correct thing to do as each passing minute brought more and more people onto the streets of Whitechapel.

On arrival at Goulston Street he held a conference with other officers as to whether the graffiti could be covered up until it was light enough for a photograph to be taken, or whether a part of it could be removed. After hearing the various ideas and suggestions, Sir Charles took the decision to *'obliterate the writing at once, having taken a copy'*. The fact that he had taken the right decision is borne out by the fact that of all the officers present, only Detective Halse, from the City force, protested. However it is fair to say that because Goulston Street was in the

Metropolitan Police district, if Halse had had his way and things had gone very wrong, it is unlikely that the City Force would have insisted on taking the blame. Consequently the graffiti was finally removed at about 5.30 am.

When the true series of events are examined it does make a mockery of all those people who insist on reading something sinister into Sir Charles's actions. All sorts of wild stories abound, Warren immediately went to Goulston Street on hearing of the writing and ordered its immediate destruction because he knew it implicated, the Freemasons, a mad poet J K Stephen, Prince Albert Victor, a barrister M K Druitt and presumably Uncle Tom Cobly and all. This is nonsense, the discovery of the apron and the writing were made by PC Long at about 2.55 am. The writing was not finally erased until 5.30 am, almost two and a half hours later, this is hardly the panic stricken actions of a man who is trying to protect somebody.

In retrospect it is difficult to see what other action could have been taken. A photograph would have been ideal, but this would have meant closing off a considerable portion of the street, if all chances of reading the graffiti were to be avoided. Likewise trying to screen off the doorway would have immediately attracted attention. It is however to be deplored that an accurate copy of the words were not taken. Several officers copied down the words, but they were all apparently different!

The version given above is the most likely. Of course the writing only commands our interest if it were written by the murderer, and about that there is considerable doubt. Swanson thought that the writing was old, he describes it as *'blurred'*, but Halse describes it as *'fresh'*.

It does not seem likely that any anti-Semitic graffiti would have survived for long in an area heavily populated by Jews, but that would depend on whether or not it was recognised as being anti-Semitic. As the writing stands it does not make any sense at all, and it does seem as if no one has recognised this fact. If, as it has been often suggested, the writer was trying to blame the Jews for the murders, why not just write *'The Juwes done it'* or something equally uncomplicated? Why this tortuous excursion into English grammar with double negatives etc. For some people, the very fact that it makes no sense - makes sense! John Wilding in his book *'Jack the Ripper Revealed'* explains it like this. Jack the Ripper is two people, J K Stephen and M J Druitt. Normally Stephen did the killing, but that night Druitt murdered Liz Stride (thus explaining why her murder was so different to the rest), and Stephen wanting to taunt the police wrote the message as an anagram, for if you re-arrange all the letters you get, *'F G Abberline. Now hate M J Druitt. He sent the woman to Hell'*.

This is all very exciting and appears to be the answer, until you approach the situation with a little common sense. Wilding admits that sitting in the comfort of his own home *'it took me a considerable time to work out the exact wording, even with so few letters.'* That being so look again at this incredible claim.

1.   If Stephen usually did the killing, and the graffiti was written as a result of Druitt murdering Stride only a matter of a couple of hours beforehand, this means the graffiti couldn't have been worked out in advance. Is it likely that a man rushing from one murder to another with hardly time to draw breath could construct such a puzzle on the run so to speak?

2.   If it took a considerable time to solve the anagram in the comfort of your own home, how come Sir Charles managed to solve it the instant he saw it and thus order its immediate destruction?

3.   Is it likely that a murderer with enough intelligence to construct such an anagram, would be so stupid as to hang around an area swarming with police to scrawl on a wall?

So if we dismiss all the fantastic claims about the writing on the wall, what are we left with? It is a very strange message and one that makes no sense at all, however I have seen something similar. Many years ago I was taking a statement from a Chinese in Hong Kong. The man concerned was a minor Civil servant employed by the Crown, and he was making a statement about some Communist agitators who had come over from the mainland to stir up trouble in Hong Kong. Looking at the intense concentration he was displaying, and the obvious struggle he was having with a written language not his own, I was impressed with the effort he was making. However when I came to read the statement it was absolute gibberish, it made no sense at all.

The difficulty was he was concentrating so hard on each word he was overlooking the fact that the sentences were nonsense. All his creative powers were being used up with the construction of unfamiliar words, he could not be worried about if collectively they made any sense. Look at a child's writing and you will see something similar. The Goulston Street graffiti has the same sort of flavour about it. I can almost see in my mind's eye some person laboriously writing out each word, scattering a few capital letters here and there as needed, and then stepping back to admire his handiwork.

I'm not saying that murderers don't scrawl on walls, but they generally do it to get a message over, look at Heirens for instance *'Stop me before I kill again'*. Short and straight to the point. The other point that is often overlooked is the size of the writing, it was very, very small. Surely if a deranged killer wanted to proclaim his message to the world he would have scrawled it in letters a foot high, apart from the difficulty of someone writing that message in the dark (try it yourself), it was only by pure chance that it was spotted at all. The truth about the Goulston Street graffiti will never be known, but I think on balance the chances are that the killer did not write it.

If the graffiti can be consigned to the *'out'* (or at least pending) tray, the piece of apron is very much at the top of the *'in'* tray. It was positively identified as such, by matching the remnant to the apron worn by the victim. The segment was wet with blood and faecal matter and it appeared that the murderer had cut off a piece of his victims clothing to wipe his hands, discarding it when he had finished. The importance of this clue should not be overlooked, for it gives the first definite indication where the murderer was, we know he was in Mitre Square and we know he was at Wentworth dwellings in Goulston Street. It is therefore possible to make a very good guess as to the killer's route on leaving Mitre Square. We are assuming he would try to avoid all the main roads as much as possible.

Leaving the scene of the murder go straight across the square to the passageway leading to St. James Place. This is a fairly safe assumption, the only other two exits from Mitre Square, Church Passage leading to Duke Street, and the main entrance leading to Mitre Street, were both regularly patrolled by the police, it wouldn't do to meet them coming in when the killer was going out. (There was also a public urinal in St. James Place where the killer could wash his hands and dry them on the piece of apron he had taken away with him). From St. James place turn right into Duke Street, cross over and into Stoney Lane. Go right up Stoney Lane until you reach Middlesex Street (Petticoat Lane) turn right then first left into New Goulston Street. This takes you into Goulston Street, turn left, cross over and you're right on top of Wentworth Dwellings. Now this might sound like a long journey but in fact it is only about 400 yards using this route to get from Mitre Square to Wentworth Dwellings, and the only two main roads, Houndsitch and Middlesex Street are quickly crossed.

From there the trail runs cold, no other clues were found. Major Smith of the City Police did write in his memoirs of finding a sink in Dorset Street where the murderer stopped to wash his hands, he knows this because the bloodstained water was still gurgling down the drain when he arrived. This however seems very unlikely, first if Major Smith did find a sink with bloodstained water in it how could he possibly connect this with the murderer, secondly why did Major Smith wander six yards off the road to investigate a sink in the first place? The other point about this mysterious sink is that they were not equipped with plugs, water was pumped into the trough you washed in the running water, and it ran away down the drain. For any water to be bloodstained it would have to have been contaminated just that second. Try it yourself, stain your hands with ink, wash them under a running tap, and see how long it takes for the stained water to disappear. It happens in an instant, which means Major Smith would have to be practically looking over the shoulder of the person washing his hands to have seen what he says he saw. Remember he was a City policeman and unlikely to know the whereabouts of every sink in Whitechapel. Major Smith, worthy gentleman though he undoubtedly was, did exaggerate sometimes!

Finding the rag at the Wentworth Dwellings, however, does give a strong indication that the lair of the killer could be close by. When you take into account that Martha Tabram was found murdered only a couple of hundred yards away to the east, it does look increasingly likely that Jack the Ripper lived nearby. The police at the time obviously shared this view, for they mounted an intensive house to house search, backed up by a leaflet campaign in which some 80,000 handbills were printed and distributed in the area. The handbill itself gives an interesting insight into the sort of person the police were looking for.

POLICE NOTICE
To The Occupier

On the mornings of Friday, 31st August, Saturday 8th and Sunday, 30th September, 1888, Women were murdered in or near Whitechapel, supposed by someone residing in the immediate neighbourhood. Should you know of any person to whom suspicion is attached, you are earnestly requested to communicate at once with the nearest Police Station.

Metropolitan Police Office, 30th September, 1888.

The line *'should you know of any person to whom suspicion is attached'* gives a clear indication that they thought that the killer was going to be of the type portrayed in the media, a skulking, furtive figure, clutching a blood stained knife and cackling maniacally. What they didn't appreciate, and what is now known about the appearance of these killers, is that they are anything but suspicious. They are often, bland ordinary people who you wouldn't look twice at. In fact the most frequently heard comment as the person is being led away in handcuffs is something along the lines of *'but he's such a nice man'*.

This leaflet merely reinforced the public's perception of the killer, anyone thought to be suspicious would immediately be confronted, but good old Joe Public who lives around the corner wouldn't be given a second thought. This is borne out by the fact that on two occasions men disguising themselves as women in order to trap the killer were pounced upon (one was a police officer and the other an enterprising reporter), and scuffles ensued.

We cannot be too smug about this as police even today are appearing on television after various crimes asking the public to report anything suspicious. It is a fact that more crimes have been solved by people reporting things that they have thought *'odd'* rather than suspicious. There was an attempted robbery in Italy several years ago that was foiled when a passer by noticed a tourist apparently photographing his lady friend against the background of a bank. When he *'helpfully'* pointed out that the church next door made a far better backdrop he was told in no uncertain terms to go away. This he thought decidedly odd and he mentioned this to the local policeman who he was sharing a coffee with. The policeman wandered over and recognised the erstwhile photographer as a known bankrobber. It transpired that the horizontal stripes on the woman's dress were being used as a scale to calculate the exact dimensions of the bank to aid a future robbery.

The house to house inquiries were well underway by the 13th October. It is interesting to note that the area to be examined was reduced to an area approximately a half mile square. To the North the area was bounded by Quaker Street, to the East, Dunk Street and Great Garden Street, to the West, the City of London Boundary, and to the South, most interestingly, by Whitechapel Road. What makes this area of supreme importance to anyone seeking an answer to the Whitechapel Murders, is that out of the five murders popularly supposed to have been committed by Jack The Ripper, Nicholls, Chapman, Stride, Eddowes and Kelly, at this point in the investigation only one, Chapman, had actually taken place in this area. With the discovery of Kelly's body a month hence, this still only brought the total to two.

We must begin to ask ourselves whether the police had some sort of evidence to suggest that their man lived in this area. Unfortunately most of the written results of house to house inquiries up to this point are now missing (there is nothing sinister in this; records do get *'weeded'* on a fairly regular basis, but all highly frustrating) so we cannot say with any certainty what this evidence might have been. However given that the murder sites covered such a comparatively large area, I believe that it is significant that this concentrated effort was aimed at such a small area.

This mammoth task was completed on the 18th October and once again nothing new was found.

On the 3rd October a milestone event took place in the search for the Whitechapel Murderer. The police published a poster containing both the *'Dear Boss'* letter received by the Central News Agency on the 27th September, and a postcard, again sent to the Central News Agency and received by them on the Monday morning, 1st October. The postcard read:

"I wasnt codding dear old Boss when I gave you the tip. youll hear about saucy Jackys work tomorrow double event this time number one squealed a bit couldnt finish straight off. had not time to get ears for police thanks for keeping last letter back till I got to work again.

Jack the Ripper"

The postcard was tastefully decorated with what appeared to be a large bloodstained smear over the writing.

This postcard has probably caused more controversy over the years than any other communication supposedly written by the killer. The people who want it to be written by the Ripper point out that it mentions the double killing and therefore contains information only the real killer would know. This overlooks the fact that the news of the double killing was all over the East End on the Sunday 30th September, and since the postcard was postmarked the 1st October, could have been posted at anytime after the last collection on Sunday. It is also pointed out that this card is signed the same as the *'Dear Boss'* letter, Jack the Ripper, and since that letter hadn't been made public, this proves they were both written by the same person. This is nonsense. The *'Dear Boss'* letter was received on the 27th September and spent two days in the offices of the Central News Agency before being forwarded to Scotland Yard. There must have been simply hundreds of people who could have seen it at the Agency or at the Yard.

As to the claims that the handwriting is the same, this is not the case. The letter is a perfectly formed script, this is a rather untidy scrawl. Of course if the answer to this is that the killer disguised his handwriting, what on earth for? Disguising your handwriting only makes sense if there is a danger of someone recognising it. If we assume the letter is the author's normal handwriting, why on earth would he bother to disguise his writing on the card? Surely if the killer did write both, it would be in his own perverted interests for the handwriting to be the same, thus proving their authenticity?

I believe the case against the card being genuine is stronger than the case for. For a start the information is inaccurate. It states *'had no time to get ears for the police'*. The only point in including this is because the letter promises to *'clip the lady's ears off and send to the police officers'*. However judging by the severe and extensive mutilations performed on Eddowe's body, there was plenty of time to clip the ears and just about any other part of the anatomy if required. True Eddowes did have one ear lobe severed, but this hardly constitutes an ear, and if the lobe was standing in for the ear, why wasn't it sent to the police as promised?

The other thing about the postcard which gives it away is the style of writing. At first glance it appears to be an uneducated form of writing liberally peppered with words like *'codding'* and *'saucy'*, but a closer examination shows this not to be the case. For a start it is spelled correctly, I defy any fourteen-year-old today to write that out without making one spelling mistake. Look at the word *'Squealed'*, not a simple word for an illiterate person to handle, you would expect something like, *'skweeld'* or even *'Sqeeled'*. Secondly all the contractions are correct. For instance the writer has contracted *'was not'* correctly into *'wasnt'* (albeit without the punctuation). Surely an uneducated person would contract it phonetically and write it as *'wasent'*. Similarly with *'youll'* and *'couldnt'*.

The author has tried to give an impression of rough illiteracy by leaving out the apostrophes and the capital letters at the start of a sentence. But almost unable to help himself he has inserted all the full stops and made sure the pro-noun *'I'* is correctly rendered as a capital letter. This postcard is almost certainly not written by the same person who wrote the letter. It does however give strong indications that it is written by someone who is familiar with grammar, and is entirely comfortable in using the written word. He has made a rudimentary attempt at trying to hide this, but has only succeeded in highlighting his proficiency. For these reasons I would judge this to be the work of a reporter rather than a policeman.

The importance of these two communications wasn't so much in their content, but in the fact that for the first time the public learned of a new name for the Whitechapel Murderer, from the time the police poster was published and for ever afterwards he was referred to as Jack the Ripper.

The press reaction to the two murders was instant and predictable. Newspaper boys scurried along streets, risking death from horses' hooves to ply their wares. One resident of the West End wrote to *The Times* to complain of the almost continual noise coming from these urchins shouting out the news of yet another '*Orrible Murder*'. Sales of newspapers soared, whereas before a paper might publish one edition a day, now a third and fourth edition were not unheard of, as the presses in Fleet Street rolled to satisfy the masses craving for the printed word. Not all that appeared in the papers was concerned with the actual murders themselves. Articles appeared in the Jewish Chronicle to assure people that the Jews could not be responsible for the killings as mutilation of a corpse was particularly abhorrent to those of the Jewish faith. The edition of the 12th October mentioned the Goulston Street graffiti as being a deliberate and unwarranted attempt to connect the Jewish population with these murders. It is interesting to note that if the writing on the wall was well known to the press, it rather undermines the conspiracy theorists who maintain this was some kind of great secret.

The gentlemen of the press seemed to have discovered a new hobby, playing the City police off against their colleagues in the Metropolitan force. The *Star* for instance noted:

'The City police from the Major (Smith) downwards, try to oblige the representatives of the press rather than try to frustrate them in their enquiries, like Sir Charles Warren's men.'

This was perhaps not quite fair, after all the City police had only just become involved with the discovery of Catharine Eddowes' body, the Metropolitan police had previous dealings with the press, and had not always found them helpful, indeed on some occasions have found them very un-helpful, the '*Leather Apron*' fiasco being but one instance. What was definitely lacking was some sort of press liaison between the police and the press, but this was far in the future.

The *Pall Mall Gazette* took this opportunity to comment on the fact that in the middle of all these murders, the newly appointed head of the CID, Dr. Robert Anderson, wasn't even in the country. He took up his post the day Polly Nicholls' body was found, and then went on sick leave to Switzerland the following week, leaving on the very night Annie Chapman was murdered. He only returned to his post after a great deal of pressure had been brought to bear on him to do so, arriving back in the country on the 6th October. When he left on sick leave he appointed Chief Inspector Donald Swanson to head the inquiry, and wrote at the time,

"I am convinced that the Whitechapel murder case (Anderson assumed Tabram to be the first victim of the Ripper) is one which can be successfully grappled with if it is systematically taken in hand. I go so far as to say that I could myself in a few days unravel the mystery provided I could spare the time to give undivided attention to it".

Those words no doubt returned many times to haunt him in the coming months.

On his return to England both the Home Secretary, Henry Matthews, and the Commissioner, Sir Charles Warren, left him in no doubt that they now expected him to make good his boast. Anderson replied, *'I will hold myself responsible to take all legitimate means to find him.'*

In retrospect Anderson was not a good choice to head the CID, and if his predecessor James Monro had still been in office, greater progress might have been made. His lack of understanding of the basic problems concerning police operations are evident in his recommendations. The first, that all known prostitutes on the streets after midnight should be arrested, no doubt caused vast amusement at the local police stations. Where on earth the manpower was supposed to come from to carry out this Herculean task was not made clear, and apart from the fact that it would probably take the best part of two days to arrest all the prostitutes, where were you going to put them? You would need a cell block the size of a large army barracks. After this idea was tactfully rejected, he next came up with the brilliant solution of telling all the prostitutes that the police would refuse to protect them. Writing later his pomposity shows through when he says:

"However the fact may be explained, it is a fact that no other street murder occurred in the Jack the Ripper series"

trying to give the impression that his return had stopped the killings. With a lawyer's logic he carefully disguises the fact that the murders didn't cease, it's just that Mary Kelly was murdered indoors and not on the street.

Despite all his bluster he was forced to admit on the 23rd October in a memo to the Home Office *"that despite five murders* (he again includes Tabram) *being committed, the police do not have the slightest clue"*. It is very noticeable that when Anderson is extolling virtues, it is always *'I'*, and yet when admitting failure (as in the Home Office memo) this is changed to *'we'*. It is also very revealing that Anderson although ousting Monro from the job as head of CID was not adverse to picking his brains, although Monro's job as adviser on Political crime to the Home Office, meant he had absolutely nothing to do with the investigation.

Anderson clearly belonged to the *'I succeed'* but *'We fail'* school, and his later writings are littered with tongue in cheek hints that although everyone else was fooled, he knew all the answers, from the identity of Jack the Ripper, to the author of the Jack the Ripper letters.

An interesting comment about Anderson's ability and character can be found in the writings of Lord John Spencer, Viceroy of Ireland. He wrote of Anderson that he had been:

"utterly careless when employed by Brackenbury (Director of Military Intelligence) and he seemed to be a weak creature in every respect".

Hardly the sort of comment one would wish to find on the CV of a man heading one of the most difficult and demanding investigations the police ever had to cope with!

With the excitement whipped up by the two latest killings, reporters poured on to the streets of Whitechapel searching for the merest hint, the slightest clue. A reporter from the **Star** tracked down Schwartz, the witness to the Stride attack, and published a lurid account of the interview. The fact that several important features of his statement now differed from that given to the police the previous day mattered not one whit. Reporters and private detectives hired by the newspapers searched out Matthew Packer, a shopkeeper who ran a small greengrocers next to Dutfields Yard, the scene of the Stride murder. From Packer came the tale of selling grapes to Stride and the man who accompanied her.

When interviewed by Sergeant White on the 30th September (the day after the murder) he said that he had seen nothing, heard nothing and in fact knew nothing of the murder until told about it that morning. The detective then interviewed three other people living in the same house and they all told the same story. However two days later in an interview to two private detectives everything had changed, now Packer says that he not only sold grapes to the couple but actually spoke to the man, now believed to be Jack the Ripper. And thus the legend of the grapes passes into Ripper lore. When the authorities read this new account they were especially annoyed at Sergeant White for missing such valuable evidence, but White insisted he had missed nothing. His subsequent attempts to re-interview Packer were thwarted by the two private detectives who would not let him near Packer. They did however deliver Packer to Scotland Yard where he made another statement.

However this new statement, and indeed all subsequent Packer statements vary so greatly as to make one wonder if the first incidence of cheque book journalism wasn't rearing its ugly head. In any event it is unlikely that any statement by Packer can be relied upon, in fact even his original statement that he saw nothing is open to question. If he was closing his shop at about 12.30 am, then he would have seen PC Smith and the couple that Smith had seen outside the school. According to Smith at about 12.30 am he and this couple were no more than 20 feet away from Packer's shop when according to Packer, he was putting up the shutters. It is also of note that Smith did not mention seeing Packer on the street at that time, all of which tends to suggest that Packer had in fact closed his shop about an hour before at 11.30 am. Why had he made up such a story? Well between being interviewed on the Sunday and seeing nothing, and being interviewed two days later when apparently he was almost on first name terms with the killer, the Corporation of

London had issued a reward of £500 for the killer's arrest. In those days £500 was a considerable sum of money equating to roughly £25,000 today.

All these obvious points failed to impress the papers who were still printing Packerisms up to the 27th October, when he claimed he once again saw the murderer who ... and then on the 13th November a man came to his shop and ... Anyone who had anything remotely to do with the victims or the scenes of the crimes were avidly traced and interviewed.

John Kelly, Catharine Eddowes' partner gave an interview to the *Star* on the 3rd October, but because of the several inaccuracies contained in it, it is likely that the bulk of the story was concocted by the reporter. He states that when Kate didn't return he wasn't unduly worried because he thought she had stayed with her daughter. However this is wrong, Kelly knew on the Saturday night that Kate had been taken into custody, and this was probably the reason that when news of the double murder broke he wasn't unduly worried as Kate had been safely locked up for the night. Afterwards he learned that they were trying to identify the body and the papers had published a full description of the corpse. When Kelly discovered that the dead woman had the initials 'TC' (Thomas Conway her last partner?) tattooed on her arm he became increasingly concerned, and went to the Bishopsgate police station. From there he was taken to the mortuary and identified the body as that of his long time common law wife, Catharine Eddowes. At least all the papers agreed that he was very visibly shaken by the experience.

The autopsy was carried out by Dr. Brown at the City Mortuary on the afternoon of her death. Also present were Dr. Sequeira, who had been the first medical man on the scene, Dr. Saunders the City Analyst and Dr. Phillips. Dr. Phillips was becoming quite an authority on the murders having attended Chapman and Strides inquest previously.

The details of the mutilations were just what the papers needed to boost circulation still further. One of Eddowes' kidneys was missing and the *Daily Telegraph*, the *Daily News* and the *Star* all reported this fact. It is this type of reporting that made the police very reluctant to involve the press to any greater degree. In any murder investigations, especially where the corpse has been mutilated, exact details are often withheld from the press on purpose. This enables the police to sort out the many inevitable confessions that they receive as soon as possible. If the person confessing to the crime does not possess a degree of knowledge greater than that of the press, then he can safely be discarded. By printing this detail an important weapon had been removed from the police armoury.

If the authorities hoped that by allowing so many doctors to examine the bodies, a uniform opinion might be forthcoming, they were doomed to disappointment. With the recent *'Medical man as Killer'* theory still fresh in peoples' minds, one of the questions asked at the inquest was *'Is the murderer a doctor?'* Doctor Brown gave his opinion that the murderer had deliberately sought out and removed the kidney, thus enforcing the view that the killer was indeed a medical man. Doctors Sequeira and Saunders disagreed. Their view was that killer had come across the organ by accident and just simply hacked it out. Dr. Phillips stated that there was no evidence that the killer had any medical knowledge, but that there was no evidence to show he hadn't, or indeed that he wasn't a hunter, a butcher, a slaughterman, a medical student, or a fully qualified surgeon.

Much has been made of the missing kidney in the Eddowes murder. The kidney resides at the rear of the body and is quite difficult to find, however if you just slash away, dip your hand in and pull everything out, then sooner or later you will find it. You must also take into account that various other organs in Eddowes' body had been slashed and stabbed. The pancreas and liver both showed cut marks, the womb had been cut through and removed with part of it still in the body. The killer had also slashed through the intestines, placing the bulk of them on the ground over her right shoulder, and another piece about two feet long by her left side.

Why had the killer taken the womb and kidney? Well to be perfectly accurate there is absolutely no proof that he did. The only thing that is known for certain is that they were missing from the body. It is interesting to note that the two items which were missing are quite small. In other words if you are kneeling down pulling the entrails out and slashing at them, small pieces might easily be thrown over your shoulder, while the larger pieces (the intestines) being awkward to throw, are merely taken out and dumped by the corpse. If that is the case then in all the commotion that followed it is quite possible that the two items were missed. For example, a kidney looks like a kidney, but if you step on it, it merely looks like a bloody smear. Similarly with a piece of womb, overlooked in all the fuss who knows what the hungry cat, dog or rat population might have done with it.

I cannot readily reconcile the popular picture of the Ripper scurrying away from the scene with his gruesome trophies, with a man who is so fastidious that he cuts away a piece of his victims apron on which to clean his hands.

So what does the evidence tell us about the Ripper, doctor or not? If professional surgeons who actually examined the body cannot agree, I feel there is very little chance of ever answering that accurately, however I feel we must ask ourselves the question *"If the Ripper was a doctor is it **possible** for him to have performed the operation to remove a kidney?"* The answer to this must be a resounding *'NO'*. Look at the facts, it is in the early hours of the morning, the moon is in the second day of the last quarter, the murder took place 63 feet from the nearest lamp, which because the killer was kneeling at Eddowes' right side, would have been behind him. The body wasn't spotted until illuminated by a policeman's lantern, in other words there simply was not enough light for the killer to have deliberately removed the kidney. (One of the doctors was reported to have said that there was enough light to carry out the mutilations, however it must be realised that when he said that he was surrounded by police officers carrying lanterns!)

There was one thing about this killing that was new, for the first time the killer had mutilated the woman's face. The killer had slashed at the woman's eyes and had cut down through the cheek severing the tip of her nose completely. The mutilation of a persons face has always been recognised as a sign of particular hatred, the face is what makes us individuals, it makes us unique in the world, when you destroy someone's face you destroy their very existence, you transform a human being into a shapeless blob of matter. It is one of the trade marks of a *'disorganised serial killer'*, the urge to quickly de-personalise his victim. It seemed as if the killer bore a special hatred for poor Kate Eddowes.

After the Eddowes murder the trickle of letters to the police, either from people purporting to be the killer, or from concerned citizens giving hints on how to catch the murderer, became a flood. There is no known total of how many letters were actually received, but they certainly ran into thousands, indeed so many letters were arriving with every mail that Scotland Yard had a pre-printed reply letter created to send to everyone who had put a name and address, thanking them for their interest. One slightly sinister aspect of these letters was that Mr. Lusk, chairman of the Whitechapel Vigilance Committee, began receiving them, and a sinister bearded stranger was seen watching his house. The police provided Mr. Lusk with a constable to stand guard outside his house. Then on the 16th October, just when it was thought that no more horrors could possibly be visited upon the sensibilities of the populace, Mr. Lusk received a letter *'from Hell'*.

The letter came in a small cardboard box, but it wasn't the letter that created all the excitement, for it accompanied what appeared to be half a human kidney! the letter read;

From hell

Mr. Lusk
      Sor
            I send you half the Kidne I took
from one women prasarved it for you tother
piece I fried and ate it was very nise I may send
you the bloody knif that took it out if you only
wate a whil longer
    signed   Catch me when
                   you can
              Mishter Lusk

This may seem like the scribblings of an illiterate person, but on closer examination certain points stand out. For example, the word *'preserved'* (prasarved) is quite exotic, would a truly uneducated person have used this word, in its correct context? Or would another word such as *'kept'* been more appropriate.

Although the *'e'* is missing from the word knife, at least the author knew knife was spelt with a silent *'k'*, similarly with the word *'whil(e)'*, the silent *'h'* is present. This again gives the very strong impression of someone who is not quite as illiterate as he is trying to suggest. However in this instance I rule out journalists as being the creator. For one thing no journalist could resist the opportunity of signing the letter *'Jack the Ripper'* instead of *'catch me when you can'*. The other point is the letter was addressed to George Lusk, Chairman of the Vigilance Committee, and not some faceless *'Boss'* at a News Agency. This fact alone makes me wonder if this could in fact be a genuine letter from the murderer, for this one is directed at a person who could be identified as an enemy.

An examination of the kidney should of course have removed all doubt, unfortunately it doesn't. The kidney eventually ended up with Dr. Thomas Horrocks Openshaw, Curator of the Pathological Museum, London Hospital. The first report of his findings came in a statement by a Mr. F S Reed who was an assistant to a Mile End Doctor. According to Mr. Reed, Openshaw had said the kidney *'belonged to a female, that it was part of a left kidney, and that the woman had been in the habit of drinking. He should think that the person had died about the time of the Mitre Square murder'* this account was eagerly seized upon by the press and was published on the 19th October. At last it appeared that hard fact was beginning to find its way into the papers.

Unfortunately when the **Star** interviewed Openshaw, it appeared to be a case of back to square one, for Dr. Openshaw said in his opinion *'that it was half of a left human kidney'*. He couldn't say however whether it was that of a woman, nor how long ago it had been removed from the body, *'as it had been preserved in spirits'*. From the horse's mouth, so to speak, a radically different story emerged. Gone was the positive identifications of sex, gone was the reference to drink and there is now no mention of it being removed at the time of the last murder.

Mr. Lusk, on hearing that the kidney was human (his initial reaction had been that someone was playing a macabre joke on him and that the kidney wasn't human) decided that the police had to be informed, and duly handed the box and its grisly contents over to Inspector Abberline. Inspector Abberline being cognisant of the fact that this object might possibly be from Eddowes, and thus nothing to do with the Metropolitan Police, handed it over to the City Police. The City police surgeon, Dr. Brown examined it, unfortunately his report is now no longer in existence so we are dependent upon the accounts of Chief Inspector Swanson, and the barely credible, Major Smith.

Swanson's report seems to ally itself with Openshaw, in that he says the kidney is

'the kidney of a human adult, not charged with fluid, as it would have been in the case of a body handed over for the purposes of dissection to an hospital, but rather as it would be in a case where it was taken from the body not so destined'.

In other words the absence of embalming fluid led Swanson to believe it wasn't from a hospital specimen, however it does not preclude its origin from any other source, and it definitely does not state the kidney came from Eddowes.

Smith's version stated that the renal artery is about three inches long, the kidney under examination had about one inch attached to it and Eddowes' body still retained about two inches. Also the kidney appeared to belong to someone suffering from Bright disease as did Eddowes. However in the absence of any forensic evidence to prove a definite link between the corpse of Eddowes and the kidney, the strongest word that can be used is *'possibly'*. Indeed some authorities were prepared to go even further. Dr. Sedgwick Saunders in an interview for the *Evening News* stated:

"some people have not the courage to say they don't know. You may take it that there is no difference whatever between the male and female kidney. You may take it that the right kidney of the woman Eddowes (the one remaining in her body) was perfectly normal in its structure and healthy, and by parity of reasoning you would not get much disease in the left. The liver was healthy and gave no indication that the woman drank. Taking the discovery of half a kidney and supposing it to be human, my opinion is that it was a student's antic. It is quite possible for any student to obtain a kidney for this purpose'.

In this last comment the doctor is absolutely correct, for although the absence of embalming fluid made it highly unlikely the kidney came from a corpse destined for the dissecting theatres of a teaching hospital, it did not preclude the origin being one of the many corpses being autopsied.

So did the Lusk kidney come from Eddowes or not? We simply do not know one way or the other, and there are insufficient clues to favour one solution over another. My personal belief is that if any of the Ripper letters are genuine it is this one.

On Saturday the 6th October poor Liz Stride was buried far from her native Sweden in a paupers grave in the East London Cemetery. Kate Eddowes' funeral on the following Monday was altogether a different affair. Kate's body encased in a magnificent coffin of elm complete with a brass plate with golden letters, was borne in an open hearse to the City of London Cemetery at Ilford. Crowds thronged the streets to pay their respects and the police were on hand to clear the way. A mourning coach followed behind with the chief mourners neatly attired in black. It was reading the account of this funeral in the papers that first caused a slight worm of unease to start twisting and turning in my brain.

It did not seem to be the account of a funeral of a streetwalker. None of the previous funerals came anywhere close to the grandness of this occasion. Annie Chapman was buried with very little ceremony, Liz Stride received a pauper's grave, only Mary Nicholl's funeral came close to rivalling Kate Eddowes. Was there any particular reason for this apparent inconsistency? Then the worm stopped turning and popped a question. What if Kate Eddowes *wasn't a prostitute?* At first that idea seemed ludicrous, of course she was a prostitute everyone said she was. And herein lies the error. You should never accept a statement or a concept without checking it out, that is the first thing you learn when you start to investigate. So I started to check and I found that not only was there no firm evidence to suggest she was a prostitute, but there were in fact a lot of indicators to show she wasn't.

If you look back to the statements made by Eddowes' friends and relations they all say the same thing. Kate Eddowes was not a prostitute. Now various authors have always dismissed these statements by saying that the people concerned did not wish to speak ill of the dead. This is nonsense. People who knew Smith, Tabram, Nicholls, Chapman and Stride all stated unequivocally that they were prostitutes. Remember what Tom Bates said about Liz Stride *'when she could get no work she had to do the best she could for a living'* meaning she was at the very least a part time prostitute. Prostitution in those days was seen as a necessary evil, calling someone a prostitute wasn't looked upon as speaking ill of someone. Indeed as the Kelly murder was to show living witnesses didn't hesitate to admit they were ladies of the night, as one of them said *'I am a widow and an unfortunate'.* Even census returns show prostitute as an occupation.

The more I researched the less evidence I could find that would show Kate Eddowes was a street walker. All the many books about the killings seem to have just assumed she was. Not one incident of her appearing before the courts on charges relating to prostitution could I find. Finally in the first edition of Tom Cullens' brilliant work, Autumn of Terror, I found on page 142 the first indication that she might have been a soiled dove. According to Cullen, Major Smith asserted that Eddowes was a known prostitute.

'The beat of Catharine Eddowes was a small one.... she was known to a good many constables'.

At first glance this seems to settle the matter, but let us consider this statement further. First of all it is made by a man, Smith, who is notoriously unreliable, who saw nothing in inventing any detail he was short of to make a good story. Secondly the City of London police are a very small force as they only operate in the one square mile of the City of London. Given that fact, and the statement that *'she was known to a good many constables'*, I find it incredible that none of the police officers who came into contact with her that night knew anything about her. Three constables and at least one Sergeant were involved in the arrest of Eddowes that night and yet **none of them knew her name**. When she was arrested she gave her name as *'nothing'* and on her release as *'Mary Anne Kelly'*. If she really was well known and her beat a small one, I find it unbelievable that the two constables who were supposed to have shared her beat, didn't know her.

However what I consider to be even more convincing evidence that she was not a prostitute can be found in her actions of the last few days of her life. It is known that she and John Kelly had just returned from the back breaking hop picking (if you were a really fast worker you might just earn 50 shillings for a month's work). It is known that when they only had enough money for one doss, Eddowes chose to walk to Mile End work house to flop for the night. The next day they pawned Kelly's boots. She then told Kelly she was going off to ask her daughter to lend her some money. What I see here is every method known being used to raise a few coppers, begging, working, pawning *except* walking the streets. Wouldn't it have been more likely that if she was a prostitute Kelly would have just sent her out to work for a few hours rather than pawn his new boots and leave himself barefoot? I find it incredible that they would try every avenue except street walking. It just doesn't make sense. Take the three points together. One, no one who knew her says she was a prostitute, in fact they say the very opposite. Two, this woman who is supposed to have a very small *'beat'* and is *'well known to constables'* is a stranger to four officers of what is arguably the smallest police force in the world, two of those officers walking the same beat as she was. And three, when the chips are down she uses every method known to raise money *except* the very one that a prostitute would use first! I believe the case is not proven. The prosecution have failed to present one shred of evidence that Kate Eddowes walked the streets, and the defence has raised several points which strongly indicate she wasn't.

If this is true, then why was she where she was, and why was she murdered? It was searching for these answers that finally led me to the man I believe was Jack the Ripper.

The common lodging house at 8 White's Row where Annie Millwood lived.

Photograph: 1997

*The entrance to Church Passage (now renamed St. James's Passage)
where Catharine Eddowes was last seen alive.*

Photograph: 1997

Looking down Church Passage (now renamed St. James's Passage) towards Mitre Square. The original passage was much narrower, the width of the flag stones seen on the left. Eddowes's body was found on the left of the flower bed seen behind the City of London boundary markers.

Photograph: 1997

Photograph taken from position of Catharine Eddowes's body looking towards the position of the only lamp in Mitre Square. It was situated where the no parking sign is now.

Photograph: 1997

The doorway where the Goulston Street grafitti and piece
of Catharine Eddowes's apron were found.

Corner of Wentworth & Goulston Streets looking down to graffiti doorway (arrowed).

Photograph: 1997

*Corner of Wentworth & Goulston Streets looking down to
Victoria Home (arrowed) total distance 150 yards approx.*

Photograph: 1997

39-41 Commercial Street. The site of the Victoria Home for Working Men, today it is a luggage shop. Across the road is the City Darts Pub which used to be the Princess Alice, drinking den of Leather Apron and Michledy Joe.

Photograph: 1997

Chapter Six

"thereof in the end come despondency and madness"
Robert Traill Spence Lowell

As the month of October wore on the East End held its breath. In Birmingham on the 6th October, Alfred Napier Blanchard gained a certain notoriety by being the only person to actually stand up in court and be charged with the murders. He thought it would be a jolly jape to admit to being the killer whilst imbibing freely in a public house. The authorities didn't agree. The *Manchester Guardian* points out that in spite of being remanded until the following Monday, the police did not consider his arrest to be important.

Many people had noticed a strange pattern in the timing of the murders. Tabram had died on the 7th of the month, Polly Nicholls on the 31st, Annie Chapman on the 8th and Kate Eddowes on the 30th. Would the next 7th or 8th day of the month herald another gruesome discovery? When the days passed there must have been a collective sigh of relief, nothing happened during the first week of October and nothing happened during the last week. Had the murderer left the area, had he been caught and killed by furious citizens, had he been secretly incarcerated in some lunatic asylum.

Whatever the citizenry thought, the men at the top knew differently, they knew the killer was still at large, and they also knew they were no nearer catching him than they had been two months ago. Sir Charles Warren wrote to the Home Secretary on the 6th October urging him to offer a free pardon to any accomplices of the murderer who would turn Queens evidence together with a cash reward of £5,000 (this was a colossal sum roughly equivalent to £250,000 in today's money.)

The seriousness with which Sir Charles viewed this matter can be judged by the fact that the reward offered by the Government for the murderers of Lord Frederick Cavendish and Thomas Henry Burke who were killed in Phoenix Park in Dublin by Irish terrorists, was £10,000, which means in money terms alone Sir Charles Warren at least valued a streetwalkers life as being equal to half that of a Lord! This alone makes a mockery of all those agitators who insisted that the police were not too concerned about the murders because the victims were only East End women.

The Home Secretary flatly refused to go along with the idea, stating that it was not the habit of Her Majesties Government to offer rewards, a statement totally at odds with the Phoenix Park rewards, which incidentally resulted in the guilty parties being brought to trial and hanged. The animosity between the Commissioner and the Home Secretary was beginning to be noticed in all the wrong quarters. A cartoon appearing in the October 13th edition of the *Moonshine*, showed Matthews and Warren glaring at each other over a desk, each asking the other *'Why don't you resign?'* In the background a scowling Prime Minister, Lord Salisbury is asking *'Why don't you both resign?'* There is a media saying that when the comedians start making jokes about a subject, it has gone too far.

There were many suggestions passed to the Home Office, including several from Mr. Lusk, regarding the chance of a pardon for an accomplice without mention of a reward. Unfortunately as time went on without any further murders, it became clear that the Home Office was rapidly losing interest in the whole affair. Like the typhus epidemic which was raging in the East End at the time, it was hoped that the crisis had passed and things would soon return to normal.

For the police on the ground it was a different story. On duty hours were filled with an endless round of statement taking and visiting likely hiding places for the Ripper. Butchers shops, abattoirs and slaughterhouses were all visited regularly to see if anyone knew anything. The few hours off duty brought little respite, it was difficult to sleep, appetites were diminished by the nauseous parade of raw meat and offal that became the lot of every detective. Officers began to lose concentration, they were becoming tired - they were becoming exhausted. Of all the officers, none worked harder than Abberline.

The public, ever eager to help deluged Abberline's men with statements, in all they made out over 1,600 files concerning their investigations. Even after he came off duty, he would wander the streets of Whitechapel until four or five in the morning, always hoping that it would be the night he would come face to face with the man that haunted his every minute. It is hardly surprising that he almost suffered a nervous breakdown.

Strictly speaking the Eddowes murder was the responsibility of the City Police. They worked as hard as anyone to trap the killer. An indication of just how thorough they were can be seen when a citizen wrote to the City Police that the killer might be a Jewish Slaughterman, Major Smith scribbled on the back of the letter *'Thank him for his suggestion and say that we have accounted for the times of all the butchers and slaughterers'*. Bearing in mind the number of slaughter houses in the area, this must have been a mammoth task.

It would not be fair to say there were no suspects, there were, possibly too many, it's just that all the inquiries led nowhere. There were even the usual batch of *'confessors'*, people who see a chance for fame by confessing to a crime they didn't commit. It's strange to think that this particular trait is still very much in evidence today.

The press ever needful of their duty to keep the killings at the forefront of everyone's minds, published theories as to who the killer was. *The Times* readership favoured a drug crazed Lascar, the *Daily News*, picking up on a story in an American newspaper, favoured an American. *The Daily Telegraph* hedged its bets by saying it could be an American or an Englishman who has visited America. As soon as they tired of the nationality game, they moved on to other things. A rumour started that the Ripper carried his knives in a black, Gladstone type bag. Soon every suspect had to have this essential prop, and every innocent doctor soon abandoned it.

As the days wore on a noticeable change came over the East End. Girls who had been in the habit of going around in groups, soon started going out in pairs and not long after were walking the streets on their own again. As October gave way to November people were beginning to wonder if it all wasn't a bad dream. The killings seemed to have stopped, nothing happened on the 7th October and the 30th was quiet, the 7th of

November came and went, and now something else was beginning to cause a stir in the East End, the annual Lord Mayor's parade, this year it was to be held on Friday 9th November, and all London was looking forward to it.

At about a quarter to eleven on the Friday morning John McCarthy, a shopkeeper and landlord, sent his assistant Thomas Bowyer round to one of his tenants, a pretty young prostitute named Mary Kelly. She was 29 shillings behind with her rent and a call was long overdue. Bowyer went round to her tiny one room lodging and knocked on the door. Receiving no reply he went round to one of the windows. A coat had been hung over the inside of the glass, but two of the panes were broken and reaching through the lower one he pushed the coat to one side. It took a few seconds for his eyes to adjust to the gloomy interior, but when they had they recorded a scene that haunted him to the grave and beyond. On this occasion the Ripper didn't worry about being disturbed, this time he had all the time he needed.

Of all the characters in the unfolding drama, Mary Kelly is the most enigmatic and mysterious. No one knows where she came from and you will still get an argument about where she went. According to the popular legend she was born in Ireland in Limerick. When she was young the Kelly family moved to Carmarthenshire in Wales where her father took up employment in an ironworks. Shortly afterwards Mary married a coalminer named Davies in 1879 (or thereabouts) who was unfortunately killed in a mine explosion shortly afterwards. She then went to live with a cousin in Cardiff who introduced her to the life on the streets. After spending some time in an infirmary in Cardiff she moved to London around 1884, where she found employment in a high class West End brothel, and it was during this time she was taken to Paris by a gentleman admirer.

After this she is reported as lodging with a Mrs Carthy who later stated that Mary had left her to live with a man in the building trade, popularly supposed to be Joseph Fleming. Shortly afterwards she met a market porter called Joe Barnett in a local pub and left Fleming to live with him in George Street. After moving to various lodgings in the area they finally settled in 13 Millers Court which in reality was the partitioned-off back room of 26 Dorset Street, and it was here that she finally met Jack the Ripper on the morning of Friday 9th November 1888.

At first glance this seems like a sorry tale of a respectable working class girl suffering all the bad breaks life can offer, and finally ending up on the streets. Unfortunately most of this tale comes from the evidence of Joe Barnett and he got it from - wait for it - Mary Kelly! So what if any of this is true?

Well, the part about leaving Ireland and settling in Carmarthenshire is perfectly feasible, and there were certainly ironworks, tinworks and other industries in the coastal area of Llanelli, Burry Port and Kidwelly. There were (and still are) many Irish families in this area, unfortunately not one trace of a Mary Kelly can be found. The only Mary Kellys in this area for this approximate time are either too old, mid forties, or too young, eight! There is no record of a Mary Kelly marrying a Davies or Davis at this time either, and the only death in the mines of a man of about the right age was a 19 year old miner who was killed when someone dropped a trapdoor on his head.

There was a family called Kelly living in Llanelli at this time and they did have a daughter called Mary who does not however appear on the census roles. The reason was that this Mary Kelly had moved away, and after the murder there was a rumour that it was she who had been killed. However the *Llanelli and County Guardian* of November 15th states

'Another appaling (sic) murder was committed in Whitechapel on Friday morning, the victim being a woman named Mary Jane Kelly. It has been stated that Kelly was a Llanelly woman and that she left here a few years ago. This however does not appear to be correct as investigations failed to associate her with the Town. No doubt the statement was made with reference to the Kelly family on the Wern, but all the girls are accountable for, two having left for America while the other lives with her husband near Cardiff '.

Moving on to the Cardiff part of the story, there is no record at all of a Mary Kelly being admitted to any infirmary at this time. Mr. Alan Jones of Gwent has arguably done more research on the history of Mary Kelly than anyone else and to date he still has to find a link with the victim and any part of South Wales. Likewise the story of her living in Paris for a while should be taken with a large pinch of salt. Mary Kelly had a very active imagination and for a while called herself Marie Jeanette, she actually appears on her death certificate as *'Marie Jeanette Kelly otherwise Davies'*, but there is no independent verification of her living if France.

When I started researching Mary Kelly I often used to wonder where she dreamt up the name *'Marie Jeanette'* and in a churchyard in Burry Port I once thought I had found the answer. I imagined her taking her brothers and sisters for a walk and stopping off in the churchyard to read the plaque set into the church wall, telling of the loss of a ship and the death of a niece of Napoleon just off the Burry Port sands. The name of the ship? - the Jeanette Marie! This did seem like an excellent pointer, but alas in the absence of any other information I have relegated that to the dustbin of coincidence.

The truth will probably never be known, but there are indications that she might have come to London direct from Ireland. Her landlord remembers letters coming for her from Ireland, but doesn't mention letters being delivered from any other part of the UK. There is also a chance that she had a brother, Henry, (known for some reason as Johnto) in the Scots Guards. In evidence later Joe Barnett correctly stated that the Scots Guards were in Ireland at the time of Kelly's death, a piece of information most likely to have come from Kelly herself. Another pointer to the possibility that she came straight from Ireland to London is the statement she made to a young friend of hers, Lizzie Albrook. Lizzie states that the last time she saw Mary she gave her (Lizzie) some good advice;

"Whatever you do, don't you do wrong and turn out as I have." Lizzie went on, *"she told me, too, that she was heartily sick of the life she was leading and wished she had money enough* **to go back to Ireland where her people lived."**

This seems a strange thing to say if her people were living in Wales.

Given the complete absence of hard information on Mary Kelly I believe the only thing that can be said about her with any certainty at all is that she once lodged with a Mrs Carthy of Breezers Hill around 1886, and in 1888 she was living in Millers

Court with Joe Barnett, having met (and presumably discarded) a Morganstone (Morgan Stone?) and a Joseph Fleming on the way.

Most of the information about Kelly comes from Barnett and there is no real reason for him to disbelieve it. He and Kelly seemed to have got on reasonably well together, although she did have a fiery temper especially when the worst for wear from drink.

In appearance Mary has been described as a *'short dumpy woman but quite attractive'*. Walter Dew, the policeman who later found everlasting fame as the officer who arrested Crippen, said of her:

'Often I had seen her parading along Commercial Street... usually in the company of two or three of her kind, fairly neatly dressed and invariably wearing a clean white apron, but no hat'.

She was possessed of a number of nicknames, Ginger and Black Mary being but two. Whether these referred to her natural colouring or her temperament is not quite clear. Most accounts speak of her as being fair-haired, but a witness who spoke to the **Illustrated Police News** said, *'I have known her for about five years, she had long dark hair'*. On balance though it would appear that she was fair haired and complexioned, features that were to be of the utmost importance later. It is however this very lack of an accurate picture of Mary Kelly that makes her so beloved of conspiracy theorists. One woman describes her as being *'5 feet 7 inches in height'* and yet another as *'a pleasant little woman'*. With the average height of females in those days being around the 5 foot 2 inch mark, it is difficult to justify the description *'little woman'*. However since we have the word of Walter Dew that she was a *'short dumpy woman'*, I think the balance of evidence is that she wasn't 5' 7", but rather closer to five feet. One thing they seemed all agreed upon is that she was *'rather stout'*, which leads one to believe that whatever she did go short of, it was not food.

Joe Barnett and Mary lived together without too much fuss until the evening of the 30th October. He had objected to Mary moving a streetwalking friend, Maria Harvey, in with them, whether it was because of a possible lesbian relationship, or

118

more likely that there was just not the room isn't clear. It did however lead to a quarrel, during which apparently the windows were broken, and Joe walking out. He found lodgings in New Street, Bishopsgate, but significantly he and Mary remained friends. Julia Venturney, a neighbour, spoke of their relationship:

"he frequently gave her money, he was very kind to her, he said he would not live with her while she led that kind of life (prostitution)".

The last evening of her life saw Mary entertaining both Joe Barnett and a friend at her small room in Millers Court. Barnett had called round to explain that he still had no money to give her. He stayed for about fifteen minutes, and insisted that she had not been drinking at the time. There is some confusion as to who the woman was with Mary at this time. Most sources state that it was Maria Harvey, but Barnett giving evidence at the inquest states it was *'a woman who lives in the court (Millers)'* and at that time Maria Harvey was living in New Court, a few yards down Dorset Street. According to Barnett, Mary was quite sober at this time. However over the next few hours Mary certainly changed that.

According to Mrs Cox, (by her own description a widow and an unfortunate (prostitute)) who lived at 5 Millers Court she saw Mary at about 11.45 that same evening in the company of a blotchy faced, stout man who appeared to be carrying a quart can of beer. Mary was very much the worse for drink at this time. As she went into her room with the man she called out to Mrs Cox, *'Good Night'* and then announced she was going to sing. When Mrs Cox went out again fifteen minutes later Mary was still singing, and on her return at 1 am was still going strong. Whether or not the singing continued throughout the time Mrs Cox was away it is impossible to say, or whether the blotchy faced man was still with her. It would appear though that Mr. Blotchy had accompanied her back to her room for a drink rather than sex. It is rather inconceivable that a customer paying for sex would settle for a concert instead.

The next incident was the return of Elizabeth Prater who lodged in the room directly above Mary Kelly's. She had been standing outside in Dorset Street waiting for the man she lodged with, but when he didn't turn up, went to bed at about 1.30 am. She was awoken during the night by her kitten (Paul Begg assures me it was called Diddles) walking across her face, and as she lay there she heard a cry of *'Murder!!'*. Unfortunately this was not an unusual occurrence and she did not pay a lot of attention to it. She couldn't even be sure when it was, in her statement to the police she estimates it as being between 3.30 am and 4.00 am, but then she later recalled that the lodging house light was out, so it was probably after 4.00 am, in any case she paid it very little attention and went back to sleep. Such testimony would normally have little value, but on this occasion there was corroboration.

Sarah Lewis had fallen out with her husband and had come to stay with her friends the Keylers at 2 Millers Court. Sarah Lewis had had a nasty fright earlier that evening. A couple of days earlier she had been accosted by a man in the street who had reached for something beneath his coat. What it was she didn't wait to find out and ran for it. Early in the morning of November 9th she thought she saw the same man again in Commercial Street, and again not waiting around to verify this, she hurried back to her friends in Millers Court. As she entered Millers Court she paused and looked back, although she couldn't see him, she did notice someone else. Across the street from Millers Court was a lodging house with a covered entrance. Standing there, looking up the narrow alleyway to Millers Court was a man. She described him as

'not tall, but stout, had on a black wideawake hat, I did not notice his clothes. The man standing in the street was looking up the Court (Millers) as if waiting for someone to come out'.

When she reached her friends, she found she could not sleep very well, and dozed in a chair until 3.30 am when she was awake until 5.00 am. However just before 4.00 am she heard a single loud scream of *'Murder'*. The scream she described as *'like the cry of a young woman not far distant'*, but like Mrs Prater, thought little of it. This evidence is crucial because it backs up Mrs Prater. Unfortunately it is not possible to pin the time down accurately. Sarah says she dozed until 3.30 am and heard the clock strike the half hour. However what half hour is open to question. It couldn't have been 2.30 am because at that time she was in Spitalfields just passing Christ Church and took the time from the clock. But if you are dozing and awake to the sound of a clock striking the half hour it could be the 4.30 am strike and this places the scream at just before 5.00 am not 4.00 am. If it was just before 5.00 am and it was the same scream Mrs Prater heard, this would explain why the lights in the court were out.

The other point to remember is that both women didn't attach any importance to the scream because it was a common occurrence. It has been pointed out that the actual crime of murder was comparatively rare in the East End, and that is certainly true. The previous year, 1887, there was not one single case of murder recorded in Whitechapel, but of course that didn't mean that the cry of *'Murder'* was uncommon, just the act! Therefore it is possible that the scream had absolutely nothing to do with Mary Kelly, and was simply part of the normal background noise. If however it was Mary's last gasp, it places the time of her murder somewhere between just before 4.00 am or just before 5.00 am.

The next witness is a complete mystery. Mrs Caroline Maxwell, who lived at 14 Dorset Street, testified that she saw Mary Kelly alive, but considerably unwell at 8.30 on the Friday morning. According to Mrs Maxwell, Kelly was at the entrance to Millers Court looking far the worse for drink. Some vomit in the gutter bore testimony to her fragile state. At about 9.00 am she said she saw Mary again talking to a man outside the Britannia on the corner of Dorset and Commercial Street. Now the only possible explanation for this statement is that Mrs Maxwell was confused about the days, and it was Thursday not Friday morning that she had the conversation with Mary.

There is a very small indication to this being the case. Mrs Maxwell says that when asked why she was up so early, Mary replied *'I have the horrors of the drink upon me, as I have been drinking for some days past'*. This would seem to suggest that Mary had been on a bender for a number of days and this was the result. Yet if we believe Joe Barnett that on the Thursday evening she was completely sober this doesn't make sense. However if Mary's pub crawl had ended **Thursday morning** and not Friday morning it now makes sense. The new sequence of events is now; previous to Thursday morning constant heavy drinking,

Thursday morning seen by Mrs Maxwell feeling very sorry for herself, Thursday evening seen by Joe Barnett sober and finally Friday morning - murdered! Of course we can only speculate and if it didn't happen this way we have a true mystery.

The next major occurrence is the finding of the body by Thomas Bowyer at approximately 10.45 am. The word body might be slightly inappropriate here, for what was found on the bed of Mary Kelly's room bore very little resemblance to a human being. The news was quickly passed to the police at Commercial Street Station. Inspector Walter Beck was on duty chatting to the young Walter Dew, when a man burst in with the news. Grabbing his hat and coat Beck proceeded to the scene. Finding the door locked, the Inspector followed Bowyer's example and peered through the broken window. Seconds later he staggered back, deathly pale. *'For God's sake, Dew, don't look.'* However in common with most of us given advice like that, Dew took his place at the window and peered in. In his own words *"I saw a sight which I shall never forget to my dying day."*

The only reason the object on the bed could be identified as human was that it vaguely conformed to the shape of a human being in that there was a head, a torso, two arms and two legs. Other than that there was no resemblance. The face had been extensively mutilated *'hacked beyond recognition of the features'* according to Dr. Bond, the torso had the flesh stripped away from the abdomen, which had then been opened and all the internal organs taken out. The flesh had been hacked away from the thighs so that the bone showed through, the throat, as usual had been slashed across. The body parts had been liberally spread around, Bond again:

'The viscera were found in various parts viz; the uterus and kidneys with one breast under the head, the other breast by the right foot, the liver between the feet, the intestines by the right side and the spleen by the left side of the body. The flaps (flesh) removed from the abdomen and thighs were on a (bedside) table.'

Even this nightmare horror wasn't enough for some papers with the *Guardian* of the 17th November reporting *'The fiendish assailant was not content with taking the life of his victim by severing the head from the body...'* it wasn't and others reporting that the killer had decorated the room with Mary Kelly's entrails hanging from nails in the wall - they weren't.

The police surgeon, Dr. George Bagster Phillips, arrived at 11.15 and Abberline arrived soon after. Unfortunately as often happens in times of great tragedy what occurred next was pure farce. According to Inspector Abberline, after Dr. Phillips had ascertained the woman to be beyond help, the Doctor then requested that no attempt should be made to enter the room until the bloodhounds had been sent for. These dogs had been loaned (according to the police - hired according to their owner) to assist in the tracking and capture of Jack the Ripper. They had in fact been returned some time before but this was not widely known. In consequence of this it wasn't until 1.30 pm that Superintendent Arnold arrived on the scene and ordered John McCarthy to force open the door. Joe Barnett later informed police that the key to the door had been lost some time previously but it could be opened by reaching through the broken window and pulling back the 'spring bolt'.

The room was sparsely furnished, a bed, a couple of rickety tables, a chair a disused washstand and a cupboard. The grate contained the ashes of a large fire and above this a print, 'The Fishermans Widow' (for more information on this item read Ripperana no. 16 April 96). For the first time in the murder investigations photographs were taken of the corpse in situ. There was also talk of photographing the victims eyes as there was a belief that a dying persons eyes retain the last image they see. Whether this was in fact done is not known as only two photographs of the body are now known to exist, the most famous, showing the body from the left hand side, and the other, only recently reproduced, showing the body from the other side. At the subsequent inquest mention is made of a number of photographs being taken, some by Dr Philips himself, but alas these together with detailed drawings of the room have vanished in the mists of time.

The news spread like ink in a puddle, one report stated that *'women rushed about the streets telling their neighbours the news and giving utterance in angry voices to expressions of rage and indignation'.* The news electrified the crowds lining the streets for the Lord Mayor's Procession and as the parade swung round into Fleet Street it was greeted by the sightseers streaming away and converging on Dorset Street. When it came to watching a procession of City dignitaries or looking at another brutalised corpse, there was no contest. Dorset Street was of course cordoned off but the streets at either end quickly became blocked with the crowds. At about four in the afternoon these crowds parted to let a cart bearing Mary Kelly's remains to Shoreditch Mortuary. The tarpaulin covering the cart also hid the several buckets of human debris collected by green skinned police constables. After this the windows to number 13 were boarded up and the door padlocked. Although the crowds didn't know it, Jack the Ripper had apparently dispatched two victims, Sir Charles Warren, Commissioner of the Metropolitan Police had had enough, his resignation was dated the day before, on the 8th November 1888.

The next day Abberline returned to Millers Court to begin sifting through the evidence. He searched the ashes of the fire and found the remnants of some women's clothes, a tin kettle had lost its spout, the solder melted. The ashes of the fire had still been warm at 1.30 pm the previous afternoon, and so it was very likely that the fire had been burning whilst the murder was being committed. Abberline could not find anything of interest in the fire and gave as his opinion that it had been started to provide illumination for the killer. This seems highly unlikely as a fire of this nature does not give off any light. There was a stub of candle found in the room which Abberline dismisses as being of no importance as it was too small. However there is no way he could know how large the candle was on the morning in question. In fact if the murderer had lit a candle to provide illumination, then a stub would be all you would find. If a whole candle had been found then that would have ruled it out - a stub tends to rule it in.

There has been a lot of speculation over the years as to the purpose of the fire, and why it was so fierce as to melt the spout off a kettle. So let us examine this in more detail and see if we can't come up with some logical answers. The solder in use at that time turned liquid at about 160 degrees, however it did lose adhesion at about 140 degrees, but even these relatively low temperatures are well outside what can be obtained by a fire

using old clothes as a fuel. How do we know that the
were used as fuel? Simple, remains were found in the g
the fire was still warm at 1.40 the following afternoon. (
time of death as being round about 4.00 am or 5.00   ᴜᴀt
meant the fire had to retain its heat for at least eight hours! The
only type of **untended** fire that can do that is one that smoulders.
Most reports describe the fire as being *'fierce'* a *'roaring blaze'* etc.
This is nonsense. Basic physics tells you that a hotly burning fire
consumes fuel at a faster rate, therefore for this to be burning
fiercely someone would have had to be stoking it with more
fuel, and this didn't happen. How then did the kettle lose
its spout? Again the logical answer is very simple, we are all
assuming that the spout was lost on that night, and yet there is
not one shred of evidence to support that. There was a fire in the
grate, a kettle has lost its spout, everyone assumes the two
things happen concurrently, and yet all the evidence points to
this not being the case.

Like many aspects in the Jack the Ripper case, when logic is
brought to bear a lot of the mystery disappears. The logical
answer to the fire is this, the kettle lost its spout some time
previously (presumably when Mary could afford coal or coke for
fuel), the fire was started by Mary or her companion for the sole
intention of providing a little warmth. Don't forget it was
November and the night of the 8th/9th was particularly
miserable, being wet and cold. She burnt some old clothes left by
Maria Harvey to provide a little warmth. We can't **prove** this of
course but if we look carefully there is a little pointer. **Reynolds
Newspaper** for the 18th November has a drawing of the interior
of the room. There folded over a chair are her clothes, and there
in front of the fireplace are her boots. Why would boots be
placed in front of a fire! On a rainy night as this was, to dry
them. Why would anyone try to dry boots in front of an unlit
fire? They wouldn't, so I believe its a fairly safe bet that if Mary
put her boots in front of the fire to dry it was lit, and therefore it
was either she or a companion who lit it!

Apart from the ashes in the grate, some old ginger beer
bottles and a clay pipe on the mantelpiece, the room revealed
nothing. The clay pipe, which had actually been knocked off the
mantel and smashed by one of the examining doctors, had been

claimed by Joe Barnett as one of his, so even that led nowhere. Once again the killer had struck, killed, mutilated and escaped in silence without leaving a clue. The despair felt by Abberline at this time can best be imagined.

The inquest on Mary Kelly was held on Monday 12 November at Shoreditch Town Hall. The room was packed and the doors were locked shut to prevent any more people forcing their way in. The jurors were first of all taken to see the corpse, which by this time had been reassembled, and then on to Millers Court to see the actual crime scene, it was about noon when they all returned and started listening to witnesses. Dr. Phillips gave evidence that death was caused by the severing of the right carotid artery but beyond this gave little away. Nothing was heard of the extensive mutilations and other gory details. This was possibly at the request of the police who by now were getting extremely wary of letting any more than the actual minimum of detail be known. The other witnesses gave evidence as to the last hours of Mary's life. Mrs Cox, Mrs Prater and Sarah Lewis all told their stories. Joe Barnett gave evidence of identification of the body. The face had been so terribly mutilated that he identified it by the hair and the eyes. His testimony has often been reported as being *'ears and eyes'*, but this is generally regarded as a simple case of miss-hearing.

The final evidence of the day came from the police in the form of Beck and Abberline. After hearing this the coroner, Dr. McDonald, terminated the proceedings, telling the jury that their only duty was to establish the cause of death. After asking the jury if they had heard enough evidence to enable them to reach a verdict, the foreman, after checking with his fellow jurors affirmed that they had, and they returned a verdict *'of wilful murder against some person or persons unknown'*. There have often been doubts raised about this inquest. Why was it concluded so swiftly? Why did the coroner say there was *'other evidence which he did not intend to call at this time?'* The conspiracy theorists put this down to certain proof that powerful forces were at work. However the fact of the matter is that all an inquest is for is to establish the cause of death, the time of death and whether that death was accident, suicide, murder or misadventure. The inquest on Mary Kelly, short though it was, had achieved this. There is also, as mentioned before, a very real possibility that the authorities wanted as much as possible kept out of the public domain to assist them in their inquiries. Many times in the past information leaked to the press had hampered the investigation.

After the inquest the streets were alive with rumour and speculation, and then at six o'clock a man walked into Commercial Street Police Station with an incredible story. He was an unemployed labourer named Hutchinson and this is what he said.

"About 2am 9th (the morning of the murder) I was coming by Thrawl Street Commercial Street and just before I got to Flower and Dean Street I met the murdered woman Kelly and she said to me 'Hutchinson will you lend me sixpence'. I said I can't I have spent all my money going down to Romford she said Good morning I must go and find some money, she went away towards Thrawl Street. A man coming in the opposite direction to Kelly tapped her on the shoulder and said something to her they both burst out laughing. I heard her say all right to him and the man said 'you will be all right for what I have told you'. He then placed his right hand around her shoulder. He also had a kind of small parcel in his left hand with a kind of strap round it. I stood against the lamp of the Ten Bell (deleted and Queens Head inserted above it) *Public House and watched him. They both came past me and the man hung down his head with his hat over his eyes. I stooped down and looked him in the face. He looked at me very* (end of first page of statement, signature at bottom of page George Hutchinson) *stern. They both went into Dorset Street I followed them. They both stood at the corner of the court for about 3 minutes. He said something to her. She said all right my dear come along you will be comfortable. He then placed his arm on her shoulder and gave her a kiss. She said she had lost her handkerchief he then pulled his handkerchief a red one out and gave it to her. They both then went up the court together. I then went to the court to see if I could see them but could not. I stood there for about three quarters of an hour to see if they came out they did not so I went away.*

Description age about 31 or 35, height 5ft 6 complexion pale, dark eyes and eye lashed dark (deleted) *slight moustache curled up each end and hair dark very surly looking. dress long dark coat collar and cuffs trimmed astracan and a dark jacket under. Light waistcoat dark trousers dark felt hat turned down in the middle button boots and gaiters with*

127

white buttons, wore a very thick gold chain, white linen collar black tie with horse-shoe pin. respectable appearance. (End of second page and statement signed at bottom)

'GeoHutchinson' walked very sharp, Jewish appearance. Can be identified'

This was an incredible stroke of luck, for here was a definite identification of a man seen with Kelly just before she was killed. Hutchinson knew Kelly from old so there was no chance that the female half of the couple wasn't the victim. In the Stride case a lot of people had apparently seen a couple but were not able to positively identify Stride. It also answered another question. Sarah Lewis had earlier stated that when she had got back to Millers Court she had noticed a man on the other side of the road *'looking up the Court as if waiting for someone'* this person is in all likelihood Hutchinson, as the time, place and activity all fit in with his statement. At least this was one lead the police wouldn't have to waste time and manpower following up. The following day the gentlemen of the press printed another version of Hutchinson's statement but now with even more detail. The description now reads;

"The man was about 5ft 6ins in height, and 34 or 35 years of age, with dark complexion and dark moustache, turned up at the ends. He was wearing a long dark coat, trimmed with astrachan, a white collar, with a black necktie, in which was affixed a horseshoe pin. He wore a pair of dark 'spats' with light buttons over button boots, and displayed from his waistcoat a massive gold chain. His watch chain had a big seal, with a red stone, hanging from it. He had a heavy moustache curled up and dark eyes and bushy eyebrows. He had no side whiskers, and his chin was clean shaven. He looked like a foreigner. The man I saw did not look as though he would attack another one (man). He carried a small parcel in his hand about 8ins long, and it had a strap round it. He had it tightly grasped in his left hand. It looked as though it was covered with dark American cloth (a type of waterproof cloth). *He carried in his right hand, which he laid upon the womans shoulder, a pair of brown kid gloves. One thing I noticed, and that was that he walked very softly. I believe that he lives in the neighbourhood, and I fancied that I saw him in Petticoat Lane on Sunday Morning, but I was not certain.*

Hutchinson also elaborates on his meeting with Mary Kelly stating *'Kelly did not seem to me to be drunk, but was a bit spreeish'*.

This was incredible information, for the first time in the whole investigation the police now had a workable description of the man most likely to be Jack the Ripper. There was however an insurmountable problem. Now that the papers had published a full account of Hutchinson's statement and description, the killer could either flee the area or alter his appearance so much as to make the description worthless. It appeared that once again the papers had inadvertently given the killer the scissors with which to snip through the police net.

After Hutchinson had made his statement to the police on the evening of the 12th, Abberline was immediately notified of this important piece of evidence. He hurried to the station to interrogate Hutchinson and that evening forwarded his report in writing to Scotland Yard. He says:

'An important statement has been made by a man named George Hutchinson which I forward herewith. I have interrogated him this evening, and I am of the opinion his statement is true.'

Abberline was at last given a chink in the Rippers armour and he was determined to exploit it to the full. He immediately assigned two detectives to accompany Hutchinson everywhere he went in attempt to spot the elusive suspect. They set off immediately walking the streets, but in vain. The next day though they were out again.

One week after Hutchinson made his statement, the remains of Mary Kelly were buried. No relatives came forward to bury the body, and rather than see her consigned to a paupers grave the verger of St. Leonards, Henry Wilton, paid for the funeral and she was finally laid to rest in St. Patricks Roman Catholic Cemetery in Leytonstone. She was the last victim of Jack the Ripper. Like a Caribbean hurricane he sprang out of nowhere, wreaked havoc, death and destruction then just as suddenly disappeared forever. The East End of course were not to know this and the Ripper's evil influence still prevailed. A young clerk, respectably dressed, decided on the Friday to see for himself the place where Kelly had been murdered. Unfortunately his appearance, so at odds with the rest of the inhabitants of the East End, triggered off a mob intent on lynching him and he ended the day seeking the protection of the police. The East End was not a safe place for outsiders.

The news of Warren's resignation brought cheers from the populace and the newspapers alike. Most thought he had resigned over his incompetent handling of the Ripper investigation, but that wasn't strictly true. Sir Charles had written an article for *Murray's* magazine, basically saying that he wished the police in Britain could be more like the continental police, who were under far less scrutiny from the press and politicians. This faux pas enabled his long time enemy, the Home Secretary to write a rather snotty letter reminding Sir Charles of an edict which forbade serving police officers from writing to the press without first clearing it with the Home Office. (In fact the Home Secretary got an underling to write to Sir Charles, a move calculated to infuriate him even more). Sir Charles replied that the ruling didn't apply to the Commissioner, and if it did he would be forced to tender his resignation yet again. This time the Home Secretary readily accepted it. However it is interesting to speculate that if the Ripper had been caught, the Home Secretary would never have dared to accept his resignation, so there is a grain of truth in the theory that the Ripper caused Sir Charles's downfall - he certainly didn't help! His successor was James Monro, the ex-head of the Detective branch, who had earlier quarrelled with Warren.

As time wore on it became clear that despite Hutchinson's description the police were no nearer an arrest. People were arrested, but once their stories were checked out they were released again. When a man fitting the description of the beer-carrying man seen with Mary Kelly on the night of her murder, was pointed out to a police officer, the informant was told that the police were looking for a man of an entirely different description (presumably Hutchinson's description). With hindsight this is very unfortunate as any information about a victim's last hours is vital, if only to fill in gaps and corroborate other evidence.

The peace and quiet of the morning of the 20th November were disturbed once more by the familiar cries of *'Murder'*. The victim this time was one Annie Farmer, a prostitute, who said she had been attacked by Jack the Ripper. At first she presented herself as a likely candidate to join the grim queue of Ripper victims, but it soon became evident to the police that she had inflicted the superficial wounds to her throat herself, presumably in a successful attempt to scare off a client she had cheated.

Five days before Christmas the body of another prostitute, known as Drunken Lizzie, was discovered in Poplar High Street. Despite this being over two miles from the East End, and in spite of the fact that doctors couldn't establish how she died, the inquest jury returned a verdict of murder. Much to his chagrin Sir Robert Anderson had to allocate manpower to investigate a murder that in likelihood was death by natural causes.

In July of the following year Alice McKenzie known as Clay Pipe Alice, was found murdered in Castle Alley. At least this time there seemed to be some justification in attributing this to the Ripper, as first reports spoke of a cut throat and wounds to the abdomen, and the *Times* didn't hesitate in going to press and assuring everyone it was indeed the work of the Ripper. However, on closer inspection the wound to the throat was found to have been done with a short bladed knife and the so called 'wounds' to the abdomen turned out to be scratches.

In February 1891 the body of Frances Coles was found underneath the railway arches at Swallow Gardens. Her throat had been cut and she was still bleeding when the police constable found her. An acquaintance of hers, a drunken bully by the name of Thomas Sadler was arrested and charged with her murder. At first sight the evidence against him seemed strong, witnesses spoke of him being seen in bloodstained clothing, but at the trial the evidence collapsed and he was released. It is interesting to note that detectives involved in this case went to a great deal of trouble to establish his whereabouts at the time of the Whitechapel murders, three years before, unfortunately for them he was at sea at the time. Again the *Times* thundered into print that the Ripper was at it again!!

The poor police constable, PC Ernest Thompson 240H, who found the body noticed that she was still alive, and in spite of hearing footsteps running away, obeyed standing orders to stay with the body. He was later unfairly criticised for not giving chase, and the matter haunted him for the rest of his life. In the

131

early hours of December 1st 1900, he was stabbed to death trying to break up a fight at a coffee stall.

This was the last serious attempt to attribute a killing to the Ripper, but it is extremely interesting to note that even at this early stage, so soon after the cessation of the actual Ripper killings, any death, regardless of whether or not it was a violent death, was being attributed to the Ripper. Even more revealing was the example of Annie Farmer who knew that the mere uttering of the words *'Jack the Ripper'* would enable her to scare away a cheated client. It was almost as if the reality of the Ripper murders was not exotic enough, people demanded more and more outlandish details, the accuracy or lack of it mattered not. Possibly because she was the last of the Rippers victims, Mary Kelly seems to have generated more than her fair share of the legend.

One of the first rumours to circulate about Mary Kelly was that she was three months pregnant at the time of her death, and yet as the post mortem account makes absolutely no mention of this it can be safely regarded as fiction. How did it start? A story in the ***Daily Telegraph*** of the 13th November states,

'We are enabled to state, on good authority, that notwithstanding all that has been said to the contrary, a portion of the bodily organs was missing.'

Now when you read that in conjunction with a report in the ***Guardian*** of the 17th November that *'she had a little boy aged about six or seven years, living with her'*, the pregnancy story starts to make sense. Look at it this way, the rumour mill states her child is missing, (there was no record of Mary having a little boy living with her) and couple that with *'bodily organs'* being taken away it is a very short step to change the boy of six or seven into an unborn child. Ergo she was pregnant at the time. The *'bodily organs'* mentioned in the press alluded to her heart. Dr. Bond states *'The pericardium was open below and the heart absent'*. What this doesn't tell us is whether or not the heart was absent from the body or absent from the scene of the crime. As Dr. Bond is writing post mortem notes his only concern is that state in which he found the body, ***not the circumstances of the crime***. That being the case I have always interpreted his notes to mean the heart was missing from the body, and not necessarily missing from the

132

room. In fact there is some evidence to show that this is so as other reports speak of the body as being *'complete in all respects'*. However this is yet again another point it is impossible to be certain of.

There were other incidents linked with Mary Kelly that were destined to become the stuff of legend, the blazing fire (that wasn't) the appearance on the streets after she had been murdered (she didn't) and the sinister stranger seen by George Hutchinson who apparently had just vanished into thin air.

Soon the East End Murders faded from the front pages and started to reappear in succession of books and pamphlets purporting to tell the *'True Story of Jack the Ripper'*, the first was published shortly after the murders ceased and they are still being published today - 108 years later.

It is interesting to note how many of the early works mirrored the popular theories of the time. Such apparently motiveless crimes were almost unheard of so naturally the perpetrator must be a madman. Leonard Matters in his 1929 book, *'The Mystery of Jack the Ripper'*, has a mad Dr. Stanley searching the streets of the East End to find the prostitute who caused the death of his son. This is possibly a distillation of the various rumours concerning the Ripper as a person with medical knowledge and the mysterious American doctor who wished to purchase anatomical specimens. Certainly the *'Mad Doctor'* theory was well established before 1910. It wasn't until some of the senior police officers of the day started to write their memoirs that the really fanciful theories evolved.

Sir Robert Anderson wrote his memoirs, *'The Lighter Side of My Official Life'*, in 1910 and in them he states:

'For I may say at once that 'undiscovered murders' are rare in London, and the Jack the Ripper crimes are not in that category' he goes on *'I will merely add that the only person who ever had a good view of the murderer unhesitatingly identified the suspect the instant he was confronted with him, but he refused to give evidence against him'*.

He then identifies the killer as a *'Polish Jew'*. He also mentions that the identification took place after *'the suspect had been caged in an asylum'*, thus re-stating the popular view that the killer was a lunatic. At first glance this might seem like the end of the chase, but closer examination shows this not to be so. In naming his suspect as a mad Jew, Anderson is merely re-hashing the initial belief that the killer must (**a**), be mad and (**b**), be foreign. His subsequent assertion that a witness actually identified the killer is absolute nonsense. If this was so the killer would have been immediately arrested and charged. The witness could have been subpoenaed, and whether or not he gave evidence would be un-important. If he had given evidence the suspect would have been found guilty but because of his insanity would have spent the rest of his life in an asylum, if the witness had failed to give evidence then the suspect would still have been committed to any asylum since according to Anderson, he was already in one. The bringing to trial however would have been essential to vindicate the police. No, Anderson's glib statements are pure fiction, made to show everyone just how clever he was. Don't forget Anderson had boasted that given time he could easily bring the killer to justice just before he left for Switzerland. On his recall both the Home Secretary and the Commissioner made it quite clear to him that they expected him to make good his claim which he failed to do. This was his way of letting everyone know just how clever he had been, and in part he was clever, for he made his claim in such a way that no-one could ever disprove it!

Sir Melville Macnaghten took over as assistant Chief Constable CID, Scotland Yard in 1890 and he left in the records at Scotland Yard the most important document which has come to be known as the *'Macnaghten Memorandum'*. There are three versions of this memorandum in existence, but it seems only logical to take the version written in Macnaghten's own handwriting as the definitive one. This was first described by Donald Rumbelow in 1975. The memorandum was written in 1894 as a report on a series of articles appearing in *The Sun*. The paper was confidentially stating that they had solved the mystery and that the Ripper was a Thomas Cutbush who was incarcerated in an asylum. Macnaghten wrote his memo to explain to his superiors that this was not so. It is interesting to note that in explaining why the murders stopped he says, *'A much more rational theory is that the murderer's brain gave way altogether after his awful glut in Miller's Court, and that he immediately committed suicide, or, as a possible alternative, was found to be so hopelessly mad by his relations, that he was by them confined in some asylum'.* He then goes on to say *'I may mention the cases of 3 men, **any one of whom would have been more likely than Cutbush to have committed this series of murders;'**.* He then names the three men: M J Druitt, Kosminski and Michael Ostrog. It is very important that the passage is read as it is written. Macnaghten does not say *'the killer was one of these three men'* he says any one would be a more likely suspect than Cutbush. In other words he is not emphasising their guilt he is emphasising Cutbush's innocence (at least of being the Ripper). Again given the favourite theories of the Rippers identities it is interesting to note the three suspects;

M J Druitt is listed as a doctor (he was in fact a barrister) who committed suicide.

Kosminski was a Jew who was later committed to an asylum.

Michael Ostrog is listed as a Russian doctor, who was later committed to an asylum.

In other words in these three you have just about every permutation of suspect you could possibly get! It is interesting to note that whereas people such as Anderson and Macnaghten speculate as to who the killer was they are doing so from a second hand position. Anderson was only in England for one of the murders, and Macnaghten wasn't involved at all. When you look to the men who were actually involved, inevitably you get the same answer, they didn't have a clue!

It has long been a popular pastime to decry the efforts of the police involved in the investigation. Some of the most famous cartoons of the period show the police blindfolded, surrounded by suspicious characters, or very obviously looking the other way as a knife wielding manic slaughters yet another helpless victim. In fact the police operation on the ground could not really be faulted. They did everything they could to catch the killer, it wasn't their fault it wasn't quite good enough. If there is fault to be found it is in the higher ranks of the senior police officers that it will be found. The constant animosity between the Commissioner and the Home Secretary, the lack of effective (or any) leadership of the CID at this critical time all conspired to hamper the investigation.

Sir Charles Warren was, as previously mentioned, not the ideal man to head the Met. Apart from his conflict with Matthews, his Military background placed unnecessary restraints on his men when they needed more freedom. For instance he forbade any of his men to enter public houses whilst on duty, this immediately starved them of much needed gossip and information. The City detectives on the other hand, were positively encouraged to mix with the populace in an attempt to glean any information that might prove useful. The City force also seemed to handle the press a lot better, and consequently the press tended to praise Major Henry Smith of the City force and curse Sir Charles of the Met.

Anderson was not a suitable leader for the CID. Vain and boastful, and yet quite unable to make good any of his promises, his suggestions bordered on the ludicrous. It is interesting to speculate what might have been with a *'Dream Team'* consisting of Major Smith as Commissioner and James Monro as head of CID.

With a lack of direction from on high, the investigation differed very slightly from those held during the last eighty years. Photography should have been brought into play much sooner than the last victim. Isolation of crime scenes should have been a prime requirement. The science of fingerprint analysis could have been tried. It is wrongly assumed that fingerprints were not used for identification purposes at this time. Sir William Herschel was using fingerprints as a method of identification in India as early as 1858 and had actually written to the Registrar General on 15 August 1877 drawing attention to the use of fingerprints. Another pioneer of fingerprint use was Henry Faulds who actually had been trying since 1886 to get Scotland Yard to adopt his method, he even went to the lengths of offering to undertake the work *'free of cost'*. In Argentina a murderer had already been caught and convicted using this new science.

Perhaps the most useful tool available to the police was the press. Properly handled they could have been of great use, but unfortunately relationships soon deteriorated to such an extent that in the end the press were actively hampering the police investigations. To quote Monro in later years *'the Ripper was never caught - but he should have been!'*

One of the biggest problems was the fact that the police had to check all leads, spurious or not, and thus wasted a colossal amount of time. It was pointed out that since the Eddowes murder over 1,400 letters had been received, and each had to be thoroughly investigated. It can be seen why the police were so frustrated by the press publishing every detail, for it left them nothing with which to evaluate information. After a while, with nothing new being brought to the investigation, and no new murders being committed the massive police operation was being wound down.

On the 26th January 1889, Monro told the Home Office that he was gradually reducing the number of officers engaged in the Ripper investigation *'as quickly as it was safe to do so'*. This running down of the operation led some to speculate that the Ripper had in fact been caught, and that he was being held in a private lunatic asylum, others say the Ripper was dead - his body had been found in the river. Whatever the reason the police gradually withdrew more and more men from the investigation until in 1892 they finally closed the case.

Chapter Seven

"Some poisoned by their wives, some sleeping killed;
All murdered: for within the hollow crown
That rounds the mortal temples of a king
Keeps Death his court"

Richard III

Murder is defined as the *'unlawful killing with malice aforethought'* of another human being. Murder is the worst crime that can be committed in all civilisations, it transcends the normal boundaries of criminal behaviour and encroaches on blasphemy. When you murder someone you are directly transgressing against God's will. He has deemed that someone shall live, shall exist and the murderer has gone against God's wishes, he (or she) has directly thwarted God's intentions. What kind of person commits murder? What type of character places himself so far outside the boundaries of acceptable behaviour, that he is marked with the stigma of his crime for all time? Unfortunately for those people who are responsible for the protection of the public at large anyone can become a murderer. They come in all shapes and sizes, male or female, young or old, black, white and every hue and colour known to man. Their reasons for killing are as many as the grains of sands on a beach - and none of them make sense to the relatives of their victims. If we are to commence our search for Jack the Ripper, let us first acquaint ourselves with the type of person he could be.

Although there are countless reasons given by killers for their actions, there are in fact very few *'types'* of murder. These can be broken down as follows:

ECONOMIC MURDER This is murder committed for purely financial reasons, robbery, insurance fraud and similar. A lot of the time these killings are committed almost as an afterthought, the bystander who is gunned down in the shootout with police, the nightwatchman hit just a little bit too hard.

SEX OR POWER MURDERS These are killings committed for a sexual reason, such as rape. However since rape is deemed to be not a crime of lust, but a crime of domination or power, certain murders are often called sex crimes, even when no intercourse or even attempted intercourse has taken place. Two of the most infamous killings of this type could be said to be the Jack the Ripper murders and the Jack the Stripper murders of the mid sixties.

SPREE MURDERS. These take place simply because the killer likes killing people. They are often typified by the *'sniper in the Tower syndrome'*, a killer (these are very rarely the crimes of more than one person) suddenly explodes in a murderous rage, slaughtering a large number of people before being either overpowered by the police, or more often committing suicide. The Hungerford murders of the late 80s, the Dunblane massacre and the Tasmanian massacre of 1996 are all examples of this type.

POLITICAL MURDERS. I personally believe that so called political murders by terrorists should more correctly be grouped under the Sex or Power murder category. There is very rarely any discernible political motive behind these killings and the vast majority are committed to exercise power and control over the public. Nobody could seriously expect anyone to believe that blowing two little boys to pieces in Warrington achieved anything for the IRA except the spreading of terror and fear. The vast majority of so called *'Terrorist'* (meaning political) groups are nothing but a cover for economic murder. The IRA may say that they are fighting for a United Ireland, but it hasn't stopped the leaders becoming extremely rich through drug trafficking and other economic crimes.

DOMESTIC MURDER This usually involves the family or acquaintances of the victim, and is the most common. A row gets out of hand and the wife picks up a poker, a fracas in the street after closing time ends with someone being stabbed, these are the bulk of the killings dealt with by the police.

CONTRACT MURDER. This type of killing seems to be getting more and more common, but in fact in the vast majority of cases it should more correctly be grouped in one of the above classifications. A wife might hire a killer to murder her husband, this is just a variation on domestic murder. A businessman will get someone to do away with a troublesome partner, this is just a variation on economic killing. Very rarely will you get a true *'Contract killing'*, where someone is murdered for revenge or because they are becoming a nuisance to some powerful group such as a Government.

It is fairly clear that we will not find Jack the Ripper in the Economic or Domestic murder grouping. His victims had pathetically few belongings, and the list of possessions found with Catharine Eddowes rules out robbery as a motive altogether. Likewise this wasn't a one-off flare up occurring between couples or friends, the sheer number of victims rules this out. He wasn't a spree murderer, he had no intention of going out in a blaze of glory, his motivation was to kill and escape, and similarly no attempt was ever made to attribute the murders to any particular group. There has been some speculation that because the graffiti at Goulston Street mentioned *'Juwes'* and because Liz Stride's body was found next to a club mainly frequented by Socialist Jews, the Jack the Ripper murders were an attempt to implicate the Jewish population. This is nonsense. It is equally valid to state that all the murders took place within a few yards of a Public House therefore they were committed in an attempt to blame publicans. Bearing this in mind I believe we can safely eliminate Political murder as a viable grouping.

When we first look at the Contract murder grouping however we run into our first problems. Mainly notable authorities on the Ripper murders have quite firmly nailed their colours to the Contract murder mast. Stephen Knight in his excellent book, *'Jack the Ripper: The Final Solution'* (some readers might question why I should refer to a book so totally discredited as excellent. It is worthy of praise because of the time and effort he put into it and the vast amount of new material he discovered. The fact that he allowed himself to be totally misled by certain people doesn't negate this). I'm sure most readers will be familiar with the theory, but for those of you who aren't it speculates that the murders were carried out by a consortium of killers to protect a Royal Secret. In other words they were contract killers for the Crown. This theory, slightly amended was also offered in Melvyn Fairclough's book, *'The Ripper and the Royals'*, however since Fairclough relied on the same primary source as Knight pepped up with some *'diaries'* supposedly written by Abberline, he should have known better. The truth of the matter is quite simply this, professional contract killers are just that - professional, and it must be assumed that if they were employed on behalf of the Crown (who aren't short of a bob or two) then the killer(s) would be very good at his job. The women would have simply and quietly disappeared, not killed in such a way that the whole world is still talking about it over a hundred years later.

A modern example of this type of thinking is the Kennedy assassination. No sooner had the poor man been buried than the rumours started to fly. It was the Mafia, the KGB, the Cubans, a combination of all of them, the CIA, the FBI, the Dallas Police and so on and so on. Doesn't anyone stop to think that if any of those highly professional organisations wanted Kennedy dead he would have been murdered in such a way that no one would ever know, not disposed of in such a manner that everyone and their dog is still talking about it?

The real way organisations such as these kill was revealed in 1954 when Nicolai Kokhlov, a SMERSH agent defected to the West. With him he brought various weapons that had been issued to him for the purpose of murdering anti Soviet targets. They included a packet of cigarettes that concealed a miniature pistol, on accepting a cigarette from the packet the target was quietly shot. Another weapon was an ingenious gas pistol consisting of a false cigarette that concealed a capsule of cyanide gas. The assassin clenched the cigarette in his teeth and when drawing close to his victim, broke the phial of poison with his tooth and blowing down the tube expelled the gas like a blow gun into the victims face. The assassin was advised to hold his breath whilst doing this! Crude though it may seem this method had been used to murder five people whose mysterious deaths were put down as heart attacks!

The truth of the Kennedy assassination is that it wasn't at all glamorous or mysterious, he was shot by Lee Harvey Oswald, a mentally unbalanced loner. His were not the only shots fired that day and that is where the agencies made their biggest mistake. Instead of coming out with the truth they attempted to cover up what really happened thus ensuring the conspiracy

141

theories will be around well into the next millennium. There was a conspiracy of silence, but it was done with the best of motives, unfortunately as these things do, it backfired.

We are therefore left with the category of Sex or Power murders, and it is in here we shall find our Jack lurking.

Rape has often been described as a crime of power not sex, the rapist wants to show the world that he has such awesome power that he can commit the most heinous of crimes without anyone being able to stop him, the danger is of course that soon rape will fail to satisfy this lust for power and he then moves on to the next stage. This next stage often involves imprisoning and torturing his helpless victims, finally culminating in murder. For some men the act of rape is not enough, and they move straight to the murder stage. These crimes are often the hardest to stop as the victims are usually chosen completely at random, and there is little or no evidence to bring the killer to justice - the only witnesses are usually murdered.

Peter Sutcliffe belongs to this class, his first attack on a prostitute was in 1969 when he coshed a woman with a sock full of gravel. It is interesting to note that he did not attempt to rape or molest her, he just moved straight on to the murder mode. He failed to kill her however and it is noticeable that his next attack was in 1971 when he again attacked a prostitute, but this time substituting a brick in the sock in place of the ineffective gravel. This again failed to kill the woman and for his next attack in 1975 he had graduated to a hammer, a weapon he was to use time and time again with such brutal efficiency. An interesting point to note in this series of killings is the variety of weapons Sutcliffe used to murder and mutilate his victims. A hammer, a piece of rope, a rusty screwdriver (which he had actually gone to the trouble of sharpening to a point) and lastly a knife. The only item among those used that could possibly be called a weapon proper is the knife, all the rest were normal tools. This makes a mockery of the 'ban it' brigade who want to ban the weapons used in murder and not ban the murderer. After the Dunblane murders there was an outcry for all handguns to be banned - why? After Hungerford the cry was to ban all self loading rifles, this ban although in force, didn't save one victim of the Dunblane murderer, he simply used something else. A recent

142

case where a mentally deranged woman went into a Social Security office and started stabbing people highlights this. When the kitchen knife she was using became embedded in the skull of one of her victims, she merely took a screwdriver out of her bag and used that. Murderers murder people and they will use whatever weapons they have to hand or can make, removing certain inanimate objects from circulation does not effect them in the slightest.

The other interesting point to note is the escalation, not necessarily in the violence, but in the effectiveness in the methods of killing. The gravel filled sock didn't work, substitute a brick, if that doesn't work use a hammer, and when the hammer alone proved ineffective it was coupled with strangulation or stabbing. It was almost as if he was trying out methods of killing until he found one that worked, and when he did he varied very little from it. Sutcliffe's craving for power, this insatiable lust to be recognised as something above the ordinary is highlighted by a notice displayed in the cab of his truck. It read *'In this truck is a man whose latent genius, if unleashed, would rock the world, whose dynamic energy, would overpower those around him. Better let him sleep'.* A more chilling indication of the motive for the murders would be hard to find.

It is another indication of the power murderer that the victims are very often not raped or assaulted in the usual pattern of lust murders. Quite often a substitute act will be committed on the bodies of the victim, such as mutilation, quite often with a knife. It is almost as if the knife is raping the victim, substituting for the penis. Only two of the Yorkshire Ripper's supposed victims had been the subject of intercourse (whether rape or not it was impossible to tell). One of these, Jean Harrison was later discounted, and the possibility has just been raised that the other, Helen Rytka, may have been murdered by someone else. It is very relevant to note that when Sutcliffe was finally caught he was in the company of another prostitute with whom he had attempted, and failed, to have sexual intercourse. It is also interesting that up to this point there had been nothing untoward in his behaviour with the woman. Could this inability to perform sexually be the trigger that made him kill? In other words if he managed to have intercourse would that be sufficient proof of his *'power'* and thus negate the need to kill his victims. Was he so aware of his failing in this area that with the majority of his victims he simply murdered them without any attempt at sex?

Timing is another element in the power murderer's actions that bear examination. The murderer is like a kettle on a hotplate, when it boils - he kills, but when the kettle boils depends on many variables. How full is the kettle? Is it filled with cold water or hot? How high is the heat? All these factors must be taken into account. Sutcliffe's murders stretched for five years, from 1975 to 1980 and so it is obvious that for a lot of the time he managed to control the boil factor. The actual dates of the killings reveal something else, they are totally haphazard, with no relevance as to whether he was working or not, or even if he was married or not, when the kettle boiled - he killed. Look at other killers of this type and you will find a remarkable similarity in the haphazard nature of the timings.

SUTCLIFFE 30th, 20th, 5th, 23rd, 26th, 1st, 21st, 31st, 16th, 4th, 2nd, 18th and finally 17th.

BUNDY, 1st, 12th, 17th, 6th, 1st, 11th, 14th, 14th, 2nd, 2nd, 18th, 31st, 8th, 12th, 15th, 6th, 15th, 15th, and finally 9th.

DE SALVO 14th, 28th, 30th, 30th, 19th, 20th, 5th, 31st, 9th, 6th, 8th, 23rd, and finally 4th.

GALY 16th, 24th, 2nd, 6th, 29th, 12th and finally 20th.

NELSON 20th, 2nd, 10th, 24th, 16th, 19th, 20th, 21st, 15th, 18th, 24th, 23rd, 28th, 27th, 30th, 1st, 3rd, 8th and finally 9th.

Now if you look at these figures broken down in a week by week analysis you notice that in the first week of a month there were 18 murders committed, in the second week 16, the third 20 and the last week 16. The amount of killings taking place in any one week is remarkably similar to that taking place in any other week.

What these dates show is that the *'patterns'* of killings so beloved of fiction writers are just that, fiction. David Berkowitz, Son of Sam, was asked about this very point. He was asked how he chose the dates he would go out to kill, his answer is chilling in the extreme. He replied that he went out every night to kill, it was just that sometimes it was possible and other times it wasn't. There are no series of murders carried out on the 3rd or the 23rd of each month, or alternate months or whatever. When a killer decides to strike, he strikes without regard to the calendar or the stopwatch. The interesting thing is of course that when we look at the dates of Jack the Ripper's killings, it would appear that he did just that.

JACK THE RIPPER 31st, 8th, 30th and finally 9th.

In other words the attacks seem to have taken place during a small time frame which encompasses the very end of a month and the first few days of a month. If you now look at the two attacks which I believe to be the work of the Ripper, Annie Millwood and Ada Wilson you will find that they both took place within this time frame, Millwood was attacked on the 25th and Wilson on the 28th. It might be argued that the 25th is a bit too far from the *'very end of the month'*, but don't forget this was February so it is indeed at the very end. Now add to this the murder of Martha Tabram that I also believe to be the work of the Ripper and you will find that this occurred on the 7th. Adding in the two attacks and Tabram's murder the picture is now thus:

JACK THE RIPPER 25th, 28th, 7th, 31st, 8th, 30th and finally 9th.

Now in itself this could be nothing more than an interesting coincidence, or it could point the way to the fact that the Ripper wasn't subject to the boiling kettle - he wrote his own agenda! In other words Jack the Ripper was the ultimate power killer - he killed where and when he decided he would, he could control the *'boiling kettle'*. Killers of this type are extremely rare thank goodness, for it is very often the lack of control over their homicidal urges that lead to the capture of most serial killers, if they continue killing eventually the police will stumble over them. Leopold and Loeb could be said to be this type of *'controlled'* killer. They decided they wanted to murder someone, they chose the place, they chose the time, and they went ahead and murdered their victim, with no more reason to do so than just to prove they could. Thankfully the pair were too stupid not to leave a highly incriminating clue behind at the scene of their atrocity which led to their early arrest. It is horrifying to contemplate just how many more victims might have been murdered, if they had got away with the first one.

Ronald Cooper is another example. Deciding at the early age of eleven he wanted to become a *'homosexual murderer'*, his first attack was on a young child in 1963, fortunately he failed on this occasion to kill his victim. By 1976 he was determined to carry out his plan and putting pen to paper laid out his intentions to become a famous murderer. He eventually succeeded in murdering a twelve year old boy Mark Garnett, recording the details of the horrific crime in his diary. He was caught soon afterwards by a fantastic coincidence. Mark Garnett happened to be a friend of a boy named Pohl, who had been abducted (presumably as a prelude to murder) earlier in the year. On this occasion Cooper let his intended victim go, and after the Garnett murder Pohl told the authorities about Cooper who was arrested and convicted, mainly on the evidence in his own diaries. It could be said Cooper wrote his way to the gallows. If Cooper had murdered Pohl the chances are he would never have been caught.

It is this element of control that made Jack the Ripper so very dangerous. Because he dictated the time and the place of the killings, and not his emotions, it was very unlikely that he would ever be discovered in the commission of a murder. Many authorities have put the Ripper's evading capture down to pure luck, but as a famous golfer said once in reply to a reporter that his last stroke had been very lucky, *"Yes and the more I practice the luckier I get!"* A brief look at one aspect of the Eddowes murder demonstrates this. Mitre square and Church passage (leading into Mitre Square) were patrolled by two Police officers. PC Watkins of the City force patrolled Mitre Square, and PC Harvey of the Metropolitan force patrolled Church passage. Now the *'beat'* system of patrolling has much to commend it, it does present a highly visible police presence, but its main drawback is that it does allow the determined criminal to pinpoint with remarkable accuracy the whereabouts of the police at any given time. A relatively minor point, but one that could attain immense importance, is the fact that the police were issued with the same type of boot that was in use in the Army. These boots were made entirely of leather with metal studs driven into the soles to improve wear and grip. Unfortunately it also made the boots extremely noisy, and the presence of an approaching police officer could be signalled when the constable was still a good way off indeed this was seen as such a handicap to the catching of the killer that several papers voiced the opinion that Police officers should be issued with boots with rubber soles and heels, thus allowing them to silently approach their quarry! Ridiculous as this may sound it does not negate the fact that the Police boots did give adequate warning to any wrongdoer that an officer was approaching. In the Eddowes case this fact may have given the killer the extra vital few minutes he needed to make good his escape.

Eddowes and her probable killer were spotted by Lawende and his friends at the entrance to Church passage at about 1.35 am. At this time PC Harvey was in Aldgate High Street, and PC Watkins had just left Mitre Square. PC Watkins wasn't due to return to Mitre Square for at least another 10 or 15 minutes, and PC Harvey wasn't due to enter Church passage for another 5 or 10 minutes, so the killer knew that to evade PC Harvey, all he had to do was to get down Church passage in a couple of minutes, don't forget Harvey didn't actually enter Mitre Square, just walked to the end of the passage and back. It is very probable that the killer was actually in the process of mutilating his victim when Harvey walked to the end of the passage, but keeping a cool head, and knowing the darkness hid him, he stayed put. As soon as he had finished, the killer crossed the square diagonally and left by St. James Place, just as PC Watkins entered the Square from Mitre Street. Some might say this is taking things too far, but is it? The facts are that neither constable saw the killer although by sheer geography they must have been within yards of him, and don't forget the square was extremely dark. (Mr. Paley in his new, 1995, book - Jack the Ripper The Simple Truth- is in error when he describes the square as *'fairly well lit with five lamps'*. Reference to the sketch map prepared for the inquest by the City Surveyor, F W Foster shows quite clearly that Mitre Square proper only had one lamp, and that was over sixty feet away from the corpse. There was another lamp, though further away at the end of Church passage, and another at the Mitre Street entrance to the square, but neither of these lamps would have given any illumination to the Square itself. It must also be remembered that this was the time before gas mantles were invented, the lamps consisted of a lit gas jet, and the illumination was on a par with a large candle, bearing in mind that the dirty glass on the lamp itself would reduce illumination still further. The lamps of the day just about illuminated a small patch at the base of the lamp post, hence this became a favourite place for prostitutes to wait, as it was one of the very few places they could be seen. Lili Marlene wasn't waiting underneath the lamp light by accident! (I spoke to Melvin Harris recently and he told me of some experiments he had carried out with actual gas lamps and his results confirm that they were a very poor provider of light).

There will of course be those who dismiss this as far too complicated, as endowing the Ripper with far more intelligence and planning than he actually possessed. However experience, bought with the lives of innocent victims, show this not to be the case. Serial killers are often gifted with a higher than normal intelligence, indeed this is one reason why they turn killer, frustrated with the inability of the rest of the world to see things the way they do. To take an extreme example, many of the worst offenders in the Nazi Party were highly intelligent men and women, many holding Doctorates in philosophy and science. To these people hunting humans is just the same as going fishing, or attending an Opera, a pleasurable experience that benefits from a bit of forward planning. At the height of the Bundy murders, he still managed to lure single girls into the back of his van by placing his arm in a sling and struggling with a piece of furniture, his victims would unwittingly offer to help him and end up being bundled into the back of the van. When this ploy grew stale he tried another tack. Approaching his intended victim he explained he was a police officer and that someone had tried to steal her car. She went with him to inspect the damage then agreed to ride with him to police headquarters to make a statement. On the way Bundy tried to abduct her but she fought back and thankfully escaped. Incidentally it was through analysing the Bundy case amongst others, that Police forces around the world changed their advice to rape victims. Women were always advised not to resist their attacker, but to submit to rape. This ludicrous advice sentenced many women to death as the rapist, not demonstrating his power by raping a submissive victim often murdered them as well. It is not purely coincidence that many victims who have escaped from the clutches of killers have done so because they fought back. Lorraine Vigil, an intended victim of the serial rapist and murderer Harvey Glatman, fought with her assailant even though she had been shot and wounded. She finally managed to get the gun from him and hold him at gunpoint until rescued by a police officer. By her extraordinary courage and refusal to become a victim she brought to an end the horrendous career of a serial killer. Glatman paid the penalty for picking the wrong victim in the gas chamber at San Quentin, on the 18th August 1959.

The ingenuity displayed and the careful planning and execution of these crimes should not be overlooked. The *'boiling kettle'* may tell them when to kill, but be assured that a lot of them have got the *'how'* well planned in advance. Incidentally Bundy upset a lot of Liberal thinking psychologists during a series of interviews he gave while on death row. They asked him why he had done the terrible things he had done, and sat back, pencils poised, no doubt expecting some long winded diatribe, that put the blame firmly on Society, his mother, the Government, his upbringing or just about anything else he could think of. They weren't quite ready for his frank admission that he liked raping and murdering women - it gave him pleasure. (This same type of convoluted thinking is no doubt behind the constant protestations from *'penal reformers'* who constantly decry our penal system, and point to the rate of criminals re-offending as proof that we shouldn't lock anyone up at all. I'll always remember the answer a Prison Officer (as opposed to Prison Governor) gave to this point *'Of course they re-offend'* he said, *'they're criminals that's what they do for a living!'*)

This last very important point also highlights another reason why murderers are so often not caught for many years. *'Normal'* human beings cannot understand the rationale behind a killer's thinking. They cannot accept that there can be people who take pleasure in dismembering living victims with an electric carving knife, or eating parts of their bodies. One killer was asked why he injected his still living victims with acid, his answer was quite simply *'I wanted to see what would happen'*. Why this should be so is a mystery, every age has thrown up its collections of people who are not only quite willing but actually enjoy inflicting the most unspeakable cruelties on their fellow man. Many years ago of course it was very likely that such people would find gainful, and legal employment, as torturers and interrogators. As we progress and it becomes less and less acceptable to use these methods, it is as if deprived of their pleasure in one way they will seek it in another. And yet we as a society still shut our eyes to the reality of their existence, we still try and fool ourselves that when perpetrators of such monstrosities are finally found, they will be found complete with horns, cloven feet and forked tails. When a smiling, good looking Ted Bundy is brought before the court, our horror is compounded when we hear of all the helpless women he butchered. When a pudgy but still normal looking David Berkowitz is standing in the dock, how can we accept this as Son of Sam? The clown painted face of businessman John Wayne Gacy hid a mask of sheer unimaginable cruelty. Who could have imagined the thirty seven year old civil servant at the Soho Job Centre would turn out to be Dennis Nilsen slaughterer and dismemberer of almost 20 homosexuals?

No matter how hard we try none of us can see these killers as in anyway normal. We expect them to be deformed, or with a limp, or a permanent scowl and a snarl, anything that would make them stand out from the rest of the common herd. For us to admit that these monsters are to all outward appearances, normal, would be too horrifying to contemplate. How could we retain our sanity knowing that the next person we open our door to wants to inject our living bodies with acid *'To see what happens?'* The scenario is too much for our minds to bear, so we surround ourselves with the myth that these people aren't human, but lust crazed monsters, and can easily be recognised as such. This form of self delusion also manifests itself when the victim of the crime is someone famous.

If we admit that Kennedy, the most powerful man in the world at the time could be shot by a lone, mentally unstable gunman, then what hope is there for us mere mortals. No, for someone to penetrate such a colossal security screen, it must have been a conspiracy by some all powerful factions. Kennedy himself accepted the truth, shortly before his death he said, *"If someone really wants to kill the President of the United States all they require is a tall building and a rifle."* If the victims are not famous but the crimes are, then the same is true, this is why there are so many conspiracy theories about the Jack the Ripper killings. Surely a lone killer, an ordinary man could not strike with such impunity and disappear without trace? Surely he must be protected by some high up power or secret society?

The way we see such killers, and the way in which they elude capture is very important, for they colour our perception of the sort of man we are looking for. For example, when the Whitechapel murders started, they were of such ferocity and hideousness that they could not possibly be the work of an Englishman, the killer had to be a foreigner in other words a Jew. All the early newspaper reports talk of a *'skulking figure, hiding in the shadows and leaping out to terrorise his next victims'*. And this is what people and to a certain extent the police, believed. They honestly thought that the killer roamed the streets with an evil scowl on his face, his features obscured by a cloak, in his hand a long knife dripping with blood. Is it any wonder that the actual killer managed to pass so freely about the streets of Whitechapel? When Pizer, the unfortunate *'Leather Apron'* was arrested and subsequently released, the rumour started that the killer was now a doctor. Here was another readily identifiable enemy, the upper classes. Now the killer had to be resplendent in top hat, opera cloak and of course carrying his infamous black Gladstone bag. Most witness statements from now on talk of a smartly dressed stranger, usually heavily moustached and of course carrying something in his hand. Devotees of the early Keystone Cops movies will of course recognise the archtypical villain, compare the man described by Hutchinson with one of these early movie villains and you will see he has got him down to a *'T'*, even down to the spats and heavy watchchain.

This simplified version of the villain, also coloured people's perceptions as to what he would eventually do with himself. After seeing the dreadful carnage of Millers Court no one would argue with Macnaghten when he wrote in his memoranda,

151

'A much more rational and workable theory, to my way of thinking, is that the 'rippers' brain gave way altogether after his awful glut in Millers Court and that he then committed suicide...'

Macnaghten was assuming the killer was a *'normal'* person with the morality of a normal person, and when he found out what he had done, he would kill himself out of remorse. A perfectly rational theory if you were talking about someone who had suffered a temporary blackout or breakdown, but completely out of the question if you are talking about someone like Bundy, who in his own words *'liked killing people'*. Killing people to a serial killer is as natural an act as putting on your trousers, and no one would suggest you commit suicide because you dressed yourself. The importance of this way of thinking is of course that anyone committing suicide soon after the last murder would be a natural suspect.

In all the cases of serial killers, I cannot recall a single one where the killer committed suicide out of remorse. The Jack the Stripper murders of the mid sixties are often quoted as a case where this did in fact happen. In the published accounts of these murders, all say the same thing, that the police were narrowing down their list of suspects, when one of them committed suicide out of remorse for what he had done and this closed the case. However I recently spoke to a friend of mine who was a Detective Constable on that case, and almost in passing he let slip that the suspect killed himself shortly after being bailed. The conversation proceeded when it finally filtered through what he had said. I asked him how the man could have been bailed if he was never arrested, and then he told me what really happened. The police knew who the killer was without a shadow of a doubt, but they were awaiting vital evidence to come back from the police forensic laboratory. The senior police officer wanted this man off the streets and had him arrested on another charge. When the case came up before magistrates the police opposed bail, and the very senior officer appeared in the witness box himself to speak for the motion to remand in custody. The police couldn't tell the magistrates that they wanted him held for a series of murders because as yet they still lacked the proof but they hoped that the appearance of such a Senior Officer in what was a relatively minor offence would be the nod that was as good as a wink to the magistrates. However the Magistrates completely failed to get the message and released the suspect on bail. My friend then approached him as he was leaving the court and off the record marked his card, he was told the police knew he was the killer and from now on he would be under twenty-four hour surveillance. The man went home and gassed himself. Now some readers may think this is not exactly cricket, but it undoubtedly saved further lives. The point is of course Jack the Stripper committed suicide because he knew he was going to spend the rest of his life in prison, and not through any sense of remorse.

I now believe this was the second time the Metropolitan Police knew who the killer of prostitutes was but were forced to let him go. For I have no doubt in my own mind that Inspector F G Abberline had a very good idea who Jack the Ripper was, not only did he know this, but he informed his superiors of his suspicions, and they, in their own way, confirmed them.

There have been many times in the hunt for killers where the police have been misled by their own methods. I'm sure readers are familiar with the term 'MO', meaning Modus Operandi, or method of working. This is a system that relies on the criminal working to a generally conforming pattern, a safe cracker who blows a safe using a carefully drilled hole and a thimble of nitro glycerine, doesn't generally attack his next safe with a sledgehammer. A forger who has spent a lifetime forging banknotes, very rarely changes to being a pickpocket half way through his criminal career. Many years ago this was the way that a lot of criminals were caught, the detectives got to know the individual style of a criminal and could make very accurate decisions as to who had committed what crime. One famous burglar always committed his crimes in bare feet, he claimed it gave him a better grip on the drainpipes he used for access, one night one of these drainpipes gave way, and Flannelfoot would steal no more. Unfortunately what went along with this knowledge of a criminals MO was an almost encyclopaedic knowledge of the policeman's 'patch' and it's inhabitants. What enabled these officers to make such arrests was a combination of all these factors.

As time went by, the police force changed, it became more mobile, more fluid. No longer would a detective spend his entire career on one *'patch'* as his career progressed he would be transferred from one area to another. To counter this loss of local knowledge they committed their experience to paper for the benefit of those who would come after. Unfortunately this merely led to a system of records outlining the simplest details of a criminals MO, it lacked the other ingredients of the recipe, the knowledge, the instinct. Too much reliance was placed on an MO being carved in stone, intractable and unchanging.

In the mid seventies the North of England was rocked by a series of robbery/murders of Sub Post Masters. The MO was the same in every case, the killer would break into the premises at night and attempt to rob the safe. If the occupants showed any inclination to resist they were immediately shot down. Three sub post-masters had been murdered in this way in over twenty robberies that netted the killer roughly £20,000.

When a young heiress, Lesley Whittle, was kidnapped in January 1975, no one suspected that the two crimes were in any way linked, one was robbery and the other kidnapping. What the police failed to realise was the fact that the MO was the same in both cases - it's just no-one recognised it. All the premises had been entered at night by a lone intruder. The crimes had been executed with a considerable amount of planning, and with an incredible amount of ruthlessness. That was the true MO, not that one was burglary and the other kidnapping. Possibly as a result of failing to realise that the kidnapping had been carried out by an extremely clever and ruthless man, the investigation was not a success and Lesley Whittle was murdered. Donald Neilson, The Black Panther, was eventually caught by accident, when two officers stopped to question him one night and he panicked and produced a gun.

This blind reliance on MO has caused more than one investigation to go off in the wrong direction. The Boston Strangler, Albert de Salvo, wasn't recognised as the serial killer he was for some time, because the methods used to kill his victims were different, he strangled them, beat them and used a knife. Even his victims didn't conform to any pattern, age wise they varied from 19 to 80. Even after he had been arrested, the authorities still didn't realise the man they had in custody was the infamous strangler, mainly because his MO as revealed by the records was for breaking and entering.

In the early 80s in California several young women were murdered with appalling brutality, the bodies of several of them were decapitated. When the headless body of John Murray was found in his van, there wasn't any attempt to link the killings. The motive for the women's murders had been sexual, there seemed no motive for the man's murder. It wasn't until Douglas Clark and Carol Bundy were arrested for the *'Sunset Strip Slayings'* as the murders became known as, that the truth was revealed. The murderous duo had killed Murray because Murray had unwisely voiced his opinion that Clark was responsible for the murders. This is an interesting example of serial killers quite calmly and effectively removing someone they saw as a threat.

The real MO in the Sunset Strip Slayings was the fact that the victims were picked up in a vehicle, killed by shooting and the bodies subsequently mutilated. This was the thread that tied all the murders together, the fact that not all the victims were the same sex or murdered for the same reason, was, to a large extent immaterial.

By trying to *'fine tune'* an MO too far, the investigator runs the real risk of missing a connection. I have heard one authority on the Whitechapel murders state quite confidently that Martha Tabram couldn't possibly be a Ripper victim because she was stabbed in the chest and the other victims were slashed! This is trying to read too much into minor details, very often a murderer will vary his method of killing, sometimes to find a more efficient way of killing, sometimes just for the hell of it.

A more refined version of the MO is the Psychological Profile. This is using all the available data on a series of crimes to formulate opinions as to what type of person the killer is. In fact it goes much further than this, for not only is the information relevant only to the killer, but often details of his/her background, childhood, upbringing and state of mind are offered by the profiler. An examination of the case of the Mad Bomber of New York highlights exactly what profiling can achieve.

For sixteen years during and after World War II, New York had suffered a series of bomb attacks. According to the frequent letters and notes that the bomber left, the reason for the attacks was a grievance, real or imaginary, that the bomber had with a company called Consolidated Edison. A Dr. James Brussel undertook to complete a psychological profile of the Bomber, and his results were incredibly detailed, even down to the way the Bomber would button his double breasted suit when arrested. (In fact the Mad Bomber, George Metesky, was in his pyjamas when arrested, but on changing into his street clothes, buttoned his suit exactly as predicted). This triumph of detective work had the unfortunate effect of convincing a large number of police officers that Psychological Profiling was an infallible method of catching criminals. Instead of realising that they now had another weapon to add to their armoury, they tended to discard tried and tested techniques and rely on the profile alone. This led to a unfortunate tendency to look for a suspect who fitted the profile and disregard everyone else. In much the same way the first Photofit picture used in England bore an uncanny resemblance to the criminal, the success of the first major case of profiling carried with it the seeds of its own destruction. Fortunately this was recognised in time and law enforcement officers were left in no doubt that profiling can assist in whittling down suspects, and should not be used as a blueprint for manufacturing one. For example if you have three suspects and one is black and the other two are white, having a profile stating that the criminal is a black man may help you in concentrating your efforts on that suspect. However if you are armed with the same profile you can't just go out and arrest the first black man you see because he fits!

In 1981 a team of experts in the field of profiling, pathology and two authorities on the Whitechapel murders started the *'Ripper Project'*. This was an attempt by using the latest methods, computer analysis and detection to construct a Physcological Profile of Jack the Ripper. Among the conclusions reached about Jack the Ripper were:

He was a white male, aged between 28-36 who lived or worked in the Whitechapel area.

He would have been interviewed during the investigation, but would have been dismissed as a suspect, probably because he didn't fit the 'Blood thirsty ghoul' description that was thought to apply to the killer.

He would be a quiet loner, inoffensive, withdrawn but neat and orderly in appearance. He would drink at the local pubs.

He would not have committed suicide after his last murder.

He believed the killings were justified.

These interesting conclusions are further expanded by the work done by Professor David Canter, Britain's leading Psychological Profiler, who had such success with the *'Railway Rapist'*, John Duffy. Professor Canter states *'a large percentage of serial killers live within a few minutes walk of their crimes'*. He even goes so far as to state that according to his *'circle hypothesis'* the culprit will often be found living within an area *circumscribed by his crimes*.

'One of our firmest hypotheses about a criminal's actions, an hypothesis growing in strength and clarity as our studies unfold, is that knowledge of and familiarity with an area is a prerequisite for many violent criminals'.

Jon Ogan, has used his many talents to produce 'THE WHITECHAPEL MURDERS OF 1888 AND INVESTIGATIVE PSYCHOLOGY', an extremely interesting paper on creating an *'offender profile'* of Jack the Ripper. This was first presented at the 1996 International Conference on The Whitechapel Murders in Ipswich. The paper highlights some very important results obtained from studying thousands of sexual assaults and murders. In 1946 a Chicago Police Lieutenant, Otto Erlanson, noted that in 2,624 cases of sexual assault, 82% of the offences were carried out in the same police district that the offender lived. Canter and Larkin carried out a similar study in 1993 and found out that in their study the figure was an amazing 87%. Considering that the two studies were carried out in different countries, fifty years apart the similarity of the results are astounding. An impartial glance at the studies would assume that the modern figure would be much lower due to the availability of personal transport, however this is not so. Taking a fifty year step back from Erlanson's study which places us almost in 1888, we could therefore expect to find a similar result, in other words there is an approximate 83% chance that Jack the Ripper lived very, very close to where he committed the crimes.

The mental state of the offender was also examined in some detail. Here Jon agrees with the FBI findings that in cases of mutilative homicide (where the body has been mutilated to some extent) the perpetrator had some form of mental illness. This need not have been the strait-jacket foaming at the mouth type of illness, for instance Gordon Cummins, The Blackout Ripper, suffered from mythomania (inventing tales of self importance). This does however give us an indication that our culprit will be suffering from some form of mental aberration (over and above that normally associated with a serial murderer!).

The subject of interpersonal skills was also examined. How well did the killer get on with his victims. Was he acceptable to them or was his persona such that they didn't want to spend any more than the absolute minimum of time with him? For example many of Bundy's victims spent a great deal of time with him before they were murdered, apparently completely at ease. In the Whitechapel murders though this is not the case. In every instance (apart from Mary Kelly where we simply do not know) the victim was slaughtered minutes after meeting with her killer. We know this because of the very limited time frame involved, PC Watkins patrolled Mitre Square - nothing there, fifteen minutes later he's back and there's poor Kate Eddowes lying dead. Quite obviously the murderer didn't waste much time with foreplay! This is important because it gives us an idea of the type of person the Ripper would be, not necessarily a blood lusting ghoul, but quite likely the sort of person who made you feel *'uncomfortable'*, possibly as a result of his mental condition. Donald Rumbelow, who is quite a large police officer and certainly no shrinking violet, tells of the time when he visited a man who had written to him saying he had some Ripper artefacts. When he got there he found the *'artefacts'* consisted of crudely drawn pictures of naked corpses and other distasteful objects. When the man expressed an interest in seeing a dead body Donald made his excuses and left. There was nothing overtly threatening about the man, and even if there was it is likely he could have protected himself, it was just his entire behaviour made him so uncomfortable he wanted to get out of the place - and quickly!

Using all this information and research Jon Ogan's conclusions as to the type of man the killer is likely to be is as follows:

White, Western European Male.

Found within the 25 to 35 age group.

Unmarried.

Unskilled labourer - tradesman class of occupation.

Living within a 800 metre radius of his crimes (this ties in very well with Canter who predicts him to be living practically in the centre).

Previous offences for assault, robbery and sexually related offences (at Conference this was originally laid down as 'Convictions' until it was pointed out that if he hadn't been caught there wouldn't have been a conviction. The point was accepted).

Mental Illness likely.

Possibly some form of acquaintanceship with victims.

Low interactional style. Poor work record. Poor at forming relationships. Noted selection of old, frail victims. Poor anger management control.

Taking all these facts together it is beginning to become clear that Jack the Ripper was the original Invisible Man. Like G K Chesterton's postman, everyone saw him, but no-one noticed him. While the press and the populace saw him as some kind of Comic Opera villain, complete with twirling moustaches and shiny leather bag, Jack the Ripper hunched his shoulders against the cold, and mingled with the rest of the crowd. How he must have laughed to read the newspaper accounts of his crimes, complete with lurid stories of the killer stalking through the East End like a blood thirsty Pawnee Indian. It is strange to think that he was probably a part of the very crowds that pressed in around the sites of the latest outrage, calling for the instant hanging of the killer.

Before leaving the subject of Psychological or Offender Profiling, let us remind ourselves what is its purpose. It should only be used to eliminate candidates from our suspect list, and to re-enforce actions against those who fit the profile. It is NOT meant to be a shopping list for a murderer, you cannot arm yourself with the profile and go looking for someone who fits, you have to have your 'Usual Suspects' first, and then bring the profile into play - it is the same as genetic fingerprinting or normal fingerprinting, used to confirm rather than delineate. So how do we find our 'Usual Suspects'? There is only one way - good old fashion detective work. Mes enfants it is time to exercise the little grey cells!

Chapter Eight

"In the discovery of secret things and in the investigation of hidden causes, stronger reasons are obtained from sure experiments and demonstrated arguments than from probable conjectures and the opinions of philosophical speculators of the common sort"
William Gilbert 1540 - 1603

The one thing that has caused me the most amazement over the years studying the Whitechapel murders is how little investigation has been done. Now before you draw attention to the many hundreds of books that have been written on the subject, I ought to point out that research does not equal investigation. The research that has been done on the subject is quite staggering, indeed it would appear that nothing is left to discover, except of course who the killer is. This has been possibly one of the problems, so many people have been concentrating on pure research without putting the results of that research to any practical use. For example what is the point in establishing the family tree of the victims? What possible use is it to know where they were born or what school they went to? This information can be of use in certain investigations where it is likely that the killer is a part of their life, but it is of no possible use at all in trying to establish who the culprit is in this particular case.

I have spoken to many people about this, and of course the majority of them say something along the lines of *'Well of course we'll never know for certain, it all happened too long ago.'* To some extent they are right, we will never know *for certain* but I believe it is possible to arrive at certain conclusions that are backed up by cold hard facts. Don't forget every investigation is an historic one, in other words every investigation takes place after the event, it's just in this case the gap between the crimes and the investigation is rather a long one.

So what exactly do we expect an investigation to reveal? Well you can do worse than to follow the advice of Rudyard Kipling when he wrote:

> "I keep six honest serving men,
> (They taught me all I knew);
> Their names are What and Why and When
> And How and Where and Who".

Once we have answered the what, why, when, how and the where, I believe we will have a reasonably accurate idea of the who.

A successful investigation relies on assembling as much information as is necessary to enable us to reach certain conclusions. This information will be obtained from two main sources;

ACTIVE INFORMATION This is information that is generated by the investigation, witness statements, alibis, rumours, anonymous letters and gossip.

INACTIVE INFORMATION This is information that is generated by the Crime itself weapons, wounds, forensic evidence and of course medical evidence.

Generally speaking inactive information is un-alterable. If for instance the victim has been killed with a knife, you can't change that to a gunshot just because your suspect carries a gun. If the victim was murdered at three in the morning, you can't change that to the afternoon because your prime suspect has an alibi for the morning. This isn't quite as silly as it sounds as one modern theory on Jack the Ripper blames all the murders on a certain suspect. When elementary research turned up the fact that the suspect in question was in fact in custody at the time of the last murder, this didn't faze the theorists at all. The authors of the theory now say that this particular murder wasn't done by Jack the Ripper at all - but a copy cat killer!! A more blatant example of altering evidence to fit a theory would be hard to find.

During the time of the Whitechapel murders there was very little inactive information to be had. Forensic evidence was rudimentary to say the least, only the last victim was photographed (at the scene of the crime) and even the medical evidence is contradictory and confusing. So for the main source of information on these murders we have to look to the Active Information.

Active information can be the most useful, but at the same time the most useless type of information to get. The majority of this type of information comes from that most imperfect of all evidence generators the eyewitness. Eyewitness information is notoriously un-reliable because it depends on that most imperfect of sources - the human being.

Humans are a mass of muscle, flesh, nerves and sinews, totally controlled by the human brain and this is where the problems start. It is not because the human brain is an imperfect tool - exactly the opposite that causes the problems. The human brain is far more sophisticated than the most complex computer and therein lies the beginnings of our troubles, for the brain has the ability to learn. It always causes me some amusement when so-called intelligent people seem to think that accusing someone of being prejudiced is slighting them in some way. Every human being that ever walked the earth is prejudiced in one way or the other, if he wasn't he wouldn't last long. Let me explain. If as a child you burnt yourself on a match or a fire, your brain stores the pain away, and alters your perception of life. Before burning yourself you might have laboured under the illusion that putting your hand in the fire is an OK thing to do, afterwards you are left in no doubt that it isn't. Your brain has altered the way you perceive fire, so that in future you can save yourself the pain of being burnt. You are now prejudiced against burning yourself. If your brain didn't do this, every time you came across fire you would stick your hand into it, your perception of fire would not have altered.

Now if you expand this to life in general you can see how the prejudices your brain stores away for you are vital for your survival. You quickly learn walking in front of trains is not a good idea, and leaping out of tall buildings is extremely counter productive. Now all these prejudices are beneficial, are helpful, but let's look at another case. Let us suppose that on your way home from work you are attacked and robbed by a coloured man. Let us further suppose that this happens several times.

163

Your brain now tells you that coloured men are dangerous and are to be avoided, it is doing its job to help you avoid danger. You are prejudiced against coloured men, quite naturally because your personal experience tells you coloured men are dangerous. Even though common sense will tell you that to judge all coloured men by your own very limited experience is irrational, nevertheless that is human nature.

What happens when on walking home one night you see a coloured man bending over the beaten body of another person. You might immediately jump to the conclusion that here is another incident similar to yours. If you then attack this man and drive him away, how would this appear in statement form? Would your natural prejudice against coloured men lead you to embellish your statement? Would you not be likely to accuse the man of attacking the victim, even though all you saw was a man bending over another? What if this coloured man was in fact a doctor giving aid to someone he had just seen being attacked by a white man, from his point of view he is doing a good turn and has been attacked and driven off by someone who could be the real perpetrator.

The danger is obvious, our perceptions are altered by the prejudices we harbour. Everyone has prejudices, there's nothing wrong in that, the trick is to be able to leave them to one side when we are involved in making a statement of fact, and that is very tricky. There was an advertising campaign run by a national paper some years ago which makes the point very well. It consisted of a number of photographs of a middle aged business man complete with briefcase and a boot-wearing skinhead. The various photos showed different scenes. In one the skinhead is running after the man who has a look of terror on his face, in another the skinhead is standing over the prostrate body of the man with the briefcase in his hand. Yet another shows the man being physically pushed by the skinhead. The caption to the advert states *'Only the Daily Blah gives you the full picture'* and then shows you the entire sequence of photographs. This shows quite clearly the businessman in danger from a falling piece of masonry. The skinhead shouts to attract his attention, then runs after him, and at great risk to himself pushes the man to safety. The final frame shows the skinhead helping the man to his feet and returning his briefcase to him.

Unfortunately witnesses very rarely get to see the entire sequence of events, they only usually manage to catch a brief glimpse. Now it is vitally important for the investigator to realise this, for this will dictate how much reliance can be placed on witnesses. The first thing that has to be established is *'Is the witness telling the truth or not?'* Notice I said is the witness not telling the truth, not is the witness lying. A witness who does not tell the truth may do so for one of four reasons:

1. Witness is mistaken.
2. Witness is unable to separate himself from prejudice.
3. Witness wishes to please.
4. Witness wishes to deceive.

Being mistaken is self explanatory, but let us examine reason No 2. In the case of the Jack the Ripper murders it is very noticeable how witnesses changed their statements to fit the prevailing prejudices. For example when the suspect was thought to be a Jew, every suspect was described as *'Foreign-looking'*, *'dark and sinister'*. When the rumour mill moved on to put a doctor in the frame, now the suspects became Opera cloak and top hat wearing, Gladstone bag-carrying toffs.

Statements about suspects were not deemed to be complete unless they were carrying a bag or package of some kind. PC Smith (Liz Stride) *'the man carried a paper wrapped parcel about eighteen inches by six'*. PC Spicer (arresting a suspect) *'he had the proverbial bag with him (a brown one)'* Mrs Pannier (Mary Kelly) *'he wore a black silk hat, black coat and carried a black shiny bag'*. Hutchinson (Mary Kelly) *'the bag he carried was American Cloth'*. And so on and so on. No one seemed to question the likelihood of any stranger openly carrying anything in their hands in the East End at that time. People were being set upon just because they looked suspicious, carrying something as attention arousing as a *'black shiny bag'* would have been akin to signing their own death warrant. The thought of the killer carrying anything is even more ludicrous. Would any streetwise prostitute allow a man carrying a bag in his hand to come close enough to strangle her before screaming the place down. This of course is overlooking the sheer impracticality of a savage killer asking his victim to wait a minute while he struggled with the knots on his parcel.

Reason No. 3 is also worthy of examination. Being interviewed by the police can be an extremely worrying and unsettling experience, especially if they are investigating something as serious as a murder. In these circumstances it is not unknown for the witness to say whatever he thinks the interrogator wishes to hear. A perfect example of this was the so called investigation by Social Services personnel, investigating alleged child abuse. The investigators were not trained interrogators and their method of questioning left a lot to be desired. They started from the assumption that all their suspicions were correct and all they had to do was to get statements from the children. In an appalling travesty of investigation they asked the children such questions as *'When did you see the baby being killed?'* The children naturally believed that the questioners wanted to hear about babies being killed, so they quite happily supplied *'details'*, all of which were of course total fiction, a skilful blend of their own imagination and half remembered items from the news and television programmes. Seeing their answers pleased their interrogators they carried on in the same vein, supplying even more and more lurid tales.

The Social Services were overjoyed that they had been *'vindicated'* and carried on. After several months of amassing such rubbish they proudly presented their *'evidence'* to the police, who promptly blew the whole thing out the water when they started to question the children. When one of the children realised that he was no longer being *'fed'* the information he was supposed to repeat, he promptly declared himself to be *'fed up with this game'*. The whole thing would have been laughable if we forget for one minute that on the basis of the *'evidence'* several children had been removed from their parents loving care, and the parents stigmatised by accusations that they had no chance to answer. In conclusion the Social Services regretted that *'errors of judgement had been made'*.

A child is a perfect example of this type of problem, because of their in-built wish to please adults. If you examine the testimony of Israel Schwartz, the same childlike desire is very noticeable. Schwartz has remarkable similarities with a child. He cannot speak the English language, therefore his ability to express himself clearly is flawed, just like a child. He equates the police to the type of official he knew in his own country that he has just left, the ultimate authority figure, just as adults are to children, and finally he takes the *'feed'* and supplies the information he believes the questioner wants to hear. He told the police the second man was holding a pipe, he changed this for the journalist, who is obviously looking for something more dramatic than a pipe, to a knife. The police ask for a description - he gives them one! It was almost as if any witness asked for a description or indeed any evidence, provided it, whether or not it had any basis in fact.

The last category is the witness who wishes to deceive or to put it another way, the witness who lies! Now strange as it may seem, although there are thousands of reasons for telling the truth, there are only two reasons for telling a lie. These are:

1.   To advertise.
2.   To conceal.

This may seem a rather strange thing to say, but think back to every lie you ever told, and you will find it will fit into one of those two categories. If you boast to your friends in the local pub about a passionate, but fictitious, date with an attractive young lady, you are trying to advertise. If you did in fact go out with her and your wife questions you, you will now conceal.

Now let us examine a witness who is telling the truth (as he or she honestly believes it to be) or in other words an accurate witness. This immediately leads us on to another problem, how can we establish whether a witness is telling the truth or not?

There are no hard and fast rules for accomplishing this, many detectives rely on their own *'gut feeling'*, their instinct, others rely on corroboration from other sources. Both methods have much to commend them but equally much to condemn them. The detective who relies on pure instinct as his only method comes unstuck when his instinct is wrong. He then has a tendency to alter or ignore evidence that contradicts his opinion, with disastrous consequences. The Yorkshire Ripper is a case in question. The officer in charge was so sure that the tape was genuine he wasted immense amounts of time and effort in tracking down the author, instead of concentrating on the hard evidence at hand. On the other hand the detective who always relies on corroboration also comes unstuck if the corroborating witness is also lying. The good detective is somewhere in between, using his instinct, searching for corroboration but never closing his mind to the possibility that he could be wrong.

So there you are, just starting your investigation and you are confronted by your first witness. You have his statement and you are now faced with the task of establishing the accuracy of it. I have found an invaluable aid in this case is to ask two simple questions. Is it likely? Is it logical?

Take the case of Schwartz and his statement. The first part of his statement about following a man slightly the worst for drink down the street is both logical and likely. The man's erratic behaviour is just the sort of thing that would stick in your mind. The man stops to talk to someone standing in the alleyway, again it is entirely possible that you would notice this. Now an argument starts, Schwartz might have known it was a woman or he might not, but this alarms him so much he crosses the street to avoid being emneshed in someone else's problems. So far so good, everything up to now is both logical and likely. It is now Schwartz starts to part company with reality, he is hurrying to get away from the scene of an argument, he is rapidly becoming unsettled and perhaps a little distressed, don't forget he neither speaks or understands English.

Is it logical that given these circumstances he would be able to give a detailed description of the man? The answer has got to be no. Is it likely? Again, given that the alleyway where this argument took place was so dark that Diemschutz appearing at the scene a few minutes later could not identify the shape as human, and even after striking a match to illuminate the scene, still wrongly identifies the woman as being his wife, the answer has again got to be no.

So much of the information concerning the Jack the Ripper murders could have been winnowed out by the simple application of these two questions that it is amazing no one has done it before. Arguments about the supposed medical skill or lack of it, of the killer have passed back and forth over the years. One of the main planks of the *'pro-doctor'* argument is the mutilation of Catharine Eddowes in Mitre Square. Could a non-medical person posses the skill to remove a kidney, a particularly difficult feat? They miss the main point, is it **likely** that even a fully qualified surgeon could remove the kidney, given the fact that whoever it was, was working in the pitch black, with his back to the nearest source of light which was over sixty feet away? The answer has got to be no.

Dr Sequira the first medical man to arrive at the locality at about five minutes to two, said that although the body was found in the darkest place in Mitre Square there was still plenty of light for the murderer to inflict the injuries. However we must remember that when he said this he was accompanied by several police officers holding lanterns. He also stated that the killer did not have any anatomical skill. PC Watkins who found the body is the only person to have viewed the corpse in precisely the same amount of light as had the killer, and in his statement he says *"I turned sharp round to the right, **and flashing my light, I saw the body...**"* Which seems to indicate that before using his lamp he could not see the body on the ground.

After applying this simple test let us assume that the witness fails it. We now have to ascertain whether the witness is mistaken, trying to please, unable to overcome prejudice or is trying to deceive. Let us now concentrate on the person who wishes to deceive. The universal experts on deceiving people are those who literally have to lie for a living intelligence and Covert Operations personnel.

In spite of the attempts of fiction to convince you otherwise, very rarely does a country send one of its own men to spy, or gather information about another country. The preferred method is to use a native of the country you are operating against to do the collecting for you. The advantages are obvious, you don't have to worry about your agent sticking *'out'* or appearing out of place, he speaks the language, knows the customs and is perfectly at home in his own country. However there are rare occasions when one of yours does have to *'cross over'*. To prepare your man in the event of his getting caught he has to completely re-learn his life, he now ceases to be who he is, and now becomes someone else. These new identities are known as *'legends'*. The main points of the legend are provided for him, where he went to school, his achievements, jobs etc., but what the clever counter intelligence operative is looking for is not these main features of a man's life, but exactly the opposite - the trivia.

For instance the interrogation will start with friendly chat. No subject of any importance will be mentioned, just harmless talk about childhood, what you did on your eighth birthday, that sort of thing. All very civilised. The following day will be the same, and so will the next. The day after will again start the same, but then everything changes, *"Great Uncle Harry - isn't he the one who sat on your birthday cake when you were eight?"* Great guffaws of laughter - until your interrogator slams his hand down on the desk and shouts *"But you told me that was your brother!"* You have been caught in a lie, by the end of the day your interrogator will know everything. Of course there are some interrogators who just start physically abusing you, but as Andy McNab (an SAS Sergeant captured and brutally tortured) proved in the Gulf War, it is not half so effective.

Of course you cannot use actual events from your life as background because you have to assume the enemy knows everything about you. This was ably demonstrated during the Vietnam War when the North Vietnamese were receiving information about Americans from American students and certain film stars. It wasn't military secrets they were asking for just innocent information about schools and colleges. The problem was that when a Airman told his scholastic record to his interrogators and they checked the details against their records they found that they didn't fit Airman Third Class Thomas, but they did fit Colonel Thomas. Thousands of American servicemen were subjected to the most appalling brutality during this period largely helped by treacherous Americans back home. (I feel so strongly about this that I still refuse to watch any film with Jane Fonda in it).

So what do you do? Well, the best way is to live someone else's life. Don't describe your birthday party, describe little Jimmy Watkins' festivities, provided you were present. At least that way the details will be correct. It is far easier to base a lie on fact than on complete invention.

The human mind is like a bucket when it comes to retaining information, if you keep filling it with details some will spill over. If when you ask someone to repeat a story he told you the day before and certain details are missing or are added, it's a fair bet it's the truth, but if details are changed significantly its a fair bet it's a lie. For instance your witness says *"A man drove up to the bank in a dark coloured car, got out and went inside"* and the following day says *"A man drove up to the bank in a black Rover got out and went inside"* it's odds on it's the truth. However if the story changes to *"A **woman** drove up to the bank etc."* alarm bells should start ringing. Remember details that are manufactured are the most often changed.

So we have questioned our witnesses and we can find nothing wrong with their statements. You have inactive evidence to supplement your case you are now ready to commence the investigation. When faced with a situation which does not seem to have a solution, you must look for the thing that is *'wrong'*. This *'thing'* is the pointer, the indicator that something is amiss, something doesn't gel and by following that something that you will arrive at the solution. When I was studying the Kennedy assassination I looked high and low for this elusive *'thing'* and I eventually found it in the list of objects recovered from the *'sniper's nest'* in the book depository. It was a very comprehensive list as evidenced by the mention of cigarette stubs, but if the scenario was true something was missing. The items that were relevant were *'One Carcano Rifle with a live round in the breech, three spent cartridge cases'*. This was to support the scenario that Oswald had fired three shots and had loaded the last cartridge into the rifle for another shot if needed.

Unfortunately there was something missing from this list, something that unless you were very familiar with a Carcano rifle you might not spot, and let's face it why would any Dallas police officer be familiar with an Italian rifle that was designed in the previous century. The Carcano uses a very unusual method of loading. The ammunition is first placed in a clip which is then fed into the magazine by inserting it from the top.

171

Now unlike most rifles loaded in this manner, the Lee Enfield for instance, the clip is loaded into the magazine along with the cartridges. When the last round is fed into the chamber this clip *falls out of the bottom of the rifle!* The clip hitting the ground is obviously a reminder to reload. So if Oswald had in fact fired three out of his four rounds, and loaded the last cartridge into the breech *where was the clip?* There is no other way to fire this type of rifle, unless someone is suggesting he fed the rounds in one at a time which would take a considerable amount of time. No, the only way this makes sense is if Oswald fired two rounds not three, he loaded the third round into the breech but didn't fire it, the fourth round was still in the magazine, held in place by the clip. The rifle is taken in where it is discovered that three rounds have been fired at the President not two. Now if you are to have the *'lone assassin theory'* stand up, Oswald has to fire three rounds, so another empty case is placed with the other two, the round left in the breech ejected, and the last round is fed into the chamber. The third live round is picked up off the floor, possibly with the clip, and disposed of. Unfortunately the clip should have been *'found'* at the scene of the shooting, but this was overlooked. Who fired the third bullet? Well sorry to spoil a good conspiracy theory, but it was accidentally fired by a Secret Service Agent in the car behind the President, this was the bullet that *'exploded'* Kennedy's head.

Once you have pinned down what is *'wrong'* then you can move on and find out why it is wrong, this is where the skill comes in.

Several years ago in North Yorkshire there was a brutal murder at a hotel. When the police arrived it was to find the landlady cradling the bloody head of her husband in her arms. At the foot of the stairs, surrounded by broken glass, was the barman with a severe blow to the front of his head. The story was that the landlady and her husband had been downstairs cashing up. The barman had cleared glasses from the downstairs bar and was taking them upstairs to wash, when he was struck across the head by an intruder. The landlady then took up the story. According to her version when she heard the noise of the barman dropping the glasses and falling backwards down the stairs, she was about to go into the passageway to see what was happening when she was pushed back into the bar by two men. They demanded the cash from the till, and when her husband refused to hand it over they attacked him with a baseball bat. After beating him severely, they made their getaway in a red Ford Cortina. She cradled her dying husband in her arms waiting for the police.

At first the police had no reason to doubt this account, and when two well known burglars were arrested at a nearby caravan site they thought they had the culprits. When it was established that they also drove an old Ford Cortina it seemed certain that they had the right men. However the Detective in charge of the investigation was an extremely efficient officer, and although certain in his own mind that he had the culprits, he refused to allow his personal opinions stand in the way of doing his job properly.

His first task was to re-assemble the glasses that had been dropped by the barman and lift the fingerprints from them. All the fingerprints proved to be from customers who were in the hotel that night, but *all of them had been drinking upstairs, none of them had been downstairs.* The detective had found his '*wrong thing*', for if none of the customers had been downstairs, how had the barman collected these glasses from downstairs? The answer of course was that he couldn't. Now after finding the '*wrong thing*' you now have to explain why it is wrong, and what in fact did happen.

The barman had lied, he hadn't been downstairs collecting glasses, so could he be involved? The wound to his head suggested he wasn't, and besides medical evidence pointed to the blows that killed the husband being struck by two people. However the detective realised that there was no way of telling when he had sustained the wound to his head, whether it was before or after the attack on the husband. So if the blow to the head had happened after the husband was attacked, it was possible that he *could* be one of the attackers. So if the story of intruders was false, then the only other person in the hotel that night was the wife, she must have been the second attacker. Surely though if she had viciously beaten her husband there would be some forensic evidence, she would be marked with her husband's blood, the detective thought back to the scene that greeted him when he entered the hotel that night. There was the wife cradling her dying husband and of course she was covered in her husband's blood.

From that one *'wrong thing'*, the fingerprints that shouldn't have been on the glasses, the detective eventually discovered the truth. The barman and the landlady had been having an affair, and had decided to murder the woman's husband. They had planned it so they were both downstairs and then had called the husband down. As he entered the downstairs bar, the barman attacked him with the baseball bat. He failed to kill him however and so the wife took the bat and savagely murdered her husband. The barman then showered and changed his clothes, stood at the top of the stairs with a tray of glasses and was hit across the head by the wife. The glasses fell and he lay down amongst the broken glass. Then all that remained was for the wife to ring the police and cradle her husband in her arms to mask the blood from the attack. After being alerted to the fact that all was not as straight forward as had first seemed, forensic evidence now appeared to support the true version of events. An expert in the way blood behaves when it is splashed was brought in, and he showed that the attack could not have happened the way the landlady said it did. The way the blood hit the wall showed conclusively the first attack on the husband had been launched by someone standing in front of him, and not from behind as the wife had said. If only they had taken the glasses from downstairs they might have got away with it.

That particular case is a textbook example of a properly conducted investigation. The evidence is gathered, is then checked and any discrepancy noted and explored. It would have been much easier for the detective to have taken everything at face value and put the blame on the two ex-cons, after all who would have believed them?

It will be noticed that this case also demonstrates the *'chain'* effect of evidence, one thing leads to another and each step should have some form of verification or corroboration. The glasses proved the barman was lying, this lead to a re-examination of the forensic evidence which showed the wife was lying, this led to the inevitable conclusion that they were both guilty of the murder.

This chain effect is vital in building a case. It is not sufficient to say this happened or that happened, you must show the consequences of such actions, and demonstrate how each step re-affirms your theory. You cannot for instance say *'This man is guilty because everyone thinks he is'*. You must show that if such a belief is in existence is there any validity to it, and if there is, where did this first start? Are there any other factors that corroborate this belief? You must test every statement, examine every theory until you are certain you have found the truth.

So are you now ready to travel with me to discover the identity of Jack the Ripper? Here are your guides, likely and logical, they will help you in your quest, question everything, test always, accept nothing at face value, for every statement, every piece of evidence could be nothing more than a mask, a mask that for over a hundred years has hidden the face of JACK THE RIPPER! ! ! !

Chapter Nine

"The Usual Suspects"
Film Title 1995

DRUITT

In 1987, ninety-nine years after Jack the Ripper walked the streets of Whitechapel, Terence Sharkey wrote a book detailing the murders. The last two chapters of this book dealt with all the most popular suspects, and gave odds as to who was the most likely candidate. It came as no surprise that Montague John Druitt, barrister at law, came top of the list. It is arguable that Druitt has been the favourite suspect of more authors than anyone else. Tom Cullen, in his 1965 masterpiece *'Autumn of Terror'* chooses Druitt, as does Daniel Farson, the original discoverer of the Macnaghten memoranda, Martin Howells and Keith Skinner in their *'Ripper Legacy'*, John Wilding *'Jack the Ripper Revealed'* and so on. So what was it about this man that convinced so many people that he was Jack the Ripper?

According to the Bible of Ripper research *'The Jack the Ripper A to Z'*, Druitt's life is summarised thus;

"Borne Wimborne, Dorset 1857. Educated Winchester and New College, Oxford. BA, Lit. Hu., Class III, 1880. Successful debater and sportsman (fives and cricket) at school and college; unsuccessful amateur actor (poor performance as Sir Toby Belch in school play). Steward of college junior common room. Employed as schoolmaster, Mr. Valentine's school, Blackheath, 1880. Admitted Inner Temple, 1882; called to the bar 1885, attached to Western Circuit. Joined Arthur Jelf's chambers, 9 Kings Bench Walk. Active sportsman: secretary Modern Cricket Club, 1884; hon. sec. and treasurer, Blackheath Cricket, Football and Lawn Tennis 1885. Special pleader Western Circuit, 1887. Dismissed by Mr. Valentine after being in 'serious trouble at the school' c. 30 November 1888. Last seen alive c. 3 December 1888. Body recovered from Thames on the 31 December. Verdict of coroners jury 'suicide whilst of unsound mind'. Buried in Wimborne cemetery."

Apart from the suicide, it reads like a very normal life. Much has been made of the dismissal from school for being *'in serious trouble'*, but since we have no idea at all what this trouble could be it doesn't help us much.

The name Druitt first came to prominence after Daniel Farson discovered the Macnaghten Memoranda mentioned in Chapter 6. The most important passage for pro Druitt supporters is Macnaghten's statement *'I am inclined to exonerate the last 2 (Kosminski and Ostrog), but I have always held strong opinions regarding No 1 (Druitt) and the more I think the matter over, the stronger do these opinions become. The* **truth***, however, will never be known, and did indeed, at one time lie at the bottom of the Thames, if my conjections (conjecture?) be correct.'*

Now what we as investigators have to ask ourselves is *'Is there any merit in the opinions of this man?'* Let us look at the **facts**. First of all let us not lose sight of the fact that Macnaghten was not a professional policeman, in fact his first job as a policeman was to be appointed Assistant Chief Constable, CID, Scotland Yard, in 1889, **after the last Ripper murder**. Before then he had been an overseer on his family's tea plantations in India, hardly a suitable grounding for taking up the post of a very senior police officer. I point this out not to denigrate Macnaghten in any way, but to remind us that any personal opinion he may have on the subject can only be based on rumour and gossip, he had absolutely no first hand knowledge of the case at all.

Macnaghten further emphasises in his memoranda, *'From private information I have little doubt but that his own family suspected this man of being the Whitechapel murderer; it was alleged that he was sexually insane.'* What private information could this be? Nobody knows, however we may take an educated guess. Both Macnaghten's and Druitt's families were of the same upper middle class background and it is a fact that rumours and gossip tend to circulate more freely within your own class structure. For example Druitt's family was blighted with mental problems, his mother spent a great deal of her time in an asylum, and in fact committed suicide whilst incarcerated in one in 1890. His sister attempted suicide and spent time in an asylum, and his eldest sister did kill herself in her old age. When Druitt's body was recovered, and his brother received a note from him stating *'since Friday I felt I was going to be like mother, and it would be best for all concerned if I were to die'*, the conclusion that Druitt had also gone insane would be difficult to resist.

If you add this information to the fact that his cousin, Dr. Lionel Druitt, had a surgery in the minories in the late 1870s and that Druitt visited him there, you have all the ingredients for a perfect suspect, insane, knew the area, a professional man, remember what the papers were saying, and committed suicide after the last murder. How many families could resist the temptation to add all this up and claim that one of their relatives was Jack the Ripper? We all have *'I thought there was something funny about Uncle Tom'* stories to tell. Obviously it would not be something they would be proud of; but I'm quite sure the gossip would start soon enough.

Don't forget it was a common belief at the time that the murders in general, and Kelly's in particular, were so horrible, that the suicide of the guilty party was expected daily. Remember what Macnaghten said in his memoranda *'A much more rational and workable theory, **to my way of thinking**, is that the Rippers brain gave way after his awful glut in Miller's Court and that he then committed suicide'*. In other words practically anyone committing suicide after the last murder would have been nominated, Druitt was a godsend.

However is there any other reason that Druitt might have committed suicide? I believe the answer to be yes. Druitt was dismissed from his school on the Friday 30th November. Why? What did he do that was so serious that it called for his dismissal and yet **did not involve the police?** For example it is unlikely that he committed any *'normal'* offence such as assault, dishonesty or offences of that type. However bearing in mind the presence of young boys and the obvious desire not to involve the police in any way, it does suggest that the offence could have been of a sexual nature. Let us suppose that Druitt was discovered in an act of an improper nature with one of the boys entrusted to his care. His instant dismissal would have been certain. But what of Druitt? Might this not have led him to question his own sanity? Might he not believe that the curse of the Druitts was now upon him? He spends the whole weekend brooding on his conduct. His career both as a schoolmaster and as a barrister are now finished, what is there left for him? He cannot return to his

178

family and admit his shame, far better to settle the matter once and for all. On the Monday he writes his notes, one to his brother, and one to the headmaster. Why write to the headmaster if he was killing himself because he was the Ripper? It is far more likely that he would write to apologise for his behaviour. Unfortunately this letter was never recovered, if it was as I suspect I would imagine the headmaster would have destroyed it immediately he had finished reading it. Having done that he then takes the last lonely walk to the bridge.

This of course is supposition, but it is likely and it is logical. Are there any indicators that this is in fact what happened? I believe there are, look at what Druitt wrote, *'Since **Friday** (this had to refer to the day he was dismissed) I felt that I was going to be like mother....'* In other words according to Druitt he only felt he was mad since the previous Friday, surely if he were committing suicide because he was the Ripper he would have felt distinctly off colour for many months before that. Don't forget this dismissal took place three weeks after the last murder, his must have been the slowest conscience on record.

Add to that Druitt's behaviour after the last murder, but before his dismissal, there is nothing there to indicate that he was in any way unbalanced. At the 19th November meeting of the Blackheath Cricket, Football and Lawn Tennis Club of which he was its Hon Treasurer and Secretary, he proposed *'that an acre of land be taken behind the Grand Stand at a similar proportion of rent to that paid for the present land'.* This doesn't really tie in with a serial killer who is so eaten away with remorse for his actions that he is going to kill himself in a couple of weeks. If he had proposed that the land be put aside for burying murdered prostitutes you might have a point!

Supporters of Druitt as Ripper also point to another piece of *'evidence'*, The Bachert Story. This story involves one William Albert Bachert, who as you will recall took over the Chairmanship of the Whitechapel Vigilance Committee from George Lusk. Apparently in March 1889, Bachert was badgering the police over the running of the investigation. He was informed by the Inspector in strictest confidence that the investigation was being run down because the Ripper was dead, he had drowned himself in the Thames at the end of 1888.

This story is offered as conclusive proof that Druitt was the Ripper. However let us investigate this claim. The story originated with the famous Ripper author and authority, Donald McCormick, who says that he got it from one Dr. Thomas Dutton, an amateur Criminologist who was living in the area at the time of the murders. However since the story is not backed by any hard evidence, but only the hazy recollections of a very old man, it is not prudent to place too much credence on it.

Even if this story was true, then what does it prove? It proves that Bachert was told that the Ripper had drowned himself; it doesn't prove that this was so. If this is the case then why should an Inspector of Police tell such a tale? A clue to this may be in the character of Bachert himself. Bachert, to put it bluntly was a nuisance, a nobody who thought he ought to be a somebody. Not content with being a member of the Vigilance committee, he had to make sure that he was always noticed. In September he had written to the newspapers expressing horror at the murders, hardly an exclusive feeling. He next appears on the 2nd October with a lurid tale of a *'suspect dressed in morning coat, black hat and carrying a black bag (of course!), asking passers-by where he could find some prostitutes'*. Needless to say this highly suspicious suspect was never traced.

After getting the position of Chairman of the Committee, he continued to pester the police at every opportunity. It was on one of these forays he was allegedly told the tale of the Ripper's suicide. He next crops up as a reserve juror at the inquest of Frances Coles. Wynne Baxter the Coroner, refused to call him to sit, presumably as he was acquainted with Bachert's reputation as a troublemaker, a reputation he was to re-enforce by protesting against the exclusion, claiming he had been deliberately excluded because he would *'enquire too closely'*.

A further indication of the man's character can be judged by the fact that he was later brought up on charges of counterfeiting, acquitted, and theft, convicted. It is also pertinent to ask if he was given the alleged information in the strictest confidence, why did he break that confidence by telling Dr. Dutton? If it did happen that Bachert was told this tale, I believe it to be nothing more than an enterprising police officer repeating a rumour to get rid of a nuisance. The quickest way to make a no-body feel important is to let him in on a secret.

If the story of the Ripper drowning himself was a rumour, where did it start? Who knows how these things begin, but look at the facts. The papers had hyped up the Ripper to be amongst other things a doctor, a professional man, obviously insane, who would do away with himself; and bearing in mind there were no more murders after Mary Kelly, this seemed a likely scenario. The next thing is that a professional man, from a family with a long history of mental illness, commits suicide at the beginning of December and he fits like a glove. The fact that Druitt was a barrister *not* a doctor didn't matter (even Macnaghten refers to him in his memoranda as a 41 year old doctor instead of a 31 year old barrister).

What is certain is that contrary to what some authors would have you believe, it was not a generally held belief that Druitt was the Ripper, especially by *'the Chiefs at Scotland Yard'* as one book would have it. Not one police officer, senior or otherwise, who was directly involved in the investigations has put forward that the Ripper committed suicide or that the Ripper was Druitt. In fact if you read what Inspector Abberline had to say on the matter he is quite categorical. In an interview he gave to the *Pall Mall Gazette* in March 1903 he says:

'You must understand that we have never believed all those stories about Jack the Ripper being dead, or that he was a lunatic or anything of that kind'.

And that as they say is straight from the horse's mouth.

However not content with the inaccurate and unsubstantiated Macnaghten memoranda, pro Druitt supporters have scavenged around to find more *'proof that Druitt is their man'*, a description would of course be nice, and in an article in *The People's Journal* of 27th September 1919, they find one.

The article itself is a strange affair, being written by *'A Scotland Yard man'* in memory of a Detective Stephen White who had died a few days previously. Detective White was one of the CID officers who was actively working on the Ripper investigation, and the article is supposed to be a report filed by him, it states:

"For five nights we had been watching a certain alley just behind the Whitechapel Road. It could only be entered from where we had two men posted in hiding, and persons entering the alley were under observation by the two men. It was a bitter cold night when I arrived to take the report of the two men in hiding. I was turning away when I saw a man coming out of the alley. He was walking quickly, but noiselessly, apparently wearing rubber shoes, which were rather rare in those days. I stood aside to let him pass, and as he came under the wall lamp I got a good look at him.

He was about five feet ten inches in height and was dressed rather shabbily, although it was obvious that the material of his clothes was good. His face was long and thin, nostrils rather delicate, and his hair was jet black. His complexion was inclined to be sallow, and altogether the man was foreign in appearance. The man was slightly bent at the shoulders, though he obviously was quite young - about 33 at the most - and gave one the idea of being a student or professional man. His hands were snow white, and the fingers long and tapering.

As he passed me at the lamp I had an uneasy feeling that there was something more than usually sinister about him (the article goes on in much the same vein describing how sinister the man was, and ends thus) as he turned away, one of the police officers came out of the house he had been in, and walked a few paces into the darkness of the alley. 'Hello! What is this?' he cried, and then called in startled tones for me to come along. At the end of the cul de sac, huddled against the wall, there was the body of a woman, and a pool of blood was streaming along the gutter from her body. It was clearly another one of those terrible murders. I remembered the man I had seen, and I started after him as fast as I could run, but he was lost to sight in the dark labyrinth of East End mean streets'.

Now I have gone to some length to reproduce this article as it is important not so much for its content, but as an example of the lengths some authors will go to twist facts to fit theories. It is of course an almost perfect physical description of Druitt, even down to the part about the suspect being *'a student or a professional man'*. Having established that this report bolsters their case enormously, we now have to ensure that everything fits Druitt and no one else.

The first hurdle to be overcome is why didn't Detective White make this statement known at the time. Simple, Detective

White was a Special Branch officer and couldn't make his presence known to the police on the ground as that would jeopardise his own operation. This may seem plausible until you recollect that at first Detective White is described as *'one of the officers who had to spend weary nights.... looking for Jack the Ripper'*. Later on however when it suits them, White is now described as *'a Special Branch Officer whose presence on City Police territory would have proved an embarrassment'*.

You will no doubt have noticed that by now White is described as being on City Police territory. This is necessary because Macnaghten later writes in his memoirs *'No one ever saw the Whitechapel murderer, unless possibly it was the City Police PC who was on beat near Mitre Square'*. The fact that Detective White was a Sergeant in the Metropolitan Police doesn't even slow them up, this is explained away as *'this leaves only one possible explanation, he was referring to Stephen White'*. I admire the definition of *'one possible explanation'*.

This also leads us on to which murder could the article be referring to? The fact that none of the details in the article bear any resemblance to actual events, doesn't deter them for one moment. Because the article mentions a *'very cold night'* and because the coldest relevant night was the 30th September then of course *'there could be no doubt that White had managed to get a good look at a man leaving the scene of the crime minutes before Catharine Eddowes' body would be discovered'*, meaning of course this is supposed to refer to the Mitre Square murder. This of course is abject nonsense. Of all the murder sites, Mitre Square is the least worthy of the title *'cul de sac'* (bearing in mind of course that the fact that the area in question is a cul de sac is absolutely vital to the story) as you will recall, Mitre Square had three separate entrances and exits, and a relatively large open space cannot be described as an alley which *'could only be entered from where we had two men in hiding'*.

Let us investigate this article with the help of the skills we have acquired from Chapter 8. First is the article logical? Is it likely? Forget for a moment all the twisting and turning that the pro-Druitt supporters have done and let us just concentrate on the article.

Detective White was there to take the report of his two detectives who were watching the alley. Is it likely that whilst making this report they would overlook the fact that a man and a woman had just gone up the alley? Is it then logical that when the man returned alone, they would make no comment? Is it then *likely* that after the man has gone you then go up the alley to check? If you had no suspicion of the man, and by letting him go you prove you haven't, would you then risk blowing your stakeout by wandering up the alley? No, this whole account is fiction, but like most fiction has a very faint grounding in fact. Let us see if we can throw a little light on this mystery.

First of all what murder could this account be referring to? Obviously if the detail of the cold weather is accurate, then it has to refer to the Stride murder the same night. Here we have our first indication that we might be on the right track, for Detective Sergeant White, H Division, *was* involved with that murder. He was the officer who took the statement from Matthew Packer, the imaginative greengrocer. The other point is of course that out of all the murder sites only Dutfields yard where Elizabeth Stride's body was found could be described as a cul de sac. The other point of similarity is that the article mentions two other detectives. There were also two other detectives involved with Packer, the two private detectives who took him off to the newspapers to tell his story. One final point, the article talks of blood running in the gutter, only in the Stride murder was blood actually seen to be running in the gutter.

So given all these points of similarity, Detective White, two detectives, cul de sac, cold night and blood running in the gutter it is glaringly obvious the article is very loosely based on the Stride murder.

What else can we glean from the article, well it is fairly certain that the suspect is supposed to a lunatic, it mentions *'there being something more than usually sinister about him'* (what is the usual amount of sinister I wonder?). He also wears rubber soled shoes, and the whole tone of the article is the lone voice knowing who the killer is yet being powerless to stop him. The article is signed *'A Scotland Yard Man'*, why? Why not sign it *'A police officer'* or a *'retired police officer'*, unless of course the author isn't and never was a police officer - but thought he ought to be!

184

Examine if you will Doctor Forbes-Winslow, who has been previously mentioned. He was of the opinion that the killer was a lunatic, and that's where the police should look, a not un-helpful suggestion, but then he goes and spoils it all with a constant barrage of advice to the police. Issue the men with rubber boots, I know who the killer is, if you give me six men I'll go and arrest him. All this coupled with a constant stream of invective against the police for their failure to capture the Ripper, and a willingness to forge letters sent to him so that they appeared to have been posted at the height of the investigations, made him a thorough nuisance. He let the press know in no uncertain terms that the police were fools, and that he should be heading the investigation at Scotland Yard.

Of course there is absolutely no proof that Forbes-Winslow wrote the article but I would say if it were later found out to be so, I wouldn't be too surprised!

I firmly believe that the only reason Druitt ever made it on to Macnaghten's suspect list is that he was repeating a rumour he picked up when he joined the force, some six months after the murders ceased. Something very (eerily so) similar happened with the Jack the Stripper murders in the sixties. After the last murder had been committed a famous sports personality was found shot to death in the back of his car, apparently a suicide. This man was a very popular figure, appearing on children's TV, opening fetes and hospitals, and appeared to be an all round good bloke. Shortly after his death however, rumours started circulating that he wasn't such a nice fellow after all. I remember talking to a man who had served in the RAF with him and he told me of an incident which demonstrated his capacity for brutal sadism. It wasn't too long before someone pointed out that the murders had stopped, and soon the rumours were that *he was the killer.* Even today you can still find some detectives who served mainly at a junior level, who will swear blind he was Jack the Stripper. The tragedy was, of course, that he was totally innocent of the crimes, he had got into trouble with some East End gangsters, borrowing money from them and refusing to pay it back, banking on his high profile to protect him. It didn't and he was murdered. Co-incidentally the real killer did kill himself after his card was marked by the investigating officers.

185

To sum up, what is the case against Druitt? Well, quite simply there isn't one. The only indication that he is the Ripper is an inaccurately repeated rumour, written by a man who wasn't even in the police at the time, a man who later wrote in his autobiography,

'I never kept a diary, nor even possessed a notebook, so that, in what I write, I must trust to my memory, and to my memory alone.'

There is not one scrap of evidence, not one witness, not one police officer who was involved with the investigation, who says that Druitt was the Ripper!

Before we leave poor old Druitt to enjoy his rest it is interesting to compare Druitt with the Offender Profile drawn up by Jon Ogan.

Living within an 800 metre location of crimes.	No
Previous convictions for assault etc.	No
Mental Illness	Possibly
Acquaintanceship with victims	No
Poor Work record	No
Poor at forming relationships	Judging by the amount of social positions he held, and the team sports he played - No
Poor Anger management control	Hardly.

Whoever and whatever else he was Montague John Druitt was not Jack the Ripper!

KOSMINSKI

In 1987 the grandson of Chief Inspector Donald Swanson (the officer who took over control of the Whitechapel Murder Investigation when Anderson left for Switzerland) inherited an interesting book. It was the memoirs of Sir Robert Anderson, entitled *'The Lighter Side of My Official Life'*. What made this particular copy so very special was that it was the personal copy of his grandfather, and in the margins and on the endpapers Chief Inspector Swanson had pencilled some notes of his own.

On page 138 Anderson wrote:

"... I will merely add that the only person who ever had a good view of the murderer unhesitatingly identified the suspect the instant he was confronted with him; but he refused to give evidence against him".

To complement this passage Swanson had added in pencil at the bottom of the page

"because the suspect was also a Jew and also because his evidence would convict the suspect, and witness would be the means of murderer being hanged which he did not wish to be left on his mind"

In addition Swanson made a further note in the margin which read,

"And after this identification which suspect knew, no other murder of this kind took place in London."

Turning to the endpaper Swanson's pencilled notes continued:

"Continuing from page 138 after the suspect had been identified at the Seaside Home where he had been sent by us with difficulty in order to subject him to identification, and he knew he was identified. On suspect's return to his brother's house in Whitechapel he was watched by police (City CID) by day and night. In a very short time the suspect with his hands tied behind his back, he was sent to Stepney Workhouse and then to Colney Hatch and died shortly afterwards- Kosminski was the suspect DSS."

This Swanson Marginalia, as it became known, was first reproduced in full in Paul Begg's masterful account of the murders, 'Jack the Ripper - The Uncensored Facts'.

This was an astounding discovery made even more important when you recall that the second man mentioned in Macnaghten's Memoranda was a Polish Jew named Kosminski. Could it be that here at last the truth was finally out?

Aaron Kosminski was a Polish Jewish Hairdresser who emigrated to England in 1882, he was about twenty four years old at the time of the murders. In July 1890 he was admitted for treatment at the Mile End Old Town workhouse, it was noted on admission that he had been insane for about two years. Three days after his admission he was discharged to his brother's care. On the 4th February 1891 he was re-admitted to the infirmary and three days later sent to the Colney Hatch Lunatic Asylum.

His admission to the asylum was because of his increasingly strange behaviour. A witness stated:

"that he goes about the streets and picks up pieces of bread out of the gutter and eats them, he drinks water from the tap and he refuses food at the hands of others. He took up a knife and threatened the life of his sister. He is very dirty and will not be washed. He has not attempted any kind of work for years".

In April 1894 he was noted as being *'Demented and Incoherent'* and on the 13 April 1894 he was transferred to Leavesden Asylum for Imbeciles.

He stayed at Leavesden until his death from gangrene in 1919. In his final years his condition deteriorated, he suffered from hallucinations and became noisy and troublesome. Reading his medical record for the last months of his life it is clear that he suffered greatly from bed sores, these ulcerating and eventually causing the gangrene that killed him. Given the agony he must have been in I think it is no wonder that he became *'noisy and troublesome'*.

There are so many features about Kosminski that make him the ideal suspect, that it is no wonder that he is a favourite *'candidate'* of many researchers. At least two Television programmes about the Ripper have elected him the guilty party (The Secret Life of Jack the Ripper and Crime Monthly). He is a barber (many barbers still practised as pseudosurgeons on the Continent) he is a Jew, he is insane and he died in an asylum. Unfortunately it is when we start looking at him under a microscope that the case starts to fall apart.

The first thing that needs to be established is that Aaron Kosminski is the Kosminski referred to by both Macnaghten and Anderson. A thorough search by previous researchers have shown that Aaron is the only Kosminski (or any variant of the name) to have died in an asylum in England and Wales since 1888. So it is clear that Aaron Kosminski and Macnaghten's and Anderson's Kosminski are one and the same.

Macnaghten, the man who never referred to notes but relied solely on his memory, wrote about Kosminski in 1894 in his famous memoranda. In it he states that Kosminski lived in the district where the murders took place, and was detained in an asylum in 1889. Macnaghten believed that at the time of writing (1894) Kosminski was still alive. He ends the entry by saying that Kosminski strongly resembled the *man seen by the City PC near Mitre Square.* The Scotland Yard version of the memoranda also contains the added line, *'There were many 'circ' (circumstances) connected with this man which made him a strong suspect'.*

Comparing Macnaghten's Kosminski with the real Kosminski, we now begin to see that the two do not tally. Aaron Kosminski was detained, very briefly in an asylum in 1890, not as Macnaghten states in 1889. Furthermore this detention was only for three days, his next incarceration in an asylum was in 1891, from where he was moved to Leavesden in 1894. Since Macnaghten wrote his memoranda in 1894 it is possible that the moving of Kosminski might have jogged his memory, and caused him to include Kosminski as a suspect. In fact the part in the memoranda where he says he believes Kosminski to still be alive is the only accurate statement made about him. The part about Kosminski bearing a strong resemblance to the man seen by a City PC near Mitre Square is pure Macnaghten, no City PC saw any suspect near Mitre Square on the night of the double murder. It is possible that Macnaghten is here confusing the sighting by PC Smith of the Metropolitan police who described a man he saw with Liz Stride in Berner Street the same night - but that's what happens when you rely solely on your memory!

So if Macnaghten's reference to Kosminski is a combination of faulty memory, recent events and an active imagination, what is there to be said about Anderson's part in nominating Kosminski?

To be absolutely fair to Anderson he doesn't actually mention Kosminski by name in his memoirs. Anderson's memoirs were first published in serial form in Blackwood's Magazine, the most interesting part of which is as follows:

"For I may say that 'undiscovered murders' are rare in London, and the Jack the Ripper crimes are not in that category I will only add here

that the 'Jack the Ripper' letter which is preserved in the Police Museum at Scotland Yard is the creation of an enterprising London journalist."

as a footnote to this extremely interesting paragraph he added,

*"Having regard to the interest attaching to this case, I should almost be tempted to disclose the identity of the murderer and of the pressman who wrote the letter above referred to, **provided that the publishers would accept all responsibility in view of a possible libel action.** But no public benefit would result from such a course, and the traditions of my old department would suffer. I will only add that when the individual whom we suspected was caged in an asylum, the only person who ever had a good view of the murderer at once identified him, but when he learned that the suspect was a fellow-Jew he declined to swear to him".*

When the memoirs were published the same year this section was slightly altered, but the gist of it is the same.

This is an astounding revelation, for here is the Officer in Charge of the Whitechapel Murder Investigation from 6 October 1888 to the closing of the file in 1892, stating that not only was the murderer known, but that he was safely *'caged in an asylum'*, where he had been positively identified. Unfortunately it is complete nonsense.

Why then did Anderson write it? The answer is quite simple vanity. Anderson, it will be remembered left England on the day that Polly Nichols was murdered, and handed over operational control of the investigation to Chief Inspector Swanson. In his hand over notes Anderson made the boastful comment that he could:

'in a few days unravel the mystery provided I could spare the time to give undivided attention to it.'

On his return to England, Warren left him in no doubt that he now expected Anderson to make good his boast, something which Anderson spectacularly failed to do. Ever after he continued to make broad hints that he knew who the killer was. Inspector Littlechild writing to the famous journalist George Sims in 1913 added a hand-written addition to the bottom of his letter *"He probably got his information from Anderson who only 'thought he knew'"*.

Anderson's memoirs came under the scrutiny of no less a person than Winston Churchill, the then Home Secretary, in 1910. Churchill had to decide whether or not the memoirs contained confidential information, and if they did, whether to stop Anderson's pension. His report to the Commons is illuminating. He decided that to stop Anderson's pension because of the memoirs would not be fair, because far from being full of juicy tit-bits they seemed:

'to be written in a spirit of gross boastfulness.. .in the style of "How Bill Adams won the Battle of Waterloo". The writer has been so anxious to show how important he was, how invariably he was right, and how much more he could tell if only his mouth was not what he was pleased to call closed'.

These comments by one of Britain's greatest son's are extremely illuminating, but are they accurate? Look at what Anderson says about the suspect's identity, and then states that it's only the publisher's refusal to accept responsibility in any libel action that prevents him from talking. This is absolute nonsense. Certain people cannot be libelled, a minor, a dead person and a certified lunatic. If Anderson's suspect was already caged in an asylum, he was safe from any action. The only other person that might wish to bring action would be any journalist accused of writing the letters, then don't name him, but even if you do I doubt very much if any action would ensue as writing letters is not a criminal offence.

To then state that no public benefit would result from naming the killer, defies belief. Jack the Ripper had caused one of the biggest manhunts in history, had plunged an entire section of London into terror, and had cost the taxpayer a fortune in extra police expenditure. I think informing the public that they were now safe from the murderer would definitely come under the heading of *'public benefit'.* Naturally Anderson had to include the information about the witness to reassure everyone that he actually had proof of the suspect's guilt, but he then spoils it by saying the witness refused to testify.

This is legal nonsense. To bring an indictment against a suspect you have to convince a magistrate that you have evidence of guilt. The police could go to the magistrate with their witness and obtain an arrest warrant. The witness could be forced to attend any trial by serving him with a subpoena. Whether or not the witness did testify is irrelevant, the accused would be found not guilty by reasons of insanity, and incarcerated in any asylum. The police would have got their man, the public would have breathed easier, and the witness would not have to testify. Anderson had to make this point so that he could avoid having to put his money where his mouth was.

This is all very well and good, but why did Swanson appear to endorse Anderson's comments in his marginalia? This is much more difficult to understand, but I believe we must first of all examine the marginalia for accuracy. When we do this, we find it as far off the mark as Macnaghtens attempts.

Swanson states that the suspect was identified at *'the Seaside Home'*, this refers to the Convalescent Police Seaside Home in Brighton, but this didn't open until March 1890! In other words Jack the Ripper was at large for eighteen months after the last murder - why didn't he kill again? In the case of a *'sane'* killer there could be many reasons, but a lunatic? Then to release him just because the witness refused to identify him is ludicrous. Again the police could have had him committed. Swanson ends up by saying that after a short while the suspect, with his hands tied behind his back, was taken first to Stepney Workhouse and then to Colney Hatch where he died shortly afterwards, and Kosminski was his name.

This is totally wrong, we know that Kosminski didn't enter Colney Hatch until 1891 and far from dying shortly afterwards lived until 1919. Swanson has it in his mind that something did happen to Kosminski in 1890, and it did, he was interred in Mile End Workhouse for three days. The whole Swanson marginalia, like Macnaghten's, seems to be half forgotten recollections of real events, but distorted by time. If Kosminski was Jack the Ripper, you can bet that any police officer involved in the case, as Swanson was, knowing the truth, as Swanson claimed, would have the facts off pat.

Interestingly enough the Swanson marginalia does clear up one mystery - who was the witness? Swanson says that Kosminski was watched day and night by *City CID*. As the City force were only involved in one of the murders, Catharine Eddowes in Mitre Square, and the only witness involved in that murder who was a Jew and who claimed to see the suspect was Lawende. Bearing in mind that at the time Lawende stated that he would not know the man again, one wonders how reliable his testimony would be two years later.

Why then does Swanson back up Anderson? I believe it was out of a sense of misguided loyalty. To put it bluntly Anderson had made a fool of himself by making these wild statements. Anderson was being described by politicians as the author of *'Anderson's Fairy Tales'*, by police officers such as Littlechild (who was a Special Branch Officer and had absolutely nothing to do with the Ripper investigation) as someone who *'thought he knew'*, and by Winston Churchill as someone who writes in a *'spirit of gross boastfulness'*. In other words it seemed as if everyone was labelling Anderson as a vain, boastful man, who could not produce the goods when asked.

Swanson was very fond of Anderson, he even witnessed Anderson's will after they had both retired. Swanson used to send affectionate Christmas Cards addressed to *'his old master'* until Anderson's death. Is it too far fetched to believe that Swanson saw his chance to back up his old friend's assertions by annotating his copy of Anderson's memoirs? He couldn't come right out and say so publicly because that would have been very quickly proved wrong and so intensified the ridicule aimed at Anderson, but by jotting down a few lines just to tell the world that Anderson was right after all was possibly the last favour he could do for an old comrade. Who knows, the only thing that is known for certain (or as certain as we can be) is that Swanson did write the marginalia, his handwriting has been verified, and that his facts are totally wrong, make of it what you will.

Once again a suspect who seemed so promising has under closer examination proved to be nothing more than a convenient peg to hang the label Ripper on. Kosminski was a poor individual who heard voices in his head that told him the only safe food was that taken from the gutters. He was well known in the Whitechapel area, and given that he never washed, was presumably avoided whenever possible. He never worked and so was always without money. He cannot be a credible suspect. Why would any prostitute knowingly go with a garbage eating lunatic, who never washed and was always without money? The point about Jack the Ripper was that he was so normal he was never suspected - right up to the moment he strangled his victims.

No, it is time to let poor Kosminski throw off the unjustified label of Ripper, he had a pretty miserable life by all accounts and died a most agonising death, let him at least rest in peace.

PRINCE ALBERT VICTOR.

The idea that the grandson of Queen Victoria could be Jack the Ripper was first put forward by Dr. Thomas Stowell in 1960. Over a private lunch with the famous criminologist, Colin Wilson, he proposed that Prince Albert Victor had committed the crimes whilst under the influence of syphilis. Many years after this meeting, Dr. Stowell published a paper called *'Jack the Ripper - a Solution?'* in the Criminologist for November 1970. In this article he called his suspect *'S'*, but with enough details provided so that *'S'* would be identified as Prince Albert.

This story was further elaborated by an American author, Frank Spiering, in his book *'Prince Jack'* published in 1978. In this book Spiering makes many references to *'confidential'* and *'secret'* papers that only he has access to, a ruse that was to be used many times in the future by authors wishing to publicise their books. (see Murder & Madness The Secret Life of Jack the Ripper by Dr. David Abrahamsen *"Based on heretofore unrevealed information from Scotland Yard"* - a claim totally denied by Scotland Yard!).

Spiering alleged the following: Prince Albert Victor was suffering from syphilis and being treated by the Queen's Physician, Dr. William Gull. Because of the way the disease affected his brain, and because Prince Albert had seen deer being gutted in Scotland, he thought he would go out and do the same with prostitutes. After he was caught there was a cover up and Prince Albert Victor was committed to a mental home near Sandringham where he lived for many years after his reported death in 1892.

The whole idea is preposterous of course, but who said the gods didn't have a sense of humour. At about this time it was revealed that two cousins of our present Queen reported dead during World War II, had in fact been confined to a mental home where they had only recently passed away. This of course lent validity to the claim that Prince Albert Victor's death had been faked, and he too had been spirited away to a mental home. Another event that pointed to the Prince's obvious guilt was the fact that the Ripper file had been closed by Scotland Yard in 1892 when the Prince had died. I know that the theory was that he didn't die in 1892, but it's all part of the cover up. The best part about conspiracy theories is of course that when you come to an obstacle to your theory you just shout.

'Well that proves there was a cover up !'

Spiering's book was based on *'secret'* notes made by Doctor Gull in which he laid out the whole plot. These notes were seen by Spiering in the New York Academy of Medicine. After he had seen them, they mysteriously disappeared and have never been seen since. Of course their disappearance proves of course that there was a cover up ...

The whole story wasn't helped by the fact that Prince Albert Victor didn't help himself by being associated with some decidedly weird people. His one time tutor was J K Stephens, the decidedly mad poet and woman hater, who incidentally is also a suspect. He was also supposed to be a homosexual and his involvement in the Cleveland Street Scandal of 1889, during which time a male brothel was raided, didn't help matters. This incident was also investigated by Inspector Abberline, and again ended in frustration for the Detective when the principal characters were protected by the establishment.

However leaving all this aside, there is not one shred of evidence that connects Prince Albert Victor with the murders, and if you examine the story you will find it full of holes.

Let us first of all examine the syphilis theory. It takes normally between twenty and thirty years for syphilis to start affecting the brain, so even supposing that Prince Albert Victor caught it at the lowest end of the scale, it would make him about four years old when he contracted the disease. Even if he suffered from a rare strain that acted within eight to ten years, the symptoms are not indicative of a mass murderer. According to 'A General Textbook of Nursing' by Evelyn Pearce the symptoms are

'irritability, slight loss of memory, apparent loss of interest, inability to concentrate and attacks of depression. The patient will develop delusions of grandeur - he may order expensive articles for which he cannot possibly pay.'

Now this may be the perfect description of a Victor Meldrew with a shopping complex, but I don't think we can call it an accurate thumbnail sketch of Jack the Ripper! One of the most famous sufferers of this disease was Lord Randolph Churchill, and far from turning him into a homicidal maniac it just reduced him to a shambling shuffling imbecile. Lord Randolph has also been put forward as a suspect.

Apart from this there is also the unfortunate fact that when he was supposed to be butchering prostitutes in Whitechapel he was hundreds of miles away in Scotland, facts attested to in the various Court Circulars. The final nail in the coffin of this particular theory is the fact that in 1891 he was created Duke of Clarence and Avondale. Is Spiering actually suggesting that they lock him away in an asylum in 1888, drag him out in 1891 to make him Duke and send him off on some Official visits to Europe, then on his return incarcerate him back in the asylum again? The question is rhetorical.

However having a Royal angle on a story is just too good to let pass (deja vu perhaps) and alternatives to this theory have been put forward as credible options. Perhaps the most famous is the Stephen Knight book 'The Final Solution'.

According to this theory, Prince Albert Victor wasn't the killer, but he was the cause of the murders. Apparently he married a commoner who bore him a child, and when the establishment got to hear of it, they decided to take action. Calling upon the Freemasons to help, they snatched the child away from the child's nurse, who happened to be Mary Kelly, incarcerated the poor wife in an asylum (the asylums must have been overflowing with people supposedly involved with the Ripper) and performed a lobotomy on her to make her forget. The operation was performed by Dr. William Gull, (again) who then went on with a coachman named Netley to murder the prostitutes. The reason for the killings was that the prostitutes were going to blackmail the authorities.

Meanwhile the child was given to Walter Sickert, the famous painter, to look after. He later married the child and had a son by her named Joseph Sickert. Many years later Joseph Sickert told the story to Stephen Knight who went on …. Credit must be given to Joseph Sickert, not only did he manage completely to fool Stephen Knight, but even after the story was shown to be complete rubbish, managed to convince another author, Melvyn Fairclough *(The Ripper and the Royals)* all over again! This time of course he was going to tell the true story. He apparently had a falling out with Stephen Knight and didn't tell him the real thing!!! As I write this Joseph is still alive in the East End willing to tell his yarn to anyone who will listen, by this time of course he is as much a part of Ripper lore as the infamous black bag!

Let us try and scotch these rumours once and for all. When people get involved in wild theories such as these they do so out of a sense of self protection. The answer must always be that there is some terrific conspiracy behind these things, that is why they are never solved. We have to believe that all powerful forces are at work, because the alternative is that these things are carried out by Joe Bloggs, mister average, and that is even more terrifying, how can we live with the knowledge that the next person we meet in the street might want to slash our throats and disembowel us? Living with a fear like that would drive us mad.

If only they stopped for a minute and listened to what they were saying. Don't they understand that if there is such an organisation that is all powerful, that can make things happen (and there are) or hide things from public view for ever, that they would carry out such a simple task as removing five prostitutes from the face of the earth far more efficiently than this. Don't you think that with all their resources they could do it in such a way that no one would never know? They certainly

197

wouldn't do it so as to attract more attention, more books and now even conferences and television programmes a hundred years later. I read recently of a man who murdered his wife fifteen years ago. She just disappeared one day and that was that. It was only recently when someone dug up the garden and found the remains that the truth came out. Now if an *'amateur'* can do that don't you think an all powerful organisation could do it equally as well?

It is very noticeable that the conspiracy theorists never let the facts stand in the way of a good story. For instance Dr. Gull who was supposed to have been wandering around Whitechapel murdering prostitutes was seventy two at the time of the murders, and had recently retired from practice after suffering his second stroke!! A semi invalid geriatric doesn't really fit the bill.

The interesting thing is that so caught up in their own little world of secret conspiracies, and powerful secretive organisations, that as soon as one brick is pulled from their wall, the theorists immediately substitute another. For example *'It couldn't have been Prince Albert Victor, he was in Scotland'* Answer *'Well of course he had help, his old tutor J K Stephen'.* And so on.

Let us make a list of all the conspiracy theorists favourite people and dismiss them once and for all. Jack the Ripper was not:-

Prince Albert Victor, his father the Prince of Wales, Queen Victoria, she would not have been amused at being nominated, her doctor Sir William Gull, J K Stephen, Lord Randolph Churchill, Robert Anderson (yes even the head of CID has received a nomination!) John Netley and any other person vaguely connected with anyone on this list, or any combination thereof!!

JOSEPH BARNETT

The April 1982 edition of *True Crime* magazine, had a very interesting front cover. In large, red letters it proudly announced that *'We name Jack the Ripper'* Inside a short article named Joseph Barnett, friend of Mary Kelly, as the murderer. The article was written by Bruce Paley, an American (its amazing how many

Americans have written books on the murders) and the important thing about his suspect was that here at last was a believable candidate. He had all the attributes that the real killer would have, an intimate knowledge of the area, an association with at least one of the victims, and he was Mr. Grey - no one would notice him amongst the crowds.

In 1996 Bruce Paley finally brought out his full length book, expounding his theory that Joe Barnett was indeed the Ripper. There was another book on the same suspect written by Paul Harrison in 1991, but it appears to be a mere expanding of Bruce Paley's original *True Crime* magazine article of 1982, without any new or exciting information.

Briefly the history of Joseph Barnett and Mary Kelly is as follows. Barnett met Kelly in a bar in Commercial Street on Friday 8th April 1887. They met again the following day and agreed to live together, they lived together for over a year, ending up in Millers Court. On the 30th October Barnett and Kelly had a row during which a pane of glass in a window was broken, (the window in question, the smallest one nearest the drainpipe, actually had two broken panes, whether they were both broken on the same night is unclear) and Barnett moved out. The cause for the row has never been established, first of all Barnett states it was because Kelly was going back on the streets again and he didn't want that, then he says it is because she moved another prostitute in with them. Considering the room was only twelve feet square and with one bed this was obviously too much of a squash.

He apparently remained on friendly terms with Kelly, often visiting her and giving her money, it will be remembered that on the last day of Kelly's life Barnett visited her at Millers Court to apologise for not having any more money. He stated that he left Kelly at about 8.00 pm and never saw her alive again.

There was a witness, Maurice Lewis, who says that he saw Kelly drinking in a pub, The Horn of Plenty, later that evening. However he identifies her drinking companion as a man called:

'Dan, a man selling Oranges in Billingsgate and Spitalfields market, with whom she lived with up to as recently as a fortnight ago'.

Unfortunately this causes a bit of confusion, Joe Barnett was not known as Dan at all. Bruce Paley insists he was, but the only reference I can find to this is the statement by Maurice Lewis. Another point that indicates that *'Dan'* is not Joe Barnett is that he is described as *'a man selling oranges in the markets'*. Joe Barnett had lost his job in the market round about July 1888, so hadn't been selling oranges for upwards of three months. The other point that eliminates this person as being Joe Barnett is the fact that at 8.00 pm he has no money, neither does Mary Kelly. So where in two hours does he get the money to go to a pub?

So is there any logical explanation for Maurice Lewis's statement? I believe there is. Joe Barnett had a brother called Daniel or Danny, who lived just a few yards away at the Victoria Home for Working Men on the corner of Wentworth and Commercial Street (according to the records he was still living there as late as 1891, a little over two years after the murder). Danny Barnett was also a porter at the market, but unlike Joe, still had his job (again according to the records he still had the same job in 1891, and he bore a physical resemblance to Joe. Is it beyond the realms of possibility that the tailor was confused between Danny and Joe Barnett? Another point to remember is that because of the working conditions of tailors in those days, a lot of them suffered with bad eyesight, making an identification in a smoky, crowded bar late at night with possibly poor eyesight is not the most reliable way to do it.

In the absence of any other evidence that Barnett was with Kelly later on that night, I believe we must give Joe the benefit of the doubt when he says he returned to his lodgings after leaving Kelly that Thursday night.

Paley's case is that Joe Barnett wanted Mary off the streets, and so set about frightening her into giving up her life. He did this by murdering prostitutes and when this finally failed, murdered her.

He offers very little evidence to back this up, only assertions that Barnett hated prostitutes and blamed them en masse for dragging Kelly down into the gutter. Paley further offers Barnett's changing his story as to why he and Kelly split up, referring to this as *'lying'* to the police, and points out that he stammered and *'evidently laboured under great emotion'*, when giving evidence at the inquest. He also offers the *'Case of the Vanishing Key'* as his main piece of evidence. We shall return to the key in a minute, but let us take the other points first.

HATRED OF PROSTITUTES

This really doesn't make any sense. Barnett frequented pubs and places where he would naturally come into contact with prostitutes. He met Kelly, a prostitute, and after only one day decided to set up home with her. He knew exactly what she was and had no illusions about her moral standing. Kelly told him she was still seeing other men whilst they were living together, but apparently this didn't trouble him too much, after all they did live together for about eighteen months.

LYING TO THE POLICE

The term *'lying'* infers a wish to deceive someone. Barnett first told police that they broke up because she was walking the streets again, which indicates that she may have temporary suspended her streetwalking, and then later changes this to the quarrel being about moving a *'bad woman'* in with them. But are the two stories totally incompatible? Surely the point is they argued about something, had a fight and Barnett walked out. If Barnett wanted to deceive someone wouldn't he try and deny that there had been **any** quarrel at all regardless of the cause. The important part of Barnett's statement from an investigator's point of view is that there was a quarrel. Now if Barnett had first of all said there was a quarrel and then later denied it, that would have been interesting.

POOR SHOWING ON WITNESS STAND

I think this is the weakest charge that Paley makes. Let us not forget that Barnett had recently identified the remains of a woman he evidently cared for at a mortuary. The corpse was so mutilated that according to Barnett he *'could only identify it by the hair and eyes'*. I cannot believe that anyone being questioned about such savagery being committed to a loved one would do anything but *'labour under great emotion'*. If he had appeared confident and calm and totally at ease in the witness box, that would have interested me much more.

THE MYSTERIOUS KEY

One of the main planks of Bruce Paley's theory about Joe Barnett is the *'Mysterious Key'*, it is so important to his theory that it is found in the index to his book, and is accorded several mentions. The main point he makes is that the door to Mary Kelly's room was locked, therefore the murderer must have locked it, and hence the murderer must have been in possession of a key. The only person apart from Kelly to have a key would be Barnett, QED Barnett is the killer.

This theory falls flat on several points. First of all, according to Abberline the lock was of the *'spring bolt type'*. This means that it operated in the same manner as a Yale type lock, in other words the door could be fastened securely by merely pulling the door to, the bolt would be shot home automatically. This fact is given extra weight by Barnett's testimony that after the key went missing, he and Kelly used to open the door by reaching in through the broken window and operating the bolt from the inside. This statement by Barnett suggests that it was the lower of the two broken window panes that was broken on the night of the quarrel. It is only possible to reach the spring bolt through the upper broken pane, though with considerable difficulty. If Barnett and Kelly had been in the habit of reaching through the broken window then it must have been prior to the quarrel on the 30th October as Barnett moved out directly afterwards and Kelly was dead nine days later.

Paley uses Barnett's testimony to suggest that the door was in fact fitted with two locks. One a spring bolt type and the other a conventional warded lock that required a key to both open and close it. Otherwise he states why didn't the police merely reach in through the broken window to slip the bolt to gain access to the room? The reason why they didn't was because they couldn't - which means the door had to be fastened with a warded lock!

This is nonsense. Let us look at the facts. The room was first entered by a photographer to take a photographic record of the victim. Entry was gained by removing the entire window. At this time Barnett was not present at the scene so how could he tell the police of his window method of entry? Picture the scene, the door is locked and entry has to be made. There is no external indication what type of lock is fitted, so naturally rather than waste time they applied Ocham's razor to the problem and removed the window. (Ocham was a man who was presented by an incredibly complicated knot and was challenged to untie it. After studying the problem for several minutes he took out his cut throat razor and sliced through it!) Paley insists that if this was the case surely once the photographer entered the room he would have slipped back the bolt to let the police in? Again this is not taking into account the actual situation.

In all likelihood the photographer, provided by City Police, would have been under strict instructions not to touch or disturb anything. This seems a likely event given that the police were not proceeding with their investigations until the bloodhounds had arrived. Secondly the sights inside that room must have been straight from hell. Walter Dew describes it as a sight that he would take with him to his grave. I cannot in all honesty see anyone spending any more time in there than was absolutely necessary, I certainly can't see a photographer edging past the mounds of butchered flesh to see if he could fiddle with the door. I think it is reasonable to assume that he would get in, do his job, and get out as quickly as possible.

Of course there are those who will say that if it was a Yale lock it must have been obvious from the *outside* what lock it was, and surely the police would attempt to open it somehow? A reasonable assumption if the lock was a Yale type - I do not believe it was.

Linus Yale was an American inventor who launched his familiar cylinder barrelled lock on the world in 1853. By 1888 they were being used all over the world and would certainly be in use in England. However they were expensive, costing anywhere between 12/6 and 18 shillings. It is inconceivable that McCarthy would fit a lock costing that much to a door of a room that was being rented out for a few shillings a week.

The type of lock that I believe was fitted to the door was a type known as a Night Latch. These locks had been in use since Georgian times and were very popular. Kenrick and Sons Ltd. of West Bromich show examples of this type of lock in their catalogue for 1887. In appearance it looks just like a normal warded lock, the only clue to it being a spring bolt type is that there is no keyhole on the inside. The inside face of the lock has two knobs, one is milled at the edges and turning this draws back the bolt, and the other slides vertically and is used to fix the bolt in an *open position*. From the outside you have the normal escutcheon over the key-hole, and thus from the outside it is impossible to tell what type of lock it is. The cost of this wonder of English engineering - three shillings! Is it logical or likely that someone with an eye on a shilling as Mcarthy obviously was, would then go to the further expense of fitting another warded lock? I think the answer has got to be no.

This leads us to another point. If the lock was a Kenrick type and closed automatically, surely this points to the murderer being one of three people.

1. Someone let into the room by Kelly.

2. Someone with a key.

3. Someone who knew how to slip the bolt using the broken window.

The last two classes of person seem to definitely implicate Barnett, but here again we are assuming facts not in evidence. For example for the last two cases to be relevant you are assuming the door was *locked in the first place.*

There is absolutely not one scrap of evidence to show that Mary Kelly actually locked her door. But is there any evidence to show that she didn't? I believe there is. Let us look at this *'reaching through the window and slipping back the bolt'* theory.

Contacting the Federation of Master Builders I was able to apply some sort of scale to the famous photograph of the outside of Mary Kelly's room. This shows the two external windows, including the one with the two broken panes of glass, a drainpipe and the entrance door to the room. The top of the door is curved not straight, which tends to indicate the door was originally fitted to the building and not added as an afterthought. This means we can assume a door height of about 5' 9".

The photograph shows the top of the window at the same height as the door, which means that allowing for a few inches for the door frame etc., we can arrive at the top of the window being about 5' 10" from the ground. If you consult the testimony of Thomas Bowyer presented at the inquest this pinpoints precisely which panes were broken. He states:

"...I went around the corner and there was a broken window in the farthest window".

It is at this point that Inspector Ledger of G Division who made accurate plans of the crime scene, realises that this last statement makes no sense at all. Bowyer has referred to a pane of glass as a *'window'*. Inspector Ledger interrupts Bowyer's testimony, and produces his plans. Bowyer consults the plans and continues:

"I refer to the plans and I mean the farthest pane of the first window, the small one ..."

This testimony without a doubt shows that of the four panes of glass in the smallest window, the furthest one, either upper or lower left is broken. Later on the testimony of Dr Phillips identifies precisely which are the broken panes. He states:

*"There are two windows in the court. Two of the panes in the window nearest the passage were broken and finding the door locked, I looked through the **lower** broken pane...."*

Therefore as Bowyer's testimony confirms the broken pane is either upper or lower left, and Phillips speaks of the lower broken pane it is obvious that the broken panes in the window must be lower left and upper right. The other pane referred to by Phillips cannot be upper left because that is too far from the door to make it possible to slip the bolt by reaching through.

This now puts the broken pane of glass at approximately 5' to 5' 8" from the ground. With Mary Kelly's height being estimated at approximately 5' 3", I take this estimate from people who knew her as being 5' 2" and also the description of her as a short, dumpy woman and the intervening brickwork between the broken pane and the nearest point of the door being at least 18", allowing for standard size bricks and mortar of 1/4" thickness, it can now be seen that putting your arm through a window, surrounded by sharp broken glass, reaching right over and slipping the catch is not such a simple matter as everyone has assumed it to be. It was going to be quite a struggle for someone of Joe Barnett's height 5' 7", but for someone of Mary Kelly's height it was all but impossible. I constructed a mock up of the corner of Mary Kelly's room, and I could not just put my hand through the broken pane and slip the latch. If anyone wishes to duplicate this feat, please do as I did and use tracing paper to simulate glass - it's much safer.

However there is a way Mary Kelly could have done it. Using the drain pipe for support and standing on the window sill, clearly visible in the picture, and reaching in with your left arm, it is now much easier, though certainly not simple! How do we know Mary Kelly didn't do this on the night she was murdered?

Mary Ann Cox described her return on the night of her murder. Mary was drunk and accompanied by the man with the quart pail of beer. She entered her room with the man. Surely if Mary Kelly in her drunken state had started clambering over the window sill and hanging off the drainpipe, Mary Cox would have mentioned it? Remember Mary Kelly and the man entered the court just in front of Mary Cox, and she saw them both go into the room together. Apart from anything else there just wasn't the time for a drunken Irish prostitute to start performing feats of balancing derring-do. So is it logical or even likely that Mary Kelly would leave her room unlocked? The answer has got to be yes.

The Kenrick lock (and others of that type) were all able to lock the bolt back in the unlocked position. Mary Kelly had absolutely nothing of value in her room. An inspector involved in the Ripper investigations writes in his report:

'I thought I had sealed off the area of the crime, my men were stationed at every point, yet within a matter of minutes the place was swarming with onlookers. They had cut through peoples houses and backyards for it is a fact that the people here do not lock their doors'.

Surely the logical step for her to take if she had lost her key, would be simply to leave the door *'on the latch'*, once inside she could release the bolt and lock herself in. This is a far more logical and likely scenario than Mary Kelly balancing precariously, often drunk, on a window sill trying to open the door without slicing her arm off.

So if we are correct in assuming this, the last two categories of killer, simply do not apply. This only leaves the first category, the killer was let in by Mary Kelly - or does it. Look at the sequence, Mary Kelly returns to her room drunk with a man carrying a quantity of beer. It is fair to assume that they both drunk this together, in which case she is now extremely drunk. Later on she goes out again (Hutchinson's statement) and takes another man back to her room. Is it not likely that on both these occasions Mary Kelly kept the door on the latch so that her customers could let themselves out, without having to fiddle in the darkness with a latch handle? In other words when Jack the Ripper called he found Mary Kelly lying in a drunken state on her bed *and her door unlocked!!*

I hope this has now dispensed with the *'missing key'* mystery, another one of those dark corners that reveal all when the beam of logic is focused upon it.

Bruce Paley finishes his book with a Chapter on *'The Case Against Joseph Barnett'*. Unfortunately in doing so he very selectively picks his evidence. He puts forward the theory that basic anatomical knowledge could have been gained by his cleaning fish! I can assure Mr. Paley that fish gutters do not stand around carefully dissecting fish and examining their contents. The knife goes in, cuts up and everything inside comes out, the work is piece work, you are paid by the amount you do, not by the care with which you do it

Paley sites the description of the killer as fitting Barnett, possibly, but a description of 5' 8", medium build and a moustache could also fit 99% of the population of the East End - including the women!!

Even when he attempts to fit his suspect to the *'Offender profile'* it doesn't work. Yes of course he fits some of the categories, but then so would thousands of other people. Paley has forgotten that the *'Offender Profile'* should be used to whittle

207

down suspects, not to find someone who vaguely fits and then blame him.

The case against Barnett collapses on all these points. There is no credible motive, he was not seen by any witnesses, and all in all he just does not fit the mould of a killer. He comes across as a man who held down a good steady job for many years, had good family connections with his brothers around him, loved the wrong girl and lost her to a vicious killer.

JAMES MAYBRICK

James Maybrick came to prominence as a suspect when a book called 'The Diary of Jack the Ripper' was published in 1993. I am always suspicious of 'diaries' as it is almost unheard of for a killer to keep a diary *at the time of the killings*. Many killers have recorded their deeds afterwards and some have actually written about what they intend to do, but I have never come across a contemporary record. The basic flaw with this is that to the killer he is doing absolutely nothing wrong, nothing out of the ordinary, so why would he record it? Would you keep a record filled with accounts of how you dressed each morning?

When I read a description of the actual diary for the first time and understood that it was an old scrap book with the first batch of pages torn out, I really became suspicious. Why would anyone with the wealth, power and position that Maybrick enjoyed bother with an old scrap book? If what he was doing was so important for him to record he would have bought a brand new book, handsomely bound, probably with his name in gold lettering on the front.

The diary was supposed to have come into the possession of a man called Michael Barret who said that an old friend had given it to him in a pub. Watching a TV programme about the Diary, I turned the volume down when Barret was on to concentrate on his body language. I got the distinct impression he was not telling the truth. Later on it was revealed that he had lied and that the Diary actually came into the possession of his wife who .... I'm sorry at that point I really had to give up.

There has been much discussion on the authenticity or otherwise of the Diary. Some experts say this, others say something else. To my mind they are all academic, the fiasco of the Hitler Diaries proves that you listen to *'experts'* at your peril. Whether the diary was written by James Maybrick or not is immaterial, a fact largely overlooked by the majority of people involved in all this. What is material is *'Is James Maybrick Jack the Ripper?'* after reviewing the evidence I have to say no.

Too much emphasis is placed by the pro lobby on silly things. For instance in the Mary Kelly photograph, blood has splashed on the wall and dribbled down. Because this is vaguely in the shape of the letter *'M'* this is held as being proof as referring to the name *'Maybrick'*. This is absolute nonsense. A list of Catharine Eddowes' effects, returned to the Scotland Yard by an anonymous person in 1987, refers to an empty tin box. The diary makes a vague reference to a tin box and this again is seized upon as proof, because we didn't know about this item until 1987! This is piffle. Just because the list wasn't returned until 1987 didn't mean it didn't exist! It had to be somewhere all that time. And since the list was made at the time, presumably other people knew of its existence and may have mentioned the items found in some other publication.

I have no doubt that we will open our papers one day and it will be revealed that the whole thing is a hoax. James Maybrick away you go.

THE LODGER

In 1995 a new Ripper book called *'The Lodger'* was published. Written by two authors, Stewart Evans and Paul Gainey, it purported to reveal the true identity of Jack the Ripper. (the book was subtitled *'The Arrest and Escape of Jack the Ripper'*). It was an important book because for the first time for a long time the suspect was a complete newcomer, someone no-one had ever considered before. On the dust jacket the book promised to reveal the identity:

'of the man the police believed was Jack the Ripper. He was the prime, if not the only suspect, at the time of the murders'.

Heady stuff indeed, and along with thousands of others I passed over my money for this latest offering. However, after reading the book I was left with a profound sense of disappointment, for I could not see any justification in the claim that his man was the prime suspect of the police, indeed it appeared to me as if the exact opposite was true.

Following on the book, another edition was published this time titled *'Jack the Ripper - the First American Serial Killer'* (which is factually incorrect there were several serial killers in America before 1880, Thomas Piper who murdered three women and a little girl in 1873 amongst them). At the same time David Jessop made a programme for Channel 4 TV which was broadcast in the *'Secret History'* series in July 1996. Again the programme relied heavily on the *'fact'* that the suspect was the first choice of Scotland Yard. When Mr. Jessop made this programme he also took his cameras to the First International Conference on the Whitechapel Murders, which was held in Ipswich in April 1996.

During the two days he spent filming there he met some of the world's leading authorities on the Whitechapel Murders, and many of them expressed contrary opinions to those put forward in the book. One thing that came out of the conference was the fact that when Mary Kelly was murdered this *'suspect'* was in fact in Police custody on a morals charge. This was quickly explained away in the second edition of the book by dismissing Mary Kelly as a Ripper victim!

The conference was the first opportunity for experts and enthusiasts from all over the world to meet and discuss the Murders in depth, and there were some extremely valuable contributions made, unfortunately when the programme was screened all footage of the conference and all mention of it was edited out.

The background to the new suspect is simply this. Stewart Evans, one of the authors was offered a bundle of letters that used to belong to the famous reporter, G R Sims, who was passionately interested in the murders, and had covered them at the time. One of the letters was from a retired policeman, John Littlechild, and it makes interesting reading. It says in part,

"I never heard of a Doctor D in connection with the Whitechapel murders but amongst the suspects, and to my mind a very likely one, was a Dr. T (which sounds much like D). He was an American quack

named Tumblety and was at one time a frequent visitor to London and on these occasions constantly brought under the notice of police, there being a large dossier concerning him at Scotland Yard".

There is a lot more in the letter where Littlechild speculates on the identity of the Jack the Ripper letter writer, ascribing them to an enterprising journalist named Bullen or possibly his chief a man named Moore. One further interesting point is the hand-written note at the end of the letter in which Littlechild adds,

"except that I knew Major Griffiths for many years. He probably got his information from Anderson who only thought he knew".

It is obvious from this letter that Littlechild was replying to a request for information from Sims as to the possible identity of Jack the Ripper. The mention of a *'Dr. D'* is highly suggestive as this ties in with Mcnaghten's mention of a Dr. D who had committed suicide. Mention of Griffiths and Anderson also indicates that Sims was querying the Polish Jew theory.

Now at first glance this letter seems to be vitally important as it introduces an entirely new player into the game - the mysterious Dr. Tumblety. However when the facts are analysed the whole theory starts to look decidedly shaky.

For a start who was Inspector Littlechild, and what part did he play in the Ripper investigation? The answer is that he was the head of Special Branch from 1883 to 1893 and played no part in the Ripper investigation. Littlechild's main area of interest was the funding by American sympathisers of the Irish terrorists known as the Fenians. (sounds familiar) Because a lot of Americans used Liverpool as their landing port in England, obviously special watch was kept on this area of the country.

Tumblety was a shady American quack doctor, who had dabbled in pornography and abortions. He had a chequered past that included him being arrested by the American Secret Service in connection with the assassination of President Lincoln. His character was that of a show off, and if he felt that he was not the absolute centre of attention - he took steps to make sure he was. At one time he launched a bitter tirade against an actor who was, Tumblety said, slandering Tumblety by his outrageous performances. Tumblety deluged his friends and papers with letters condemning this actor, and inviting them to go to the theatre to see for themselves how his good name(?) was being besmirched.

However when some of his friends took up his invitation to go to the theatre and see for themselves, it was obvious to them that the man cavorting about on stage with the ludicrous make-up was none other than Tumblety himself!

Tumblety was supposed to have a great hatred of women, especially prostitutes, stemming from the fact that his first wife was, unbeknown to Tumblety, a prostitute who quite happily carried on her profession after her nuptials. However this evidence of a great hatred for women comes from a single source who recalled something said at a dinner party one night, hardly incontrovertible evidence.

Tumblety's background however does give us a clue as to how he came to the attention of Special Branch. Tumblety was a known Fenian sympathiser, and so would automatically come under Special Branch observation. With his background of a previous arrest in connection with a political crime, Lincoln's assassination, it is hardly surprising that he came in for some very close scrutiny indeed.

The theory is that Tumblety was arrested on charges of indecent behaviour with several men, he was bailed on these charges, promptly skipped bail and fled the country. He was followed by Scotland Yard detectives in hot pursuit across the Atlantic, and his home in America was kept under observation by a very obvious Scotland Yard man, complete with loud check suit, bright red whiskers and obligatory thick soled boots! He apparently eluded his pursuers again and ended his days in St. Louis, dying in 1903.

The problem with the book is that it uses the well known ploy of mentioning something and then accepting that as hard fact. For instance, the book quotes a story which appeared in the *'The Globe'* for Wednesday 10th October. The story entitled *'Detectives on a new scent'* tells of someone who may have come from Liverpool and may have stayed in the East End of London leaving a bag behind in a hotel. The bag contained several pornographic pictures, clothing and other items which according to the paper *'is forming the foundation of a most searching inquiry'.* The story ends with the words:

*'It has been **suggested** that the mysterious personage referred to landed in Liverpool from America, **but this so far is no more than a suggestion'***

However the very next line in the book states:

'This remarkable story, showing that the CID were seeking a man from America....'

Quite clearly the story doesn't say anything of the sort. In fact it goes out of its way to point out that this is no more than a suggestion. It is interesting to note that the pro Maybrick camp also use this story as the bag in question was shown to belong to a Mr. Micbrac, obviously Micbrac is just another way of saying Maybrick - obviously! The next instance of turning news reports into facts comes with a report that a lady in Batty Street reported one of her lodgers disappearing after the double murders of the 30th September. However despite lurid tales of blood soaked clothing this particular story fizzles out. Despite this the house at 22 Batty Street is now definitely labelled Tumblety's East End hide out, *even though there is absolutely nothing to connect him with this address!*

And so on and so on. The book fails to convince in many areas, the first of which is that there is not one shred of evidence to link Tumblety with any of the murders in any way shape or form. The only time Tumblety's name is linked to the killings is after he has fled Britain and is returning to America where the press reports him as being a suspected Jack the Ripper. The way those reports are written however convinces me that Tumblety himself may have had more than a small part in their creation. Don't forget at the time just about everyone was being accused, and suspects arrested on a daily basis - only to be released again through lack of evidence.

The only time Tumblety's name is linked with the killings by an official, is when a retired police officer who had absolutely nothing to do with the investigation writes in 1913 that in his opinion Tumblety is a good suspect. I hardly think that this solitary mention makes him Scotland Yard's prime suspect. I find it rather strange that all the police officers who were actually involved with the investigation make no mention of him whatsoever. Why should Littlechild think Tumblety is a good suspect? Lets look at the facts. Littlechild is investigating American supporters of the Fenian terrorist organisation. Tumblety is known to be a supporter and has in fact been arrested by the American Secret Service in connection with a political crime.

This I would suggest, would make him a prime candidate for Special Branch keeping a very close eye on the man. But what do they find? Instead of a dangerous and romantic international terrorist, a rather pathetic self publicist who wanders around the East End committing acts of gross indecency with men. A truly warped and twisted character and I presume someone who must seem like an ideal candidate for the warped and twisted murders of Jack the Ripper.

As for Scotland Yard pursuing their man across the Atlantic, this is patently nonsense. If Tumblety was released, presumably because the police had absolutely no evidence tying him to the Ripper killings, what was the point in pursuing him? What were they going to do with him if they caught him? Tell him they still had no evidence, but that they're still looking? I've no doubt detectives did cross the Atlantic but I maintain they had nothing to do with Tumblety being the Ripper. As for the so called detective keeping watch on Tumblety in America, such an outrageous costume and manner of behaviour suggest only one man Tumblety himself. His previous performance as Tumblety pretending to be an actor, pretending to be Tumblety seems to create a precedence. The final proof of what I surmise comes from Littlechild himself for in his letter to Sims he states.

"Tumblety was arrested at the time of the murders in connection with unnatural offences and charged at Marlborough Street, remanded on bail, jumped his bail, and got away to Boulogne. He shortly left Boulogne and was never heard of afterwards."

In other words Littlechild states that after Tumblety had left Boulogne he vanished. So who were these Atlantic hopping

Scotland Yard detectives supposed to be chasing? Surely if they were after Tumblety, and if a Scotland Yard detective was patrolling outside Tumblety's house in America, Littlechild would know? After all he is the only police officer who ever suspected Tumblety.

The whole scenario fails to convince in any quarter, but the following points particularly disqualify him.

Character. Tumblety was a publicity-seeking quack who would do anything to ensure that he was always the centre of attention. The last thing Jack the Ripper wanted was to draw attention to himself.

Geography. There is nothing to show that Tumblety had any sort of base in the East End apart from his arrest, this only proves he visited the East End. Even if we stretch all the points and agree that he was the mysterious lodger at 22 Batty Street this actually makes him less of a suspect. Batty Street runs parallel with Berner Street. We know that Jack the Ripper was in Mitre Square and we know he was outside Wentworth dwellings in Goulston Street where he dropped the piece of apron. What on earth was a man travelling from Mitre Square to Batty Street doing in Goulston Street which is the opposite direction? From Mitre Square the quickest way would be to cross Aldgate and go down Jewry Street. Left into George Street, right into Minories, left into Swan Street. Right into Mansell Street left into Great Prescott Street, go to the end cross over Leman Street into Hooper street, through the tunnel, left into Back Church Lane. Turn right into Ellen Street and either left into Berner and right at Fairclough or left at Providence and right into Fairclough. If however he wasn't particularly worried about using the main roads he could just walk up Aldgate and Whitechapel High Street, turn off into Commercial Road and right into Batty Street.

Corroboration. There is absolutely no corroboration for Littlechild's statement anywhere else. Nothing points to the man's guilt, nothing indicates even in the slightest degree that Tumblety had anything at all to do with the murders. In summary then Tumblety must join the ranks of the other impostors. Charlatan he most certainly was, sexually twisted and unstable, definitely, egocentric con man, absolutely, but Jack the Ripper? Never ! !!!

Over the last few pages we have looked at some of the most commonly accused suspects. They have ranged from mad Polish Jews to heirs to the throne, with quack American Doctors along the way. This is by no means an exhaustive list, it would take an entire volume to list all of those, and more are being added every day. Yet we have discarded them all, mainly through lack of that most essential of ingredients - proof.

The proof we seek is not the same as required by a court of law, it is very unlikely that any evidence of that kind will ever be forthcoming, but surely there must be some pointers? Some indications that something was wrong with someone? Something that will link in with something else to provide a very reasonable indication that our man is found?

There is.

In all the millions of words I have read, the hundreds of thousands of words I have exchanged with fellow enthusiasts, no one has ever put forward the name of the man I believe was Jack the Ripper.

That man is George Hutchinson.

Chapter Ten

"When you have eliminated the impossible, whatever remains, <u>however improbable</u>, must be the truth"

Sir Arthur Conan Doyle 'The Sign of the Four'

George Hutchinson is one of the most mysterious characters in the whole Jack the Ripper saga, not through any intention I'm sure, but merely because no-one has ever bothered to find out more about him before now. In his book 'The Ripper and the Royals', Melvyn Fairclough claims to publish the first photograph ever seen of George Hutchinson. He also includes an interview with Reg Hutchinson, George's son. Unfortunately I believe he has the wrong man entirely.

For a start Fairclough's George Hutchinson's full name is George William Topping Hutchinson and this is not the name he is referred to either in the papers, understandably, or in his statement, not understandably. It is common practice in statements to refer to the person either by the whole of the person's name, or at the very least by his first name and all initials. This is done for the obvious reason of correct identification. The statements are signed George and Geo Hutchinson again with no other initials. There is also the fact that George W T Hutchinson is the wrong age. George Hutchinson is referred to in all the papers that gave his age as being 28, George W T Hutchinson was only 22 at the time. (By a strange coincidence he was 22 on the 1st October, the day after Eddowes was murdered) It is difficult to see how such a mistake could have been made, there is a great deal of difference between someone who is just 22 and someone who is 28.

The world renowned document examiner, Sue Iremonger, has also investigated whether or not this is the correct George Hutchinson. She compared the marriage certificate signature of George W T Hutchinson, with the signature on the statement made by George Hutchinson, and has concluded that they are not made by the same person.

I believe the correct George Hutchinson was born on the 10th ʊ ᵢ December 1859 at 43 King David Lane, Shadwell, only a couple of miles from the heart of Whitechapel, the road is still there to this day. His father, Joseph Hutchinson, was a licensed victualler. He is registered as George Hutchinson with no other names, this at least compares with the name on the statement and his age would be 28 at the time of the murders. Not a lot can be found out about George except that in 1881 he was working as a barman in the *'John of Jerusalem'* public house at 1 Rosaman Street, Clerkenwell only a mile or so from the scene of the murders in Whitechapel.

He then turns up in 1888 as residing at the *'Victoria Home for Working Men'*, situated at 39 to 41 Commercial Street, Whitechapel. Nothing is known about what happened to him after that except that just over two years after Mary Kelly's murder he had left the Victoria Home and apparently vanished. It is probable that he had lived in the Whitechapel area for some years before the murders as he stated that he had known Kelly for several years beforehand.

It has often been said that the key to the Ripper murders was Mary Kelly. She was a landmark victim. She was younger and prettier than all the others, she was killed indoors and she was the last victim. It was also noticeable that the worst mutilations were performed on her body, it was as if the killer had finally snapped, lost every shred of self control he possessed and completely and utterly destroyed her. Mary Kelly wasn't just murdered and mutilated, Mary Kelly was wiped out, she was expunged, and after the Ripper had finished, it was as if she had never existed. Remember Barnett, the man who had lived with her for eighteen months, could only identify her by her hair and her eyes.

So what was it about Mary Kelly that triggered the killer lust in the Ripper? What was so special about her, what did she do?

Mary Kelly was the sort of person I would classify as a user. They use other people to make their own lives more comfortable. Rudyard Kipling brilliantly described this phenomenon in his poem *'Martha's Sons'*. In this poem he refers to the two sisters, Martha and Mary. When Jesus visits their home, Mary is all agog and listens to the prophet spellbound.

She absent mindedly orders her sister Martha to wash Jesus's feet for him and Martha tired of being bossed around, angrily refuses. In the poem Kipling tells of the two types of people who inhabit the earth, the sons of Mary, who tend to lounge around ordering the sons of Martha to do all the work. One stanza goes:

> *'Raise ye the stone or cleave the wood,*
> *To make the path more fair or flat,*
> *Lo! It is black already with blood,*
> *Some son of Martha spilled for that!'*

It describes perfectly the type of person Mary (Coincidence ?) Kelly was. She naturally expected the world to revolve around her, and probably because of this - it did! I'm not saying that she did this deliberately, she probably didn't even realise what she was doing, but she did it all the same. If you like, you could say she had natural leadership abilities.

Look at the way she led her life. She always had someone in tow to look after her and provide for her. Even when she left one man and moved on to the next, her ex-lovers still apparently kept calling on her and giving her money. Examine Barnett's testimony, he tells of one of her ex-lovers, possibly Joe Fleming, who still called round occasionally to give her money. Look at Barnett's own situation. At the end of October he and Kelly have a row, whether it was about Maria Harvey staying with Kelly or whether it was about Kelly going back on the streets is neither here nor there, the fact is Barnett and Kelly had a blazing row and he stormed out. Yet only a few days later he calls round to apologise that he hasn't got any money to give her! You would have expected Barnett to have stormed out never to darken her door again. After all he picked her up in a bar there must have been plenty of other fish in the sea.

Again we have the situation with Kelly's rent arrears. McCarthy collected the rent on a daily basis, this avoided tenants running up arrears and then doing a moonlight flit. Yet for some reason completely unexplained McCarthy allowed Kelly to run up twenty-nine shillings in arrears! This was unheard of. Either he was completely under her spell, or else he knew that she had plenty of men friends who would bail her out. No other explanations seem probable.

Most of the time this attitude is irritating but relatively harmless, just a case of someone being a bit *'bossy'*. If the person being used realises it, it is annoying and often these people place themselves outside of the users influence, they form new relationships or just simply ignore the users existence. However there are times when the user unwittingly travels in dangerous territory - often without being aware of it.

Users adopt many different strategies to get their own way, but the most common is to flatter the *'victim'*, make them feel different, special. I'm sure we have all experienced this type of behaviour or witnessed it in some way. Who amongst us has not heard the mother coax her baby to eat his food with such as lines as *'There's a clever boy, now I wonder if you are clever enough to manage just one more spoonful?'* It may not seem like it but the mother is using empty flattery to get her own way. Of course as time goes on the type of flattery changes, it now becomes the helpless female standing beside her broken down car saying *'I'm sure a clever man like you will know just how to fix it?'*

Of course in these circumstances it is all very harmless, but what happens if the person you are flattering takes the flattery as a sign of something more? What happens if the user inadvertently picks on someone for whom a simple word of praise takes on an entirely new meaning - one that was never intended. What sort of person would behave in that manner? Well they could be termed obsessives, or as we now label them - stalkers.

Basically a stalker is a person who not only has lost touch with reality, but doesn't even live in the same world as the rest of society. A simple smile bestowed upon a crowd of people at random by a film star is translated by the stalker as a secret sign that proves the bestower is madly in love with them.

One such stalker who terrorised a news reader for many years had even constructed his own code book, which set out the secret method by which the news reader and her secret admirer were communicating with each other. For instance if the newsreader said the word *'London'* this was translated by the code book to mean *'I love you'*. The word Birmingham meant *'Meet me'* and the next place name after that was the location for the meeting. Of course when the newsreader didn't turn up, the stalker bombarded his victim with demands to know why she had failed to keep their appointment! The extent to which reality is lost to these people is shown by the fact that when the police pointed out to the stalker that this *'code book'* had in fact been constructed by himself, they were treated to a scornful reply *'Of course he had written it - under secret telepathic instructions from the news-reader. Didn't they know anything?'*

There is no communication with these people, because the world you inhabit is entirely different to the one they presently reside in. Unfortunately the only safe way to deal with these people is to lock them up and throw away the key. It is difficult to understand the lengths these people go to delude themselves. Confrontation, pleading even violence fails to work because of this complete lack of any rational thought. One stalker was arrested by police and was asked why he terrified his victim by parking outside her house every night, and knocking on her door every hour to inquire whether she was all right. The stalker was genuinely baffled by this, and could not understand why his victim was not grateful to him, *"Doesn't she realise"* he said, *"that while I'm there I'm keeping all the murderers and rapists away?"*

I believe that Mary Kelly made the mistake of directing her charms on George Hutchinson. It may have been something trivial, but I believe he took it completely the wrong way. George Hutchinson had an obsessive personality, and he began to stalk Mary Kelly.

Of course it is easy to make such a claim, but is there any proof. Is there any indication at all that this might be so? I believe there is. Martin Fido makes mention in his excellent book *'The Crimes Detection and Death of Jack the Ripper'* (page 88).

*"This might explain Barnett's uncertain feeling that she (Mary Kelly) was frightened of someone, **not necessarily the Ripper"**.*

Then again in Paul Begg's *'Uncensored Facts'* (page 148).

Coroner   Have you heard her speak of being afraid of anyone?

Barnett   Yes; several times

Begg then asks the question *'Who was it that Mary Kelly was afraid of?'*

Barnett's deposition at Mary Kelly's inquest again gives us an indication that she was afraid of someone,

"She seemed to be afraid of someone..."

So who was Mary Kelly afraid of? The first obvious answer is the Ripper, but as Begg points out this is not necessarily so. If she was afraid of the Ripper, surely she would make that clear when talking to her friends and Barnett. But time and time again we keep coming back to the testimony of various people that she was afraid of someone else. Of course she was not to know that Hutchinson and the Ripper were one and the same. I believe that Hutchinson was the archtypical stalker, who in the early stages causes discomfort rather than fear in their victims. This soon turns to a sense of unease, and then shortly to terror. In the early stages the stalker is seen as *'creepy'* rather than dangerous, a nuisance rather than a threat.

Mary Kelly's behaviour, her sense of unease and of being afraid of someone, is typical of the behaviour of a stalking victim. There are other pointers to Hutchinson being obsessed with Mary Kelly. Stalkers, at least in the early stages, refuse to see any other side to their victim, other than that created by them. Their victims can do no wrong, they are pure and blameless. Attempting to point out the bad aspects of a victim's character drives the stalker into a rage. The logic they use is their own twisted variety and therefore unassailable. The victim is spotless because they are the object of the stalker's obsession. For if the victim had any faults the stalker would not be obsessed with them, but since he (or she, there are female stalkers) is obsessed with them, they are therefore spotless. This is the type of logic that a stalker uses, and because it is so far removed from any semblance of normality, it is impossible to argue against.

Later on, after many rebuffs, the stalker's reasoning changes. Because the victim is pleading to be left alone, it is obvious that they are totally in the wrong, because it is impossible for the stalker to be in the wrong. In this case the victim has to be destroyed and now the love obsession turns to a hate obsession.

When a stalker fixates on someone, it is possible that the object of their desire is out of reach. They may be very wealthy people who move in different social circles and can afford physical bodyguards. It may be that their victim does not live in the same area as the stalker, and therefore the stalking is done at a distance. In this case the stalker often ascribes characteristics present in his victim to people who are more accessible. For instance if a stalker becomes obsessed with a blonde film star who is physically out of reach, he may side track some of his obsession to other blonde women. The problem is of course it is the stalker's perception we are dealing with - not reality. For instance a stalker may be fixated on Marilyn Monroe, but because she is dead and totally out of reach, he may fixate on other women he believes share similarities with Miss Monroe. In reality these other women may not bear any resemblance to Miss Monroe, *but in the eyes of the stalker they do!* In other words he may look at a brunette and see a blonde.

When the stalker moves into the *'hate'* mode of his obsession, things become very dangerous indeed. For not only is the object of his obsession in danger-so is anyone who - *according to the stalker* - bears any similarities to the original victim. This explains why quite often a series of killings appears to be totally random, with no similarities in the age or even sex of the victims, and nothing else to link the victims together.

The danger these people pose to society cannot be over emphasised. In the love mode they might kill anyone they see as a threat to their victim, in the hate mode they might kill anyone they see as resembling their victim. Luckily it is still comparatively rare for stalkers to physically harm anyone, but when they do the results can be spectacularly bloody. A young man walked into a gunshop in California and purchased 3,000 rounds of shotgun ammunition. Armed with several bandoleers full of shotgun cartridges, an automatic rifle and several hand guns, he drove to his victims place of work. His obsession of several years duration with Laura Black, a young computer operator, was about to move into the hate mode.

On his arrival he shot down everyone he saw, this included pumping three shotgun rounds into the girl he had previously insisted was his wife. His final score was over thirty people wounded and seven dead. It was this case that finally moved California to pass the world's first anti-stalking laws. Since then many people have fallen to the murderous rages of deranged people - John Lennon was another.

How can you recognise a stalker? The simple answer is that you can't. They come in all shapes and sizes, colours and creeds, young and old. Generally speaking the majority of them are male, but there are murderous exceptions. The only stalking case in Britain that has so far led to murder concerned an Indian woman who became obsessed with a West Indian driving instructor. After making the man's life a misery for many years she finally arrived at a solution. The man was not able to come to her because he was married, solution simple - remove the wife. Using her undoubted powers of persuasion, she got her sixteen year old son to murder the man's wife. The poor man's nightmare didn't end there as the police, in yet another example of sheer incompetence, charged the husband with the crime. The case got as far as a trial before the charges against him were dismissed.

The one pointer that might help future identification of such people is that an overwhelming majority of them tend to be paranoid and like most paranoids they tend to arm themselves against their imaginary enemies. By a strange coincidence the weapon of choice of these people is a knife!

There are indicators that Hutchinson complied with the general profile. His reluctance to see Mary Kelly in any but the best of lights is shown by his description of her as *'slightly spreeish'* when he met her in Commercial Street on the last morning of her life. Other witnesses say that she was extremely drunk at midnight, and this was before she shared a quart of beer with a customer. Her general state of sobriety when Hutchinson saw her two hours later can best be imagined, but I would say that *'extremely drunk'* would be a more accurate description than *'slightly spreeish'*, but of course in Hutchinson's eyes she could do no wrong.

So if we accept that indicators point towards Mary Kelly being a *'user'* of people and that George Hutchinson was an obsessive personality, a *'stalker'* we can see that the combination of these two people's lives would lead to explosive results, as indeed it did. What was the pattern, what were the sequence of events that turned George Hutchinson into Jack the Ripper? It is possible that they went something like this.

By the beginning of 1888 it was obvious that Mary Kelly didn't want anything to do with George Hutchinson. She had shown a remarkable willingness to take up with anyone she took a shine to she moved in with Barnett after knowing him for only two days, she also had various other paramours in tow at the time, but apparently none of this affection came Hutchinson's way. In his statement to Abberline he describes his previous relationship with Kelly as *'having given her some money in the past'.* Hardly a basis for happy coexistence.

To anyone else this coolness would indicate that Kelly didn't *'fancy'* him, but to Hutchinson's obsessive personality this could only mean one thing - someone was preventing them from getting together!

This may sound an absolutely ludicrous thing to say, but this is the way that a stalker thinks. His twisted reasoning tells him that he is infatuated with his victim, therefore his victim obviously feels the same way, if they are not together someone must be stopping them.

Time and time again this type of twisted logic crops up in cases of stalking, usually the stalker goes no further than threatening the supposed obstacle, but sometimes they erupt into murderous fury. Ralph Nau was twenty nine years old (exactly the age group highlighted by profilers for Serial killers and stalkers who kill) when he butchered his eight year old stepbrother with an axe. The boy's crime? According to Nau he *'came between'* Nau and the gymnast Nadia Comaneci whom Nau had seen on TV. This wasn't the end of the horror, police also believe he had murdered two other people for the same reason, but were unable to get enough evidence to charge him.

It is pertinent to note that when stalkers kill, they invariably choose the most blood thirsty method they can find. The weapons are axes, knives, shotguns, they don't seem to use poison or strangulation, it's almost as if there has to be a great bloodletting to wash away their obsession. Even when *'normal'* methods of killing are used, such as firearms, they always seem to go just that little bit further. When Mark Chapman stalked and finally killed John Lennon he made sure the bullets he used were of the vicious expanding *'dum dum'* variety. Shooting wasn't good enough, the body had to be exploded, ripped apart, utterly destroyed.

So who was preventing Mary Kelly and George Hutchinson from being together? The answer was obvious and supplied by Kelly herself. Her background, supplied by herself, told the sad story of a decent, respectable Irish girl, far from her native Ireland gradually sinking into the abyss. She told of being bought to Wales when she was young, how she married a decent hardworking collier who was so tragically killed, leaving her a widow with no means of support. How illness forced her to spend many months in an infirmary in Cardiff and how on her release from there, she was dragged into a life of degradation and vice by her cousin.

In all likelihood this is a complete fabrication, she probably came to London and the brothels direct from Ireland, and followed the dreaded trail East as her age crept up and her looks began to fade. As discussed before there are very strong indications that this was the case. However who amongst us has not embellished our past in attempt to appear in a better light to our peers?

Of course Hutchinson swallowed this tale hook, line and sinker, to him it was obvious who was to blame - prostitutes! It is possible that the brutal murder of a woman by her husband early in February 1888, opened Hutchinson's eyes to how he could achieve his aim of getting rid of prostitutes. Towards the end of the same month, on Saturday the 25th, Mrs Annie Millwood was viciously stabbed very close to where Hutchinson was staying at the Victoria Home for Working Men.

A month later on the 28th March another attack took place, this time Ada Wilson was the victim and she lived at 9 Maidman Street, about three quarters of a mile from where Hutchinson lived. It could be pointed out that his attack took place too far away from Hutchinson's lodgings to blame him for it, but that is to miss an important point, Maidman Street is only a few yards from the Whitechapel - Mile End Road, and that was the main road to Romford! In his statement Hutchinson said that he had been returning from Romford when he met Kelly. There is no reason to suspect him of lying over this point, but is there any reason to suspect that he was a regular visitor to Romford?

There is one very good reason to believe that Hutchinson might have made regular trips to Romford - work. Hutchinson had no steady employment in the East End. The papers describe him as being variously *'a labourer' 'an out of work groom'* and other occupations. We know that at the time of the killings he was doing some kind of work. The Victoria Home for Working Men only took you in if you had some sort of income, however sporadic, and Romford might well have been the place he earned it.

1888 in Romford saw three events that would explain why an out of work unskilled man would travel there. One was the sale of the Mawney Manor House Estate, which released 265 acres for development. Romford couldn't supply all the required labour so a lot came in from the outside, including the East End of London. The second was the opening of the Victoria Cottage Hospital in May 1888, and this too had provided work for East End men. Thirdly were the disastrous floods that practically wiped out the centre of Romford. These happened in August and so provided many more jobs well into the Autumn and Winter of 1888. One interesting piece in the local paper mentions an East End labourer arrested in a Romford pub on suspicion of being Jack the Ripper!

For the attacks on Wilson and Millwood to have occurred at this time and place it is almost inconceivable that they have never been linked to the Ripper killings before now. They are the classic pre-murder attacks carried out by so many serial killers. This is when they are experimenting, this is how they practice killing. How many times have we heard the police say *"This man must be caught before he kills"*. This isn't just rhetoric, the police know that these types of vicious attack don't go away - they get worse. For those of you who still do not accept that these two attacks were part of the Ripper series, two questions need answering.

a. If the attacker of Millwood and Wilson was not Jack the Ripper, what became of him? Are we to assume that someone just decides to stab two women for no reason whatsoever and then returns to stamp collecting or some other pursuit.

b. If the attacker was not Jack the Ripper what were the Ripper's previous crimes? I cannot think of one single instance where a serial killer has started his life of crime with murders, every one has graduated to murder through a succession of other crimes.

The other thing to take note of with these two attacks is the similarity between these attacks and the later murders, the MO.

a. All the attacks took place on single women who were alone at the time of the assault.

b. There were no witnesses and no clues left at the scene.

c. All attacks took place at the beginning or at the end of a month.

d. All the attacks took place in a very small geographical area.

e. A knife was used in all attacks, causing multiple stab wounds in all cases.

Taking all these similarities into account I think we can say with fair conviction that the same man carried out all the attacks.

From Hutchinson's point of view the first two attacks were totally unsatisfactory - he failed to kill his victims. It is interesting to note that the wounds on the first two victims changed slightly, the first attack was concentrated on the *'lower part of the body'*, this evidently didn't work as the victim wasn't killed outright. The second attack was aimed at the woman's throat, but again this failed to kill outright as the woman managed to scream. The third attack, on Martha Tabram, combines both these methods with an addition of a third - strangulation. Tabram's body was shredded with thirty nine separate stab wounds, this was evidently overkill, for none of the other murders used such a ferocious attack.

228

Martha Tabram's murder is interesting for another reason. There have been various attempts to pass off her murder as being the work of more than one person, and thus not being part of the Ripper's total. The reasons given for this, centre on the possibility that two weapons were used, for a lot of people two weapons mean two assailants. Unfortunately having raised this possibility they fail to examine the matter closely enough. For a start the majority of wounds on Martha Tabram's body could have been caused by an ordinary pocket knife. The assaults on Wilson and Millwood were carried out by someone using a 'clasp' (folding or pocket) knife. The only wound on Tabram's body that could not be attributed to an ordinary pocket knife was a deep stab wound in her chest.

Now compare Tabram's injuries to those suffered by the wife of the driving instructor who was murdered at the instigation of the woman who was stalking him. The driving instructor's wife had suffered,

'fifteen stab wounds, and the assault had been so ferocious that **one of the two knives used had sheared in half** . . *she had also been strangled'.*

There is no doubt that there was only one attacker of the driving instructor's wife who used two knives, and yet these injuries are practically identical to those suffered by Tabram. So to suggest that Tabram could not possibly be a Ripper victim because of the two weapons used, no longer holds up. It is also very noteworthy that Abberline thought Tabram to be a Ripper victim.

Even though the Ripper had succeeded in actually killing someone, the method required further refining. The multiple stab wounds were not necessary, all that was required was to strangle the victim, slash the throat, just to make sure, and then the body was available for any mutilations the insane mind of the killer deemed necessary.

After Tabram, both Nichols and Chapman fell prey to the murderous Hutchinson, both killed for the same insane reason that because they were both prostitutes they were somehow responsible for the downfall of Kelly, and of course preventing Kelly from joining Hutchinson.

Stride is discounted from the tally of Hutchinson's victims, for reasons already stated and also for one other. A serial killer is like a predatory animal, it will stake out its hunting territory and very rarely stray beyond it. Even in such cases where killings take place scattered over a wide area, it will often be found that the killer has in fact moved his home base, in other words his territory has changed. One of the most striking examples of this is a travelling German serial killer. He also murdered prostitutes, and for a long time no connection was made between slayings not only all over Germany, but in America as well.

When the murderer was finally tracked down by a persistent German detective, they discovered that all the murders had taken place around the murderer's lair. In Los Angeles the killings were centred around a cheap hotel the killer had used as a base during his stay in the city. The discovery of these murders was a source of high embarrassment to the Los Angeles police department. The killer was a well known author and had approached the police department as needing to do research into prostitutes in America. The police had kindly driven him around in the back of a patrol car pointing out all the known street walkers to him. They were not aware they were pointing out his future victims!

If you look at the disposition of the Ripper's victims you will find they produce an almost perfect arc with the Whitechapel High Street forming the base. Even the two attacks are not omitted from this area. Professor Canter when he appeared on a television programme about the Ripper was asked where he would expect to find the Ripper living. He held up a map of Whitechapel and circled an area with his finger. *"I would expect him to live in this area"* he said, *"and ideally living right here"* he pointed at a position on the map which pinpoints exactly the site of Hutchinson's lodgings.

The Stride murder however falls right outside the other Ripper killings. Apart from the fact the circumstances of the killing were dissimilar, the area is entirely different. It is way down to the South East. It should also be recalled that after the Eddowes murder a very strictly defined area was subject to an intensive police search. This area was so unusual in its definition that the bible of all Ripperologist's, *'The Jack the Ripper*

230

A to Z' makes special mention of it. In the 1996 edition on page 296, there is half a page on *'Metropolitan Police Area of Search'*. The passage points out that this area actually excludes areas where other suspects, such as Druitt, Kosminski and Pizer lived. The passage ends with the line,

'It is not known why so much of the 'Ripper territory' was apparently eliminated from the inquiry.'

Given the fact that Hutchinson's lodgings were practically central to this area, I believe that now we can answer that question. I am not saying that the police knew that Hutchinson was the man they were after, of course not, but I do think that they had a strong reason to deduce that their quarry lived in this very small area.

So discounting Stride as a Ripper victim we now move on to Eddowes as the next to fall prey to the Ripper's murderous ways. However Eddowes was not killed for the usual reason, Eddowes' murder was for an entirely different purpose altogether - self preservation.

Eddowes' murder was very unusual, it broke the pattern of the other murders to a certain extent. It was the only murder that took place outside the Metropolitan area, though still only a few hundred yards from Hutchinson's lodgings, it was the only murder where a genuine clue was left, the piece of apron in Goulston Street. Also it is the only murder where the victim had previously stated to a third party, the Superintendent at Shoe Lane lodgings,

*'I have come back to earn the reward offered for the apprehension of the Whitechapel murderer. **I think I know him!'.***

Catharine Eddowes wasn't murdered because she was a prostitute (there is absolutely no evidence to support this contention, *'The Jack the Ripper A to Z'* again *"we have no direct evidence that she did prostitute herself"*) she was killed to ensure her silence, Catharine Eddowes was blackmailing Jack the Ripper!

Let us look at the facts and see if they support such a contention. Eddowes and her common law husband Kelly were hop picking in Kent in the Autumn of 1888. It was a normal thing for hard up inhabitants of the East End to do, the work though backbreaking and hard, did allow them to earn a few shillings in the relatively superior conditions of the Kent country side. Most of the workers there would have come from the East End so it is entirely probable that the subject on everyone's lips was the Whitechapel murders. It is very likely that a quick witted person like Catharine Eddowes (her sharpness of mind is illustrated by the clever way she got lodgings for both herself and Kelly when they only had money for one) would have started to put a number of twos together. If so and so and been at the scene of the Nichols murder, Oh and by the way I saw creepy George hanging around, and someone else had said the same thing about Chapman's murder, it wouldn't have taken too long for the penny to drop.

What is known is that Kelly and Eddowes left the hop fields before the season was over. I appreciate that Kelly said *'we didn't get on too well, and started to hoof it home'*, but I find it hard to believe that they would have left the clean open hop fields of Kent, for the filthy streets of the East end just because they *'didn''t get on too well'* at hopping. Were their prospects any better in London? In this particular instance I believe they might have been. Certainly their behaviour suggested that they had expectations of coming into some money on their arrival; they spent all their available capital on a pair of new boots for Kelly and a jacket for Catharine in Maidstone, and when they arrived home they were penniless again.

Their behaviour after returning home follows this general pattern, as soon as they have accumulated some money they immediately spent it, it was almost as if they were merely waiting for the banks to open to draw some more out. Perhaps Catharine was. On Saturday 29th September they woke once again totally out of funds. Against Catharine's wishes, again pointing towards the supposition that she expected to get money from elsewhere, they pawned Kelly's new boots. This bought them the princely sum of 2/6d (approximately £8 by 1996 values). But yet again, without an apparent thought for the future they spent the lot in less than half a day.

Then came the afternoon parting. At about two in the afternoon Eddowes told Kelly she was going to get some money from her daughter. Her last words to re-assure Kelly about her safety. When he warned her about the killer she said,

'Don't you fear for me. I'll take care of myself and I shan't fall into his hands.'

Now we do know for certain that she had no intention of getting money from her daughter for the simple reason she did not know where her daughter was. Annie had moved away the previous year to avoid her mother's scrounging ways - and Catharine Eddowes knew this. Where then was she hoping to get the money?

But from somewhere she did get money, because by 8.30 that evening she was roaring drunk in Aldgate. Now she had no money on her when her body was found, so it is safe to assume that she had none when arrested. So once again she seems to have spent all she had. Now this is the same woman who is so careful with a penny that when Kelly had earned sixpence, she insisted on him taking a bed for fourpence while she walked to the Mile End workhouse for her own bed. Kelly had offered to do this, but Eddowes pointed out that if a man went there he would be expected to do a day's work for his bed, whereas a woman would only have to perform some menial task like picking oakum. This illustrates a very quick mind - and a totally unselfish personality. Once again she had spent all she had received, which once again points to her having expectations of more.

I am not assuming that she approached Hutchinson and accused him of being the murderer, but possibly she might have sought him out and dropped a hint that *'she knew what he was doing'*, to see what his reaction would be. Hutchinson could have reacted in two ways, if innocent he could have called her bluff but if guilty he might have slipped her a few pence with a promise of more to come. She would have insisted on a fast pay off, or she might have threatened to go to the police and claim the reward. An arrangement would have been made for a meeting later that night when Hutchinson would have more money for her.

When I first raised this point it was immediately pointed out to me that no one in their right mind would openly go up to a serial killer and attempt blackmail. Unfortunately this is not so. People do the most incredibly stupid things. I don't think anyone would deny people have been blackmailed, some certainly for the crime of murder. If you look at the case of the *'Sunset Strip Slayers'*, Douglas Clark and Carol Bundy, that's practically what happened. Carol Bundy's former lover, John Murry, confided in Bundy that he knew Clark was the killer, at the same time he must have known that in that case Bundy was also involved. The inevitable happened and Murry's headless body was found shortly afterwards.

Besides this it must be understood the terrible conditions that prevailed in the East End at that time. People like Eddowes literally had nothing to lose. One prostitute being questioned by a newspaper man was asked if she feared the killer, she answered:

'by the knife or off the bridge it doesn't make much difference to people like me. I sometimes think that a quick throat cutting might be better to slowly starving and freezing to death this winter.'

When you consider that in the previous year 304 people had died of bronchitis and pneumonia and no one had been murdered you have to concede she may have got a point. Eddowes might have reasoned that at this stage she had very little to lose.

There are indications that the arrangement had been to meet that very night. First of all the spending of all the money, keeping nothing in reserve, and secondly her strange behaviour after she was arrested. Look at her situation, she had no money, nowhere to sleep and she had just been arrested and put into a cell for the night. Surely with the temperature dropping like a stone outside, it fell to 6°C (it had also been raining), any person with half a wit would have just gone to sleep and spent a night in the cell? This must have been a fairly normal practice because when John Kelly heard about 10 pm that Eddowes had been arrested, he assumed *she was there until morning.* In his statement he says that one of the reasons he wasn't worried about Eddowes after hearing that a body had been found, was because he knew she was safe and sound in a police cell!

Yet what do we find? Do we find Eddowes going to sleep and counting her blessings? No we find her singing in her cell at midnight, just to let the sergeant know she is still awake, we find her asking to be released at 12.30 am but being refused. We find her again asking to be released at 1.00 am, and this time she gets her way. Then something very strange happens, she asks PC Hutt what time it is, *'Too late for you to get any more drink'* he replies **'No', she says 'What time is it?'** The PC tells her it is 1.00 am. For what possible reason would Catharine Eddowes have for being so concerned about the exact time? Her excuse that she *'might get a hiding for being late'* doesn't ring true, she told Kelly she would be back by 4 pm, and she definitely knew it was way past that time, besides there is nothing at all to suppose that Kelly had ever shown her anything but kindness and consideration to her. Don't forget he was the one walking the streets barefoot after pawning his boots. If he was a violent man, and if she was a prostitute, don't you think that he would have just insisted she walk the streets for a couple of hours? Then after her release she gives lie to the story that she hurrying off home by walking in exactly the opposite direction.

She is next seen about thirty minutes later in the company of a man at the end of Church Passage, a narrow alley way leading to Mitre Square from Duke Street. The three witnesses, Lawende, Levy and Harris only vaguely noticed the man, but it is Lawende's description of him which has been accepted as the most accurate, Lawende was walking a little apart from his companions and passed closest to the couple. Neither of the witnesses said there was anything remotely suspicious about the couple, they weren't struggling or anything. In fact they all say that the couple seemed to be talking rather quietly as if not wanting their conversation to be overheard. This contrasts strangely with other witnesses' accounts of prostitutes being accosted (Stride for instance) in these cases the two people involved didn't seem to care who overheard them.

It is interesting to note that all three describe the man as being slightly taller than the woman, since Eddowes was about five feet tall this would make the man about five foot three or four, I would have thought it highly unlikely for him to have been any more than five foot six. Yet the description of the man as published in the *Police Gazette* of 19 October describes him as being five foot seven *or eight*. Someone of this height standing next to someone of only five foot would positively tower over them, something that neither of the witnesses mentioned. It is interesting to note that a height of five foot five or six, matches the description of Wilson and Millwood's assailant.

Ten minutes later Catharine Eddowes was dead. When I have discussed this theory with other enthusiasts I am often told that no one would agree to meet a killer they were blackmailing in such an out of the way place as Mitre Square, but of course the point is that Eddowes didn't. She was seen with the suspect on a fairly well lit and well travelled thoroughfare, Duke Street. How did the killer entice his victim down the narrow alley to Mitre Square? I don't believe he did. Catharine Eddowes was barely five foot high and much wasted with illness, her thin body was remarked upon. It would be a simple matter to place a hand over her mouth to stifle her cries, half turn and carry her on your hip, much in the same way the old time washer women used to carry laundry. It is only a few yards down the passage and into the darkness of Mitre Square, where the poor woman could be dispatched.

Mafia gangsters used to place a final bullet in their victims mouth as a warning to other people not to talk too much. It is interesting to speculate whether the slashed eyelids of Catharine Eddowes wasn't a subconscious punishment on a woman who had seen too much.

Why did Hutchinson kill her, why not pay her off? For a start he may not have any money, but secondly, put yourself in his position. You have agreed to meet someone who is blackmailing you. One of your prime concerns is whether or not she has betrayed you to the police for the reward. Now it was common knowledge by 10 pm that night that Catharine Eddowes was being held at Bishopsgate police station, after all the news reached Kelly in his lodgings. The question facing Hutchinson was *'Did she go there voluntarily or was she picked up for some offence?'* Either way his position was by now precarious. Hutchinson might have kept a watch on the police station to see if she came out alone or with an escort. He would have followed her to the meeting place and kept watch to see if it was a trap.

This would explain why after leaving Bishopsgate at 1 am, taking about eight minutes to walk to Duke Street she wasn't seen with anyone until just gone 1.30 am.

No one has ever explained why there was so much time unaccounted for between Eddowes being released and her being seen with someone. Surely if she was there soliciting it wouldn't have taken twenty minutes to find a customer. The weather was fast approaching freezing, if she had no luck in Duke Street she would have moved on to the busier thoroughfares of the Aldgate and Whitechapel High Street. No, the reason why no one saw Catharine Eddowes soliciting in Duke Street that night was because she wasn't, she was waiting in the shadows for Hutchinson to arrive.

I cannot think of any other explanation that accords with the facts other than the one I have given. This is not twisting the facts in any way, they are there to see, untwisted. For my explanation to be wrong the following has to be answered:

1. Why did Eddowes do everything in her power to get herself released from cells on a freezing cold night when she had nowhere else to go for shelter?

2. Why was she so concerned about the precise time on her release. PC Hutt offered her an estimate (too late for you to get any more drink) but that wasn't good enough, she had to know the exact time.

3. Why on her release did she set off in the opposite direction to her lodgings?

4. It takes only eight minutes to walk down to Church Passage, why was she still there at 1.30 am, over twenty minutes later?

5. Where did she get the money from for drink on the last night of her life?

6. Why did she mislead her husband, Kelly, by telling him she was going to get the money from her daughter?

7. If Catharine Eddowes was soliciting, and was waiting at the end of Church Passage for a customer, why wasn't she noticed by PC James Harvey who was walking that

beat and must have walked within inches of her, *if*; she had been standing there?

There will still be those people who are not convinced and ask for proof. I can offer none that would stand up in a criminal court where something has to be proved beyond all reasonable doubt, but I venture I would make a fair case in a civil court where we are only concerned with the balance of probabilities. I do offer logical explanations for what have been up to now inexplicable occurrences. Also consider this, the people who were on the spot, the City Police, after following up all leads, interviewing all witnesses and taking everything else into account, were firmly convinced that Eddowes had gone out of Bishopsgate Police station to keep an appointment with her killer. If the people in the best position to know should come to that conclusion, who am I to argue?

Hutchinson was now in a quandary. This was the first killing that had been outside his control. He hadn't picked the victim, he hadn't picked the time or the place. Circumstances had done all that for him. He left the square quickly, taking with him a piece of Eddowes' apron to clean his hands. His hands were filthy, stained with blood and faecal matter, and it wasn't until he reached Goulston Street that he disposed of the rag, throwing it into a convenient doorway. It is interesting to note that he threw this away and didn't keep it. Many have theorised that the reason he mutilated the bodies was to obtain *'souvenirs'*, and many killers do in fact take away body parts and items of clothing for just that purpose. However on the one opportunity the Ripper has of acquiring an extra souvenir - he discards it. This seems to indicate that the killing of the women wasn't done for the pleasure of killing but with an extra motive in mind, such as removing them from standing between him and Mary Kelly.

The actual site of the disposal also gives a very strong clue as to the lair of the killer. It would be natural to keep the rag as long as possible, to ensure that a thorough cleaning job was done. Hutchinson only threw it away when he had to, because just round the corner of Goulston and Wentworth Street were his lodgings, a mere 500 feet away.

After this murder, and for once with a tangible clue to assist them the police delineated a very precise area of search. They must have known that the man they were looking for lived very close to where the rag was found. Unfortunately their search revealed nothing - why? Well for one thing their notices show that they are still looking for the bloodthirsty lunatic type, they ask for information on anyone *'suspicious'*. The problem was that George Hutchinson was anything but suspicious, he was just an ordinary East Ender, the original *'grey man'*.

The other reason they didn't turn up anything was that I believe Hutchinson wasn't there any more. Put yourself in Hutchinson's place, you have just murdered someone who was blackmailing you. You know that she spent the last few hours of her life in the company of the police, but you have no idea what, if anything, she has told them. The prudent thing to do would be to leave the district and lie low. If Eddowes had told the police anything it would soon appear in the newspapers, and thus warned as long as he was out of the area he might stand a chance of getting away. There was still plenty of work in Romford for an odd job man, the floods had wrecked the town centre and they were still clearing up. So George Hutchinson left the area, the Ripper had gone to earth.

September turned to October and still he stayed away. There was no need for him to kill anywhere else, it was the prostitutes in the East End that were stopping Mary coming to him, and so for the month of October no murders took place, the pattern had been broken.

At the beginning of November, he began to yearn after Mary Kelly again. In his mind, she was probably frantically worried about not seeing him for so long. This delusionary way of thinking is by no means uncommon amongst stalkers. In Jean Ritchie's excellent book, *'Stalkers'* (published by Harper Collins) she talks about the twisted logic stalkers use to convince themselves they are right.

*"For male stalkers the justification for their behaviour is often that they see themselves as protectors, believing that the woman they are pursuing needs their care, even though she repudiates it. Where their thought processes are clinically disordered, **as with schizophrenic stalkers,** they often believe that their quarry is being prevented from recognising her need by outside intervention".*

This being so, Hutchinson left Romford and started back to the East End. As he trudged through the night, he didn't notice that the weather was foul, cold and wet, all he could think about was seeing Mary Kelly again. It took him the best part of four hours to walk back and it was just on two in the morning when he walked up Commercial Street. He had decided that after such a long absence he owed it to Mary to go straight round to her room in Dorset Street. He was just passing Thrawl Street when who should be coming down but Mary. She approached him, yes this was how it should be. Instead of throwing her arms around him as she was supposed to, she asked him for money. This took him aback and he told her he didn't have any. Before he could talk to her properly she had walked past him, smelling of drink, and a more than a little unsteady on her feet.

He saw her talk to a man and they walked back towards him together. This was just the sort of thing he had to save her from, he turned and followed them. He saw them go up the narrow alley to Millers Court, and positioned himself in the entrance to Crossinghams Lodging House which was directly opposite Millers Court. After a time he saw the man leave, now was the chance he had been waiting for. He walked up the alley and quietly knocked on the door to her room. There was no answer, he tried the door, to his surprise it was open, the spring latch held back in the open position. The room was cold with a vicious draught blowing through the broken window panes, despite the old coat that had been hung over it. The atmosphere was smoky, something was smouldering in the grate, he approached the bed and called her name quietly. After several attempts he got her to wake up. She looked at him in the darkness. He explained who it was and why he had come to her. Before he could explain how he was going to take her away from all this filth and squalor, she started to swear at him.

He stood there for a minute in shocked silence, this wasn't the way it was supposed to be. Suddenly, as if someone had switched on a searchlight, everything became very clear. It wasn't a fairy tale princess lying before him on silken sheets, it was a foul mouth, drunken whore, lying in filth and cursing him to get out. It was all very clear now, when he met her in the street earlier on, she hadn't been 'slightly spreeish' she had been extremely drunk.

240

This instant reversal from all consuming love to all powerful hate is common amongst stalkers who finally realise what the situation is. Robert Bardo stalked an actress called Rebecca Schaeffer for years, professing undying love for her. Then one day he was introduced to reality when he was thrown off the TV set where Rebecca was working. His reaction to this was typical of a person who inhabits a totally fantasy world.

"I thought she didn't deserve to be a star if she had that sort of attitude, and I decided to do something about it,"

said Bardo, who left to pick up a pistol and then returned to the set and gunned down the 21 year old actress in cold blood.

Something similar happened to Hutchinson. This person who he had done so much for, this person who had forced him to murder, was now revealed as no better than any of his victims. So be it.

This murder, like Eddowes, was different from the rest. Once again circumstances had dictated his actions. He didn't bother to strangle his victim first, his mind exploded with a terrifying all consuming hate. He pulled his knife from its sheath and lunged at her.

In the last few seconds of her life Mary Kelly must have known she was going to die. In terror she pulled the dirty sheet over her face, hiding from the horror that was to be visited upon her. The knife stabbed down, through the sheet into her throat, her hand made a feeble attempt to ward off the blow and was cut about the fingers in the process.

At that moment George Hutchinson lost all form of reason. He had only one ambition - to remove every last trace of the person that was once Mary Kelly - and over the next couple of hours he certainly did his best. When the time came for him to leave the room, carefully slipping the catch on the way out so that the door locked behind him, the remains on the bed could scarcely be called human. George Hutchinson had entered Mary Kelly's room that morning, and Jack the Ripper left and journeyed into legend.

Chapter Eleven

"People in general have no notion of the sort and amount of evidence often needed to prove the simplest matter of fact".

Peter Mere Latham 1789 - 1875

Merely stating that you believe a certain person is the one you are looking for doesn't make it so, despite what numerous authors would have you believe. There has to be some sort of proof, naturally the use of the word *'proof'* is very subjective, the kind of proof that would be required by a criminal trial is simply not available. What then, what can we hope to achieve? Well we can certainly demonstrate that there are enough indications to show that a certain hypothesis is the most likely. For example if we break down the door to a locked and sealed room and find a man lying on the floor with a pistol grasped in his hand and a bullet wound to his head, we cannot prove that the man committed suicide. However if we then find evidence of depression and a suicide note written in the man's own handwriting, I believe it is a safe conclusion.

With the Whitechapel murders we are faced with the situation that there is no direct evidence, no witnesses to the actual attacks, no forensic and no hope of re-interviewing suspects. We must therefore fall back on the lessons learned in Chapter 8 and search for the *'wrong thing'*. Something we can put our finger on and say without doubt *'This is wrong, and I am going to follow this lead and see where it takes me'*.

In all the many thousands of words written and spoken about the murders I have found several items which I can unerringly point to and say with absolute conviction, *'This is wrong'*. However for the majority of them I find that there are plausible explanations. For instance, I do not wholly accept the statement by Israel Schwartz referring to the Stride murder. In this particular incident though I can with equal confidence find a reason for this being so, he was a stranger in a strange land and was over-eager to please the authorities. Given where the poor man had recently come from, I think this is a perfectly adequate explanation for his actions. Similarly Mathew Packer's evidence can be dismissed as being incorrect, but here I believe the reason was a desire by the man to get his hands on the reward being offered.

However when we come to George Hutchinson everything changes. The *'wrong thing'* about Mr. Hutchinson is his statement, it is obviously false. We must therefore establish why Hutchinson made such a statement. Remember, there are only two reasons for lying, one is to advertise and the other is to conceal. By making this statement what was Hutchinson trying to conceal or reveal?

Before we proceed we must however establish beyond all reasonable doubt that the statement is false, otherwise we will be falling into the old trap of saying something, and treating what we say as established fact.

In examining Hutchinson's statement, we are going to look at three aspects of it:

1. The circumstances of the statement, i.e. how did he happen to be in such a position to see what he says he saw.

2. The feasibility of the statement, i.e. is it possible to see what he says he saw.

3. The actual content of his statement, i.e. are the details liable to be true.

CIRCUMSTANCES

Hutchinson states that he was returning from Romford and arrived back in Whitechapel at about 2.00 am. He had just walked past Thrawl Street when he saw Mary Kelly coming down the road towards him.

These circumstances are highly suspect. Why would anyone who has been walking for the last four hours in freezing rain and cold, walk **right past** his lodgings on the corner of Wentworth and Commercial Street and carry on up the road towards Thrawl Street? It would hardly seem likely that he was going for a quick stroll before bedtime.

Some people have argued that he did that because he didn't have any money for lodgings and was just walking about. They point to the part of the statement when he refuses Kelly's request for a loan of sixpence as proof of this. But this doesn't make sense. If Hutchinson had no money for lodgings why did he return to the East End? What is the point of walking all that way from Romford in miserable conditions, just to wander round the East End all night? Why didn't he wander round Romford and save himself the long haul back? Quite often people make these statements without any actual knowledge of how human beings behave in such circumstances. If you are going to spend a night on the streets all your energy is spent in finding somewhere to sleep, you certainly don't waste any precious energy or body heat by taking part in a route march if you don't have to.

Hutchinson then says that after Kelly met a man, he followed them both back to Dorset Street and waited outside. Why? What on earth could he possibly achieve by wasting further time hanging around outside Millers Court in the early hours of the morning? Again an excuse might be that he was concerned for Mary Kelly's safety, this is nonsense. If he had any concern for her why didn't he challenge the man in the Street? Don't forget this is after the man behaved suspiciously, according to Hutchinson.

The only way these circumstances make any kind of sense at all is if Hutchinson returned from Romford that night with the express intention of seeing Kelly. That is why he was walking towards Kelly's lodgings when he met her. That is why he followed her back when she went back with a customer, and that is why he waited to see her.

FEASIBILITY

Hutchinson states that he only got an extremely brief view of the man when the couple walked past him outside the *'Queens Head'* public house. It is interesting to note that in Hutchinson's original statement he identifies this pub as being the *'Ten Bells'*, this has then been crossed out and *'Queens Head'* inserted above it. A case perhaps of his prepared story slipping a bit? He says he was leaning against the lamppost and bent down to peer into the man's face. The man looked at him *'very stern'* and the couple walked on. He then follows them to Millers Court where they pause for a moment. Kelly says she has lost her handkerchief and the man gives her a red one, they then go down the narrow alley to Kelly's room.

Why did Hutchinson halt his journey up Commercial Street to look back to see what Kelly was doing? He knew she was a prostitute and that she picked up strange men, why then did this particular incident cause him so much concern that he felt he had to wait outside the pub to get a better look at the man. He says the man was carrying a small parcel and this caused him concern, why didn't he say anything to Kelly? When he turned and followed the couple into Dorset Street he says they stopped outside Millers Court for about three minutes and had a chat. This is ludicrous, why would any customer of a prostitute, after being stared at by a stranger in the street, allow that same stranger to follow them into what has been described as the most dangerous street in the Empire, and then stand chatting to the prostitute for some three minutes, with the stranger so close he could hear a whispered conversation?

Any person traversing the East End looking for a prostitute would be extremely wary of being entrapped, beaten and robbed by accomplices of the prostitutes. They certainly wouldn't hang around chatting in the freezing rain long enough for these possible accomplices to catch up to them.

Hutchinson mentions that the handkerchief was red. This is impossible. Colours have a certain *'light signature'*, this is what makes them different from each other. However in the dark, colours lose this signature completely. This is why military camouflage experts often have one camouflage colour for daytime, and another for night. (Strangely enough one of the most effective night camouflage colours isn't black, it's blue!) In the dark colours are replaced by shades. For example in day time light green will appear light green, at night it appears grey, as do pink, white, yellow and all light shaded colours. The dark colours all appear black, such as blue, brown, dark green and red. So regardless of what colour the handkerchief was, if it was a light colour it would appear grey and if it was a dark colour it would appear black. The only way to alter this would be to have a light blue light of extreme intensity shining directly on the object, and as can clearly be seen on all the photographs of the entrance to Millers Court, it didn't even have a gas lamp at that spot! So why did Hutchinson put this little item in? Could it possibly be that a report in the press mentions one of the suspects at the scene of the Stride killing wore a red neckerchief?

CONTENT

It is however when we get down to the actual content of the statement that Hutchinson really lets himself down. His description of the man is unbelievably detailed. For ease of reference it is repeated here:

"age about 34 or 35, height 5ft 6ins, complexion pale, dark eyes and eye lashes, slight moustache curled up at each end and hair dark, very surly looking; dress, long dark coat, collar and cuffs trimmed astracan and a dark jacket under, light waistcoat, dark trousers, dark felt hat turned down in the middle, button boots and gaiters with white buttons, wore a very thick gold chain, white linen collar, black tie with horse shoe pin, respectable appearance, walked very sharp, Jewish appearance."

All that is missing from this description is how the man was twirling his moustaches and talking about throwing widows and orphans out into the snow! We are expected to believe that Hutchinson saw all this in a split second's glance as the man walked past him outside the Queens Head, in the early hours of the morning with the sole illumination provided by a single, ineffective gas lamp! The description contains just about every cliché used in describing a stage villain. It is comprised of a distillation of all the wildly inaccurate descriptions and theories that had appeared in the media up to that point. Leather apron was a Jew - Hutchinson gives this man a *'Jewish appearance'*. The killer was a doctor - Hutchinson makes him look respectable, and so on and so on.

I have spoken to many serving and ex-police officers, and without exception they all dismiss Hutchinson's description as pure fantasy. The general consensus of opinion being that witnesses generally get the sex and the height about right, but after that it's pot luck. The main points which defy reason are as follows:

1. How could he possibly see the colour of the man's eyes - let alone his eyelashes?

2. If he was paying so much attention to the man's face as to be certain about his eyes and eye lashes, how did he manage to spot that the man was wearing spats, with white buttons, and button boots?

3. Why would a man who is equipped with such a lovely warm coat (collar and cuffs trimmed with astracan) on such a foul, freezing night, leave everything so open and unbuttoned that Hutchinson could actually see his watch chain?

4. Would anyone with such a valuable collection of jewellery about their person leave it so obviously on view just before going off with a prostitute? The only thing missing here would be a large illuminated sign with *'Rob Me Here'* written on it, suspended above the man's head.

No, having looked at all these points we are drawn to one inescapable conclusion, Hutchinson lied - his statement was false!

There are however, two reasons why Hutchinson is still believed even to this day. One, on re-telling his statement, he told the near identical story again, even down to the majority of the details being the same, and secondly Inspector Abberline believed him! I believe I have the answer to both those points, first of all his statement was in part based on fact, and secondly I don't think Abberline did believe him!

I will cover the second point later, but first of all let us examine how someone can tell a lie, and then repeat it later with such accuracy that he will be believed. In Chapter 8 we looked at how people who lie literally for their lives, spies, concoct a cover story. They take circumstances and events which have actually happened, but not to them, and then merely insert them where needed. It is far easier to remember a sequence of events if they are based on fact than if they are entirely fictional. If there are differences in a story being told you will often find that the differences are those that have been invented by the person being questioned, and not in those details he has lifted from life.

When I first read the description of the man Hutchinson said he had seen, it struck me as being totally theatrical. It was if he was describing the perfect villain, an imaginary figure conjured up from someone's imagination. Then it struck me, what Hutchinson was describing wasn't a real figure at all - it was a dummy! Look at the description, everything is perfect, the overcoat, followed by the jacket then the waistcoat, all with the correct jewellery, and of course don't forget the buttoned boots with white buttoned spats.

I can almost see Hutchinson standing outside *'Stones Millinery and Mantle Emporium'* at 60 Market Place Romford, gazing with intensity at a magnificent dummy in the window display. It might have an equally well attired lady with him, perhaps with a board reading *'What the Well Dressed Gentleman and his Lady Companion are Wearing this Season'*. How many hours did he stand staring at them, seeing not two dummies, but himself with Mary Kelly on his arm? No wonder he had to return to the East End, she would be longing to hear from him just how everything was going to turn out. Of course this is pure speculation, apart from one tiny detail.

I spoke to the costume department at the Victoria and Albert Museum, and a very pleasant American lady there confirmed what I had thought. You see the chances of Hutchinson seeing someone wearing spats at two in the morning are practically non-existent. Spats are morning wear to be worn between breakfast and luncheon, no one with that amount of obvious wealth would be wearing them to chat up prostitutes at that time, but of course Hutchinson wasn't very knowledgeable in correct dress code for Victorian gentlemen.

It is interesting to note that when Hutchinson next tells his story, to the press the following day, certain details have now changed. These aren't the details based on fact, i.e. the description of the clothes (although he does add that the watchchain now carries a red stone seal, but .don't forget additions and subtractions from a story indicate accuracy) but the details that he would have had to invent for himself the features. It is very unlikely that the dummy (if that's indeed what he used) had any discernible features, so these are the points to watch very carefully, and sure enough these have totally changed.

FIRST STATEMENT	SECOND STATEMENT
Complexion pale	Complexion dark
Slight Moustache	Heavy Moustache
Dark Eyelashes	Bushy Eyebrows

It would appear that our eagle-eyed witness isn't so eagle-eyed after all. How can you possibly trust anyone who says he can describe the colour of a man's boot buttons, but changes completely the man's face? Far from dismissing these discrepancies as *'not significant'* as one author has done, I believe these discrepancies are vital to disproving the validity of the entire statement.

I believe that we have now reached the stage where we can say without fear of contradiction that Hutchinson's statements are false.

However merely proving that someone has made a false statement doesn't necessarily mean that they have something to hide. There are many reasons why someone would make a false statement, we have already considered both Israel Schwartz and Mathew Packer. We must also remember that in any situation similar to the Whitechapel Murders you will also have people who confess to the crime, although they didn't have anything to do with it. This is certainly as true today as it was in 1888, and several people did *'confess'* to being Jack the Ripper. It is to the credit of the police that they were all released, the temptation to accept one of their confessions must have been great indeed.

So apart from fear of authorities and a desire to get any reward, what other motives could Hutchinson have? He certainly wasn't an *'attention seeker'*, such a person would have leapt into the limelight at the first opportunity, not waited for three days before coming forward. It is only after you examine each reason in turn and dismiss them as being not applicable in this case, that you are left with one inescapable conclusion George Hutchinson made the statement because he was forced to do so.

Something made it imperative that he go to the police station on Monday evening and make his statement. What was it? Well, whatever it was must have happened on Monday, if it had happened earlier he would have spoken up earlier. The only event of any note that took place on Monday which had any connection with the killings, was the inquest of Mary Jane Kelly. Something happened at the inquest that forced Hutchinson into taking action. As you sift through all the statements given by all the witnesses you despair of finding a single logical reason for Hutchinson coming forward, until you get to the testimony of Sarah Lewis. Now much of her testimony regarding the mysterious stranger who had accosted her earlier in the week carries with it the faint hint of dramatic fiction, but at the beginning of her testimony you come to this interesting passage:

*"When I went in the Court I saw a man opposite the court in Dorset Street standing alone by the lodging house. He was not tall but stout - had on a wideawake black hat - I did not notice his clothes - another young man with a woman passed along - The man standing **in the street was looking up the court as if waiting for some one to come out..**"*

Unbeknown to Sarah Lewis she had caught sight of Jack the Ripper! When I first read this I tended to dismiss it as being of no importance, as a resident of Millers Court would surely know George Hutchinson who lived so close and who admitted an acquaintanceship with Mary Kelly, and would thus be able to identify him to the police. Perhaps she may not know his name but she would very likely know him well enough to give a more detailed description. Then of course I noticed I had overlooked something, Sarah Lewis didn't live in Millers Court, she lived in Great Pearl Street about three hundred yards north of Spitalfields Market. She had a quarrel with her husband and had come to spend the rest of the night with her friends the Keylers in 2 Millers Court.

Stop and consider the position Hutchinson found himself in when he learned of this. He had been spotted at the scene of the crime within an hour or so of the deed being committed. Admittedly Sarah Lewis hadn't recognised him as yet, but could he rely on his luck to hold? Hutchinson had two choices, one, he could say nothing and hope that Sarah Lewis doesn't accidentally meet him in the street or remember any more details about him, or two, he can bluff it out and concoct a story that would legitimately put him outside Millers Court at that time. Now I don't think anyone would say that Jack the Ripper wasn't a man of cool cunning, so partly because of his narrowing options and also partly out of sheer bravado, Hutchinson trots along to Commercial Street Police Station at six in the evening and tells his tale.

He realises of course that one of the first things he will be asked is why didn't he come forward earlier. He appreciates that if anyone makes the link between his coming forward and Sarah Lewis's testimony, he might have done himself no good at all. He therefore tells a yarn about making his statement to a police officer he met in the street the previous day, a Sunday. The police officer he says wasn't very interested and sent him packing. Of course, despite an intensive search this police officer cannot be found. He was lucky that no one had the wit to ask him why he stopped a policeman in the street, why not go direct to the Police Station as he is doing now? I would suspect that the police were so excited by what they thought was important evidence that in the fuss they forgot. (In case anyone thinks my answer a little unbelievable I would refer them to a recent, 1994, murder of a man who lived alone. The investigation was so caught up with forensic, taking statements and generally rushing around, that it wasn't until the head of the investigation was replaced, that a vitally important question was asked. If the man lived alone, and if he was at work on this particular day, who, the new head of investigation asked pointing at the man's phone bill, accepted the two reverse charges phone calls made on the day he was murdered. Up to now no one had noticed this vital clue!)

The statement made by Hutchinson is deemed to be so important that Abberline is immediately summoned. He interviews Hutchinson, and afterwards reports to his superiors:

"An important statement has been made by a man named George Hutchinson which I forward herewith. I have interrogated him this evening, and am of opinion his statement is true."

Now for most people this settles the matter, after all if Abberline, a highly experienced detective, was satisfied, who are we to argue? I agree totally **- *if Abberline was satisfied* - I don't believe he was!** Which leads inexorably to the conclusion that Abberline filed a false report, which is exactly what I think he did.

Put yourself in Abberline's position, here at long last is something he knows without a shadow of a doubt is wrong. I'm not saying for one moment that he knew Hutchinson was the Ripper, of course not, I believe he was too good a detective for that, but he still knew something was amiss. Like Hutchinson he has two options. One, he can say to Hutchinson *'This is a load of rubbish'* to which all Hutchinson has to reply is *'Prove it'* and walk away. Or two, he can pretend to believe him, this will at least give him some breathing space to plan his next move. I believe he took option two as the only safe course.

Naturally his main concern is to prevent any more killings, again if he suspects something, he can either lock Hutchinson up, which wouldn't work as he has no direct evidence to hold him, or he can take steps to effectively isolate him. Again he takes option two. It is a recorded fact that for two weeks after Hutchinson made his statement he was accompanied by two detectives. The official reason for these two police escorts was *'in case Hutchinson should recognise the man he saw'*. This is a little bit flimsy to say the least, if this was the real reason, why did none of the other witnesses (Mrs Long, Israel Schwartz, Joseph Lawende, Mathew Packer etc. etc.) have such an escort? It is more believable that the two officers were there to prevent a suspect offending again.

However Abberline now faces a grave problem. If he tells the truth and puts in his report that he doesn't believe Hutchinson, how long would it be before that was splashed all over the papers? Time after time, information that the police would have liked to have kept quiet appeared in the press almost as soon as the ink was dry on the official police reports. Look at what happened when they got to hear of *'Leather Apron'*. Before they could act on it, the papers were letting everyone know they were looking for John Pizer, whereupon he promptly went and hid himself. The same thing happened with the statement of Israel Schwartz, the police naturally wanted to keep the description he provided secret, but the very next day he was being interviewed by reporters. Again, when a landlady reported that a mysterious lodger had left some bloodstained shirts in her house, instead of keeping this back until the police could trap the man, the papers plastered it all over the front pages and scared him off.

There is no doubt that certain police officers were supplementing their meagre incomes by selling information to the press. Perhaps if the Metropolitan Police had been a little more forthcoming with the press they could have worked together, as it was they were constantly at loggerheads. Whatever the reason, Abberline knew without a shadow of a doubt that if he put in his report that he had any suspicions about Hutchinson at all, he could expect it to be in print the very next day.

I believe Abberline wrote out his report and took it directly to James Monro. Why Monro and not Warren? It is true that Warren resigned from his post of Commissioner on the 8th November, the day before Mary Kelly's murder, however his resignation wasn't officially accepted until the 10th, and even then he continued in office until he was relieved by Monro on the 27th November. Even so I believe Abberline would have been reluctant to go directly to Warren with his information. Warren had been the cause of Monro's original resignation and was not very popular amongst the detective branch. The detectives saw Monro as a professional policeman, one of them, and Warren was definitely not. Don't forget Monro knew and respected Abberline, he had personally ensured he was transferred to Scotland Yard, and I'm sure the feeling was mutual. Besides which if Abberline had gone to Warren he might have seen this a straw worth clutching to, and have forced Abberline's hand.

I believe that at the time it was common knowledge who was going to succeed Warren, and Abberline would see nothing wrong in going direct to Monro with the information. He would say something along the line of

'Despite what I have written in my report I do not trust Hutchinson's statement, I believe the man is lying. I have placed two detectives with him in an effort to avoid any more attacks, and I need some time to investigate further'.

I certainly don't think that Abberline would openly state and say *'I've caught Jack the Ripper'*; I think he was far too good a detective for that. Monro would of course, either by memo or spoken word, inform those other senior officers he would consider essential to be in the know. Whoever he would inform would be at the very top, a general dissemination of this kind of information would lead to a leak.

Of course this is pure speculation, there is no proof that this happened. There are however some very strange incidents that make any other explanation practically untenable. Remember what Anderson says in his memoirs:

*"I will merely add that **the only person** who ever had a good view of the murderer... "*

and again in the Macnaghten memoranda:

*"**No one ever saw the Whitechapel murderer** (unless possible it was the City PC ...."*

Now in the past when those statements have been examined, it has been from the point of trying to identify who the witness was. Was it Lawende or Schwartz, was it a City or Metropolitan PC etc. etc. The most glaring thing about these statements to me is not the quality of the witness *but the quantity*. If Hutchinson's statement was true the person he saw was obviously the killer. Hutchinson described the man down to his button boots, so why is it when two senior police officers talk about witnesses later on *they completely dismiss Hutchinson as a witness?* For if Hutchinson was accepted as a credible witness then Anderson would have said *"Two people saw the killer etc."*, Macnaghten would have said *'only one man saw the Whitechapel'* but they don't, both of them talk about there either being only one witness who ever saw the killer or none, and neither of them refer to Hutchinson.

Another interesting point which up to now has not had an explanation, is something the reporter, G R Sims, wrote on the 2nd December 1888, only five days after Monro officially took over the post of Commissioner. He wrote:

"It would be strange if the accession of Mr. Monro to power were to be signalised by such a universally popular achievement as the arrest of Jack the Ripper. From such information which has reached me, I venture to prophesy that such will be the case."

This is incredible, George Sims had private information that it was likely an arrest was imminent. Who could he have got this information from? Since Mr. Monro is mentioned, there can only be one conclusion, from Monro. If it wasn't Monro then why mention the man's name? Where did Monro get such an impression from, after all he hadn't been involved in the case at all, and yet a mere five days after taking office something gives him enough confidence to tip Sims the wink *'to watch this space'*. It is inconceivable that Monro, being naturally cautious, would have given any such impression **unless** the information came from someone Monro had the highest regard for, someone like Abberline.

If Abberline had acted in the way I surmise he did, then several things become clear. The mystery of the *'Missing Witness'*, is a mystery no longer, Anderson and Macnaghten dismissed Hutchinson as a credible witness because word had filtered through that all was not well with Hutchinson's story. Monro's conviction that something would break soon is also explained if Abberline had told him that he might be on to something. Monro, don't forget, was the one officer who always held to the belief that Jack the Ripper **should** have been caught, although he wasn't. Just the sort of thing he would have said if his hopes had been raised, but raised in vain.

Abberline was of course under the impression that he was looking for an *'ordinary'* murderer. The concept of a *'stalker'*, someone who is so obsessed with one target, and one target only was completely foreign to him. He expected Hutchinson to strike again, if he was correct in his theory, then there was a very good chance that Hutchinson was the Ripper, and this time he would be on the spot to arrest him. But of course with the object of his obsession obliterated, the Ripper faded back into the shadows, never again to appear on the streets of Whitechapel.

After a while with no new evidence coming to light, and the inquiry making no further progress, the investigation was scaled down. I believe this continued until only Abberline was left, perhaps unofficially, on the case.

In 1892 two things happened, one Inspector F G Abberline of the Metropolitan Police retired, and secondly, for no apparent reason, the Jack the Ripper file was closed. Coincidence? I don't think so.

Chapter Twelve

"We shall not cease from exploration
And the end of all our exploring
Will be to arrive where we started
And know the place for the first time"
T S Eliot Little Gidding

Was George Hutchinson Jack the Ripper? It is of course impossible to say, but I believe if the same case occurred today he would definitely be someone the police would want to interview extremely urgently. Look at the circumstances that make him the strongest suspect yet:

1. He was the only person identified as being at the scene, and at approximately the time of a murder, Mary Kelly's. We have two sources of information to confirm this, one Sarah Lewis and the other is Hutchinson himself.

2. He lied to the police with the intention of deceiving them. It is impossible for Hutchinson's statement to be true.

3. He knew one of the victims, Mary Kelly, and had known her for several years. He admitted to giving her money in the past.

4. He is the only suspect who can be proved, beyond all doubt, to have lived in the critical area, an area that the police at the time believed the Ripper lived in.

5. He is the only suspect who has the slightest connection with the only clue left by the Ripper, the piece of Catharine Eddowes' apron, he lived only a few yards from where it was dropped. There is a direct line from Mitre Square, to the apron, to his lodgings. There is no *'round about route to fool police'*.

Now we have a suspect, we can legitimately use an Offender Profile to see if it can further assist us. Remember, we are starting with a legitimate suspect and seeing if the profile fits - not trying to cram anyone we chose into a profile.

PROFILE STATES	HUTCHINSON
White male	yes
Western European	yes
Found within the 20-40 years of age category. Actual age of offenders 25-35	28 years old
Unmarried	Although it is not possible to state definitely, the indications are Hutchinson was unmarried.
Unskilled labourer	Barman & Labourer
Living within a 800 metre location of crimes	Almost exactly
Previous convictions for assault	No previous convictions because he wasn't caught, but I believe he did carry out the attacks on Millwood and Wilson.
Mental Illness	No firm proof of this, but hypothesis is of an obsessive nature.
Some form of acquaintanceship with victims.	Yes

I would submit that George Hutchinson is both a credible suspect and the type of person highlighted by Offender Profiling. I further submit that out of all the suspects he alone fulfils all these criteria.

and finally ......

As already stated very little is known about George Hutchinson, however there is one irrefutable link with him that is still in existence, his signature at the end of his statement. I took this to Andrew McNamara, a Consultant Graphologist of AMP Graphologists in Swansea. I isolated the signature from the rest of the statement so he would have absolutely no idea of who George Hutchinson was. His report is interesting, he states:

'The signature indicated **enterprise, initiative** *and ambitious drive, with a tendency to* **over protect***, or patronise perhaps in a fatherly or some other* **authoritative way.** *There is also an inner conflict with regard to* **ideals, everyday issues** *and sensual needs indicating that the writer was sensitive to the mood of the moment and socially active. The writer enjoyed* **tactile stimulation and may well have over - indulged sometimes to excess.** *There was also an aesthetic sense with literary or musical abilities.*

The writer was either depressed or ill at the time of writing as resentment, disappointment and anxiety were all present'.

To my mind the above is an almost perfect thumbnail sketch of the man called *'Jack the Ripper'*.

PS. In 1994 a man was found murdered in 4 Whites Row, just four doors from where Annie Millwood, Jack the Ripper's first victim lived. The man was a homosexual and police (who bungled the investigation, allowing vital evidence to be destroyed) believe the killer was a male prostitute. To date the killer has not been caught. The victim's throat was cut from ear to ear.

Appendix One

One of the enduring mysteries about the Whitechapel murders was the weapon involved in the killings. It was obviously a knife of some sort, but what sort is the question.

Although there were spring operated knives available at this time they were extremely rare and the chances are it was one of the two more common types, a fixed bladed knife, such as a Bowie, or a folding bladed knife. Let us look at the folding bladed knife first of all.

It is extremely unlikely that it would be of the normal penknife type, for a blade that is not locked firmly in place is probably of greater danger to the user. However there is a type of knife that has been around since the seventeenth century that does fit the bill, this is the Spanish *'Basque'* knife. This is normally recognised by the very curvaceous handle, narrowing off at either end, sometimes to a point. The blade is normally of the *'clip'* pointed type, similar to a Bowie knife. The knife is designed as a fighting knife and therefore the blade is locked firmly in place. The blade is usually about six to ten inches long and razor sharp, being designed for slashing rather than stabbing.

It is rather interesting to note that the attack on Martha Tabram has often been blamed on two attackers because two different knives were apparently used. This is false thinking. As has been demonstrated there are cases on record of one killer using two knives, but everyone seems to be overlooking the possibility of one weapon with two blades. Several folding type knives have more than one blade, often of very different size and design.

When we come to the fixed bladed designs there are many to choose from, however the chances are it was a blade of similar design to a Bowie knife. It is not generally known that although the Bowie knife is supposedly an American weapon, the majority of them were made in Sheffield. Again this is a slashing weapon, with the sharpened clip point designed for penetrating the abdomen and disembowelling

One interesting item from this era was something I came across many years ago at a country auction. I had bought a box of *'miscellaneous'* and nestling in one of the darker corners was what appeared to be an old knife in a battered leather sheath. The handle of the knife was wrapped in twine and the butt end was a wooden pommel. The knife was without quillions (hand-guards) and the blade was a thin leaf shape, sharpened on both edges. Even though it was extremely rusty the blade was still razor sharp. When I eventually got round to restoring it I found the wooden pommel was in fact a piece of hardwood shaped just like a champagne cork, and had been hammered into what appeared to be a hollow handle.

When I removed the twine from the grip it became clear that what I had wasn't a knife at all but a spear head. Talking later to a dealer friend of mine he told me some very interesting facts. Apparently during the Zulu wars (1879) souvenir collecting was just a big a business as it is nowadays. The officers, having a baggage allowance, could ship home spears and shields intact, but the ordinary soldier couldn't. Rather than miss the opportunity of making a few shillings, they hit upon a very simple idea. They took the heads off the spears and carried them home in their packs. However once home, a lot of people found they made excellent knifes and with a plug of wood and a length of twine converted them into knives instead of restoring them to spears. After all a good knife was far more use to someone than a Zulu assegai. Interestingly enough the assegai was specifically made for slashing and disembowelling, is it too far fetched to imagine a weapon forged on the plains of Africa found its way to the murky East End of London where it carried on its grisly task.

If the weapon used was a fixed blade knife then it is a certainty that the killer carried it in a sheath. The popular idea of a killer stalking the streets with a weapon in a parcel or a bag is ludicrous. For a start anyone carrying anything that remotely resembled anything of value ran the very real risk of being attacked and robbed. Secondly, one of the hallmarks of the Ripper was his speed of the attack. It is inconceivable that he should strangle someone then start fumbling around untying a parcel or rooting around in a bag for his knife.

One thing that is often overlooked in these murders is that the knife was extremely sharp. As any carpenter will tell you, you don't just leave sharpened chisels etc. just floating around in your toolbag, as any attempt to plunge your hand in to get them would probably result in you withdrawing a lesser amount of fingers than you had when you went in.

Bearing these facts in mind it is almost a certainty that the Ripper carried his knife in a sheath. There are several optimum places to carry a knife for quick easy access. One of the best places is strapped to your thigh, in World War II the British Commando knife, the Fairbairn Sykes, had two leather tabs on the sheath to enable the soldiers to sew them to the leg of their trousers. However it is unlikely the Ripper carried his there, a bit obvious I would have thought! During my time in the services I carried my knife strapped to my forearm underneath my smock. This enabled me to keep it out of the way but at the same time allowed it to be brought into action very quickly. Wearing it on a belt does make it a bit obvious that you are armed.

I hope these few facts might give you something to think about, who knows one day the actual knife may be discovered, we can all study it, take photographs, then consign the evil thing to a furnace.

Whatever happened to George Hutchinson? The simple truth is I don't know. The records for 1891 do not show him still living at the Victoria Home for Working Men (although Joe Barnett's brother Daniel is). I also cannot find any other record of him still in the area.

There are several records of a George Hutchinson dying in England or Wales up to 1955, possibly one might be our George Hutchinson, the only records which are possibly relevant are as follows:

George Hutchinson died Newark aged 69 in 1929

George Hutchinson died Bradford aged 74 in 1934

George Hutchinson died Darlington aged 76 in 1936

Since all of these men shared a common year of birth, 1860, and the George Hutchinson we are interested in was born in

262

December 1859 it may be possible that one of these is the one. At the time of writing research is continuing.

A great deal of research into the background of Mary Kelly has been carried out by Alan Jones of Gwent, and he has turned up some interesting facts. There was a Mary Kelly who resided for a time at a hostel in Bristol, who later gave birth to a daughter in Cardiff. The interesting thing about this is that one of the trustees of the home was the Reverend Samuel Barnett's brother. The Reverend Samuel Barnett was very active in Whitechapel at the time of the murders doing charity work amongst the prostitutes in the area, and his wife actually wrote the petition to Queen Victoria.

It is not beyond the realms of possibility that a girl from a Bristol refuge would be found work in London through the efforts of these two men.

On the other hand Alan Jones has also found a sixteen year old Mary Kelly whose profession is given as prostitute, in another refuge in Whitechapel in 1879. At the time of writing Alan is still continuing his research.

Appendix Two

The East End today 1996

Alas, many of the old sites are no more. Redevelopment and bomb damage have both taken their toll, and now there is very little left of Whitechapel as it was in 1888.

For those of you who are interested there are many walking tours, that will show you the sites of the murders. Be warned though a lot of the guides know very little about the murders and often pepper their commentary with incorrect facts. I would ask any of you who wish to go on one of these tours to please respect the fact that people do live in the area and to keep the noise to an absolute minimum.

The road where George Hutchinson was born is still there, but alas all the houses have long since disappeared.

Whites Row is still there, and number eight is still marked number eight. The lower floor has been boarded over and painted white, but if you look up you will see it exactly as it was when Annie Millwood stayed there. Park your car in Whites Row car park. As you walk through the car park heading north you come to a private road, and a large building, The London Fruit and Wool Exchange is directly in front of you. Turn a quarter turn to the right and you will see in this building a set of steel steps, just in front of these is a damaged kerbstone. According to the latest research done by John Stedman this is the precise position where Mary Kelly died.

As you turn South from here you come to the corner of Wentworth and Commercial Street. Today it is a luggage shop, in 1888 it was the Victoria Home for Working Men where Hutchinson lodged, as you look down Wentworth Street you can see where it crosses Goulston Street, a few yards down the road. Turn down Goulston Street and you can come to the doorway where the clue of the apron and the graffiti were found. The correct doorway is the second one down, next to the Fish and Chip shop. According to Paul Harrison in his book *'Jack the Ripper The Simple Truth'* this doorway has been demolished - it hasn't. Kevin O'Donnell's book *'The Jack the Ripper Whitechapel Murders'* has a photograph of the doorway, but unfortunately it is the wrong one!

If you turn right into New Goulston Street, cross Middlesex Street (Petticoat Lane) into Gravel Street, sharp right into White Kennet and then sharp left into Stoney Lane, this will lead you to Houndsditch. Cross over, turn right then first left into Bevis Marks. Follow this down until it turns into Dukes Place and then you are soon in Mitre Square. There is a City of London Police checkpoint just here so if you get lost ask a policeman. As you walk down Church passage you will see in front of you the City of London boundary markers and further on a raised flower bed and a wooden bench. It was just by the wooden bench poor Catharine Eddowes was found.

Bishopsgate Police station occupies the same position as it did in 1888, but the old building was destroyed during the war.

As for the other sites, Berner Street and Durward Street (Bucks Row) have long since disappeared. George Yard buildings has also vanished (Paul Harrison has again got the wrong building in his book). There is a modern block of flats there now, although the street is still in existence, although re-named Gunthorpe Street.

For those of you wishing to walk the area themselves, I can suggest no better starting point than the *'City Darts'* public house in Commercial Street, situated directly opposite the site of the Victoria Home. For some reason the name of the pub was changed from the *'Princess Alice'*, a famous pub where Mickledy Joe, *'Leather Apron's'* friend used to drink. *The Ten Bells* only a few yards up Commercial Street is where most of the victims used to drink. It hasn't changed very much since then and is very much involved with the Whitechapel murders.

Sitting there nursing your beer, it is very easy to become totally absorbed in the atmosphere. You find yourself looking up quickly at the sound of an Irish accent to catch the fleeting glance of a short dumpy woman wearing a shawl hurrying through the doors

Bibliography

Newspapers & Publications

The Illustrated Police News
The Manchester Guardian
The New York Times
The London Times
Punch
The Hartford Courant
Wolverhampton Chronicle
The Daily Telegraph
Evening News
Daily News
East London Observer
The East London Advertiser
The Llanelly & County Guardian

Books

The Jack the Ripper A-Z, written by Paul Begg, Martin Fido and Keith Skinner and published by Headline.

Jack the Ripper - The Uncensored Facts, written by Paul Begg, published by Robson Books.

The Lodger - The Arrest & Escape of Jack the Ripper by Stewart Evans & Paul Gainey, published by Century.

Murder & Madness - The Secret Life of Jack the Ripper by Dr David Abrahamsen, published by Robson Books.

The Jack the Ripper Whitechapel Murders by Kevin O'Donnell, published by Ten Bells.

The Complete History of Jack the Ripper by Philip Sugden, published by Robinson.

The Ripper File by Melvin Harris, published by W H Allen.

Jack the Ripper The Bloody Truth by Melvin Harris, published by Columbus Books.

The Crimes Detection & Death of Jack the Ripper by Martin Fido, published by Weidenfeld & Nicolson.

Jack the Ripper Revealed by John Wilding published by Constable.

Jack the Ripper The Mystery Solved by Paul Harrison, published by Hale.

Jack the Myth by A P Wolf, published by Hale.

Clarence by Michael Harrison, published by W H Allen.

Autumn of Terror by Tom Cullen, published by Bodley Head.

The Diary of Jack the Ripper by Shirley Harrison published by Index.

Jack the Ripper by Daniel Farson, published by Michael Joseph.

Jack the Ripper Summing up and Verdict by Colin Wilson & Robin Odell, published by Corgi.

Jack the Ripper the Simple Truth by Bruce Paley, published by Headline.

The Ripper Legacy by Martin Howells & Keith Skinner, published by Sphere.

The Ripper & The Royals by Melvyn Fairclough, published by Duckworth.

The Complete Jack the Ripper by Donald Rumbelow, published by Penguin.

Jack the Ripper The Final Solution by Stephen Knight, published by Harrap.

This is by no means an exhaustive list of books on Jack the Ripper, but are all recommended reading for anyone interested in the subject.

Non Jack the Ripper Books

Stalkers by Jean Ritchie, published by Harper Collins.

Forty Years of Murder by Professor Keith Simpson published by Guild Publishing.

Mortal Error by Bonar Menninger, published by Sidgwick & Jackson.

Whoever Fights Monsters by Robert Ressler and Tom Shachtman, published by St Martins Press.

East End 1888 by William J Fishman, published by Temple.

London's East End Point of Arrival by Chaim Bermant, published by Macmillan.

Other Documents and Publications

Ripperana

The Ripperologist

Metropolitan Police Files held in the Public Record Office Kew

Coroners papers on victims inquests

I'm quite sure I have referred to other sources as well, and if I have left any out it is a genuine mistake on my part.

Index

269